THE AUTHOR

TOWARDS A MARXIST APPROACH TO AUTHORSHIP

MICHAEL ROSEN

Contents

Preface 1
Abstract 3
Acknowledgements 5
Introduction 7

Chapter 1 15
Chapter 2 51
Chapter 3 97
Chapter 4 139
Conclusion 243

Bibliography 249
Appendix 273

Preface

THIS IS THE PH.D. I SUBMITTED in October 1997 and it was passed several months later. It was called 'A Materialist and Intertextual Examination of the Process of Writing a Work of Children's Literature'. As you can see, I have re-named it in a more general way, because I thought that the Ph.D. turned out to have made a more general point about authorship than the original title implied. So, yes, it is about the production of a work of *children's* literature, with the specifics that that entailed, but every form of literature will have its specifics. It's the principles that I've employed which can, I think, be employed and adapted to works across the whole range of what we call literature. That said, I have spent a good deal of my life producing and thinking about literature intended for children and I hope that people in that field will find this work helpful or interesting.

I've produced it in this edition because it isn't easy to get hold of the original copy, as there is only one. It's in the library of London Metropolitan University. It has also been archived at the British Library in digital form but the copying garbled the original, making some parts quite difficult to read.

For readers unfamiliar with the way Ph.D.s work, I should warn you that a Ph.D. has to follow certain specific procedures which I make explicit (and it is required to be such) as it goes along. I concede that some might find those procedures a little bit tedious. If life was longer I might have made the effort required to turn this Ph.D. into a more familiar form. I should say, though, that writing this thesis had the effect of producing more poems that reflected on matters that I hadn't thought about before, in particular in *Don't Mention the Children* (Smokestack Books, 2015) and *Jelly Boots, Smelly Boots* (Bloomsbury, 2016). What's more, when I was approached by Verso Books to write a memoir, there were aspects of the way I had written this thesis which made their way into that memoir, *So They Call You Pisher!* (Verso, 2017).

September 2018

1

Abstract

THIS THESIS COMES UNDER THE TERMS of Clause 3.2 in the booklet *Research Degrees, Regulations and Notes for Guidance* for the University of North London where it is stated that 'A candidate may undertake a programme of research in which the candidate's own creative work forms, as a point of origin or reference, a significant part of the intellectual enquiry.' This work, 'shall have been undertaken as part of the registered research programme.' Furthermore, it is stated that the 'creative work shall be . . . set in its relevant theoretical, historical, critical or design context.' (University of North London 1996: 6)

The creative work consists of 65 poems intended for an audience of children and the critical work of the thesis is a process of research into the sources and origins of those poems. It is therefore an enquiry that seeks to uncover how a highly specific mode of literature comes to be written.

It is my contention that descriptions of such a process are unsatisfactory unless they incorporate and combine the following four elements:

i) an examination of how the particular self under consideration (me) was formed in a specific socioeconomic, and cultural moment;
ii) an examination of how, within that moment, that self engaged with the texts made available in the institutions it occupied;
iii) an explanation of how the writing involved a synthesis of experiences – of life, texts and audiences;
iv) an explanation of how a writer reads his or her own writing.

The first two of these elements comprise the 'historical . . . context' noted above and the second two offer aspects of a 'theoretical . . . context'.

Acknowledgements

Thanks to: Harold Rosen and the late Connie Rosen for providing all of the genetic, and much of the cultural, intellectual and ideological source material; Betty Rosen for her indispensable advice and soup; Brian Rosen for his acts – brotherly and theatrical; my children Joe, Naomi, Eddie, Laura and Isaac who have brought me up to the best of their abilities; Professor Ian Donaldson whose sincerity, companionship and forbearance ensured that an Oxford University degree in English Literature could, in spite of itself, be inspirational; Joan Griffiths of BBC Schools Radio, Margaret Spencer (Meek) of the University of London Institute of Education and Pam Royds of what was then Andre Deutsch Children's Books who allied to find me an audience; Sally Feldman, the senior producer of BBC Radio 4's *Treasure Islands*, whose belief in my ability to engage critically with children's literature was the starting point for this work; Tony Watkins, Dennis Butts and Dudley Jones of Reading University who not only endured my presence on their MA course but also introduced me to Theory; K.C.H. for mixing solicitude with gentle mockery; my three supervisors – Dr Jean Webb of Worcester College of Higher Education who first made the then decidedly odd suggestion that this thesis was a feasible project, Professor Ruth Merttens of the University of North London whose supervision and cycling have been extremely challenging, and Margaret Spencer (Meek) who, twenty five years after helping my first work get seen, reappeared to help this work see the light of day too.

This thesis could only have been written thanks to the financial contribution made by Worcester College of Higher Education.

Introduction

[The] 'creative work [that] forms, as a point of origin or reference, a significant part of the intellectual enquiry . . . ' (*Research Degrees, Regulations and Notes for Guidance* University of North London 1996: 6)

. . . CONSISTS IN THIS THESIS OF 65 poems that I have written or rewritten subsequent to registration and which have now formed the bulk of a publication (Rosen 1996). As these regulations point out, the 'creative work' may be in any field – fine art, design, engineering, musical composition, dance, etc., but 'shall have been undertaken as part of the registered research programme.' In my case this set of poems was originated or reached their final draft form, at the end of 1994 and the beginning of 1995.

The regulations also request that the creative work be 'set in its relevant theoretical, historical, critical or design context' (Univ. of N. London 1996: 6). Of these alternatives I have looked mostly at the 'historical . . . context' which I am investigating in the area of how I, as the author of the work and so the work itself, was formed in history. This raises a range of theoretical questions concerning: the writing process, the relation between language and reality, the role of audience, the formation of the 'self' of the author and the relation between the work and other texts. So it is that the 'intellectual inquiry' I am embarking on consists of a set of questions around the notion of literary production. I am asking:

1) how can a set of poems, written by a particular author, be related to the following:
i) the present historical, economic and material context of their authoring;

ii) the past historical, economic and material circumstances of the author;

iii) the socioeconomic and emotional context of the author's family (or unit of upbringing);

iv) the literary and artistic context of their authoring;

v) the positioning of the author within a specific past and current literary and cultural context;

vi) the personally constructed narrative of the author's experiences, literary and non-literary;

2) How does this set of poems written by me exemplify these relationships?

3) What theoretical framework will provide an explanation for the form and structure of these relationships?

Writing as the author of the poems, I am aware of a certain irony in attempting to answer these questions. According to some I am dead (Barthes 1977). To others whatever I intend is irrelevant (Wimsatt and Beardsley 1954). And to yet others, the whole task is pointless because whatever I think that my writing-language is signifying, it is not (Saussure 1959, Derrida 1978); and anyway, in the final instance it's only the reader who knows what's written (Fish 1980). Yet again, there is for some, another supposed level of pointlessness: it is impossible for me to find out why I have written my poems – either because I am unable to see how I am enthralled ideologically within the system (Macherey 1978), or because my 'ego' will repress the real sources of my imagination (Freud 1985).

However, I, like the university regulations, am making several a priori assumptions: in my case they are that I exist, my labour exists, the objects of my labour exist (Marx 1954). Because language is available to me to describe these matters, unlike de Man (1983) I do not accept that it can be taken as a substitute for them (Bhaskar 1989 and in Shotter 1993; Ebert 1995; Callinicos 1985, 1995). The problem before me, in brief, is this: *how did this set of poems come to be written?*

Because I have framed the problem in this way, my approach to the poems will not be textual analysis in the customary literary sense. I will not be seeking to derive meaning, contradiction, irony, unity, patterning or the like from the poems themselves. Rather, I am engaged here in an enquiry into the relationship between textuality and the material, socioeconomic or ideological contexts of their production.

Most of the poems relate to childhood, both mine and an intended child audience, so one point of enquiry suggests itself: there ought to be some link between what I write and my childhood experiences. However, at the very moment of writing, I am not a child, so there must also be some connection between the life lived in the here and now and what is being written. I will take up these considerations firstly in Chapter 3 when I try to situate myself both as a child and later as a writer. Secondly, they will emerge as I look at the poems themselves in Chapter 4.

That said, I will be extremely cautious in the realm of what might be broadly called psychoanalysis. As a kind of 'Catch-22' this, in psychoanalytic terms could be because I 'repress' this approach. This may be the case, and a fuller picture could indeed be given using some of the resources of this field of enquiry. Yet, I have, for several reasons (rationalisations?), chosen to be very wary about adopting it as a method of enquiry:

1) I am unwilling to narrow explanations of the self and/or texts down to the dyads and triads of family life, the unknowable realms of the unconscious, or any schema of adult life based solely on childhood;
2) I have the feeling that some part of the gap between a piece of writing and the self, which could be occupied by psychoanalytic enquiry, would be best attempted by others, rather than me.

In broader terms, I can see there could in other circumstances be opportunities to look at the psychological significance (in the particular social formation we inhabit) of my whole artistic endeavour, e.g., trying to find answers to questions like: why do I write? why write for children? who do I think I am pleasing? why is it so important for me to 'please' anyway? what is the nature of my gratification derived from this artistic production? what is success? However, I regard these lines of enquiry too beyond the brief of this study.

Coming at the matter from another angle, it is clear that the words we use, the phrases and sequences we put them into and the forms we adopt cannot be regarded as inventions: they are borrowings, and alterings of what is already in existence: parts and wholes of texts already written or spoken,

'. . . a multi-dimensional space in which a variety of writings, none of them original, blend and clash.' (Barthes 1977: 146)

In my enquiry I will be seeking links with some of the texts and shapes of texts that I have encountered. However, in contradiction to a position that Barthes took up announcing my and my colleagues' 'death', I will assert that indeed it is of some significance as to where and how I came across the range of texts in my reading experience. Once again, I will look at this firstly in Chapter 3 as I situate myself within the world of poetry and more specifically, within poetry for children. This too, will be looked at in Chapter 4 as I look at some individual poems.

Then again, looked at from yet another perspective, it is also clear that the business of writing and speaking does not go on in a vacuum. There is a system which involves the writer (or speaker), the text (or speech), and the reader (or listener) (Voloshinov 1986). However, this is to oversimplify. The writer is him or herself the first reader and often changes the writing whilst being in that role. Meanwhile, readers and listeners making their reactions known, can have a time-linked effect on a writer's work over several years of reading and listening. The enquiry then will have to look at how these processes of reception affect what is written.

To work in these three areas, I shall proceed in the following way: firstly, in Chapter 1, I will look at some writers talking about writing poetry. I have confined this to writers working within my field i.e. those who have either written poetry for children, or writers who have sought to explain to children how their poetry came into being. As my predecessors in the field they will aid me in marking out the terrain I wish to occupy. Using some methods suggested by some of these writers, whilst avoiding pitfalls I feel they have not escaped, I will next, in Chapter 2, try to lay down the principles I intend to use in order to find the answers to that question: how did a set of poems come to be written? This will bring me into dispute with various ideas, in particular those of romanticism and post-structuralism, as the main drive of this thesis is one based on a form of materialism.

My next task in Chapter 3 will be to consider where I am coming from: on the one hand what kind of milieu did I find myself born into, and relating with as I grew up?

And on the other: what were my perceptions of the very field I have embarked on here – the writing of poetry and poetry for children? Here, I will make the assumption that I am an autonomous human subject but as Eagleton puts it, this is not 'one who miraculously conjures up him – or her – self out of nothing', but rather, it is 'someone who has been able to negotiate his or her freedom within those determinations set upon it both by nature, and by the right of self-determination of others' (Eagleton 1997: 269). In a sense, Chapter 3 then, will be a kind of autobiography, and so will pose a particular research problem: in this thesis what constitutes 'evidence'?

The legitimacy, indeed the necessity, of a researcher using his or her autobiography is one that has been argued for in the fields of anthropology, sociology and education. This 'reflexivity' (Scholte 1972) involves the observer 'apprehend[ing] himself as his own instrument of observation' (Levi-Strauss 1976:36).

In a pioneering piece of research, investigating boarding school education for girls, Okely, an ex-boarding school girl, described herself 'starting with the subjective, working from the self outwards' (Okely 1978:10) in order to grasp a different kind of truth, a different concept of lives lived than the one available from positivist-empricist methods. I am, in part, imitating her process in this thesis.

Usher reminds us that such a method 'draws attention' to the fact that 'the self that researches has an autobiography marked by the significations of gender, sexuality, ethnicity, class, etc.' (Usher 1996:38). This thesis, by its very terms of reference calls for an autobiographical approach. I am, after all offering an account of watching myself doing something, whereas

'. . . social researchers are engaging in representational practices whose outcomes purport to be truthful representations of a social reality whose members themselves engage in representational practices.' (Usher 1996:41)

What is peculiar to this thesis is that the equivalent of Usher's investigated 'members' of a 'social reality' is my self whilst the 'representational practices' they 'engage in' are, in this thesis, my poems and the process of writing them.

'Evidence' and 'data' in Chapter 3 then, will be of different kinds. Finding socioeconomic data in the post-war period can be distinguished from the process of excavating my memories of particular incidents. It will be necessary to find the socioeconomic material in order to substantiate Eagleton's comment about 'determinations'. This is available to all of us and the community of writers and readers of theses can argue with it as equals. However, much of the autobiographical material may well be, as Eagleton puts it, 'invisible to everyone but myself' (Eagleton 1997: 262).

Freeman points out that this collapses subject and object into one (Freeman 1993:5) and so intensifies the post-structuralist argument that perhaps all we have to go on are interpretations of interpretations. But Freeman asserts:

'. . . even if my "self', fleeting as it is, doesn't exist apart from my own consciousness of it, from my own narrative imagination, indeed from my own *belief* in its very existence, it is nonetheless eminently real and – within limits – eminently knowable.' (Freeman 1993:13)

This blunt assertion is the one followed in this thesis. Rose reminds us that the way we conceive of our psychological self is a material process, it is produced and assembled

> ' . . . through family albums of photographs, birthday cards, portraits, the dossier of school reports, the curriculum vitae and a whole series of practical accomplishments.' (Rose 1997:240)

This process, which I will be reproducing in Chapter 3, is analagous to archaeology, at least in that the archaeologist lives in his or her time, whilst the objects in the ground come from a previous era.

> 'The autobiographer of necessity knows as well as writes about his past from the limiting perspective of his present self image.' (Renza 1980:270)

Renza also points out an irony: it is not only the reader who is unable to verify the autobiographical evidence, the autobiographer cannot depend on readers, implied or otherwise, to 'substantiate his references' (Renza 1980: 294).

Eakin concedes that 'no one can ever confirm the existence of the self as an ultimate fact' but says that autobiographies themselves 'attest by their very existence to the reality of the autobiographical imperative' (Eakin 1985: 277). Doris Lessing in her autobiography claims that 'we make up our pasts' but then says 'you can actually watch your mind doing it, taking a little fragment of fact and then spinning a tale out of it.' (Lessing 1995:13). A little later she asserts that there are 'moments, incidents, real memory, which I do trust' (1995:13). In fact, the statement concerning 'spinning a tale' requires of Lessing and the reader to believe that it is itself a statement of truth, that there are real processes here of 'watching' and 'spinning'. She asks us explicitly to believe that there are some autobiographical moments that can be trusted but also asks us (implicitly) to trust in the realities of a) re-telling and b) self-observation. This thesis relies on these three kinds of trust: i) that there is 'real memory', ii) that some of my poems explored in Chapter 4 involve 'spinning' and iii) this process can be watched and described.

The main body of the work, (Chapter 4), will be to incorporate the ideas worked out in my second chapter into ways of analysing specific poems, twelve in all. These will not be textual analyses, but rather, considerations of different ways in which social environments, earlier texts and differing receptions have come to affect what and how I write.

Finally, in a Conclusion, I will look at the work done throughout the thesis and see whether I have been able to

1) find out how I came to write what I did,
2) establish any kind of practice or method that could be used by other writers or critics in their considerations of poetry and
3) offer any pointers towards a theory of authorship.

Chapter 1

I WOULD LIKE TO START THE process of considering the relationship between the 'creative work' (the body of poems for children) and the material, cultural and personal conditions of its construction by looking at three texts in which writers of poetry address questions of literary production. The writers I have chosen were or are concerned with young audiences either in the poetry they have written or in the discursive texts which are discussing the issue at hand. They are in chronological order: C. Day Lewis (1904-1972), Ted Hughes (1930-), and a recent American children's poet, Constance Levy (1935-). No matter what criticisms I make of these texts and no matter what implied comparisons I make between them and this thesis, I acknowledge that they are of very different status to the one I am writing here. The first two were addressed to children and teachers as creative aids to the writing and reading of poetry and the third was addressed to teachers alone with a view to inform them of poets' lives and work.

The texts by Day Lewis and Hughes have been chosen because of the poets' and their texts' pivotal positions in the discourse around poetry, children and education. Day Lewis published several books in the field, the one cited below, *Poetry for You, A Book for Boys and Girls on the Enjoyment of Poetry* (Lewis 1944) as well as *The Poetic Image* (London: Jonathan Cape, 1947) and *The Poet's Way of Knowledge* (Cambridge, Cambridge University Press, 1957). As late as 1984 this work still crops up in texts intended for teachers (Tunnicliffe 1984). Anecdotally, I can report that I myself was given *Poetry for You* by my parents (both of whom were teachers and subsequently teacher-educators) with the suggestion that it might be 'useful' or 'helpful' in my growing interest in poetry in the early sixties.

Ted Hughes took up a key position in relation to schools with his broadcasting for the 'Listening and Writing' series on BBC Schools Radio. This guaranteed him an entry into a large proportion of British primary schools. Alongside this work he has also been a judge or chairman of the country's major children's literary competition (first the 'Daily Mirror' then the re-sponsored 'W.H. Smith's') since 1964 and has in recent years helped produce three major anthologies: *The Rattle Bag* (with Seamus Heaney) (Heaney and Hughes 1982), *The School Bag* (Heaney and Hughes 1997) (with Seamus Heaney) and *By Heart, 101 Poems to Remember* (Hughes 1997) all of which are significant interventions into the field of poetry and education. The text cited below, like that of Day Lewis similarly appears and reappears in such books as *Tunnicliffe's Poetry Experience, Teaching and Writing Poetry in Secondary Schools* (Tunnicliffe 1984).

The third author I have chosen for very different reasons. I was interested in exposing this English literary tradition as exemplified by Day Lewis and Hughes to a different approach. The North Americans have long been as active, if not more so, than the British in exploring possibilities in the area of poetry, children and education and so I turned to American poets reflecting on their own practices to see if they offered different perspectives. As will be seen, the particular poet I cite, Constance Levy, struck me as someone who best exemplified some approaches that I could adopt or adapt for this thesis. However, it will not be claimed here that she occupies a pivotal, or indeed influential, position in the field.

In essence what I am pursuing here are explanations. Writers are often asked to provide explanations (or offer them anyway) of how certain pieces came into being, or to explain more generally how their creativity works. This thesis likewise is attempting to offer some hypotheses in the same area. One problem, as I see it, is one of 'necessary or sufficient' conditions. So, for example, whereas it is easy and obvious to say that it is 'necessary' to possess language in order to write poetry, it is clearly not a 'sufficient' condition. What I am looking at in this chapter are poets offering quite a few necessary conditions but not, in my view, providing sufficient ones. However, in the process of trying to provide these sufficient conditions, I will argue that two of the poets find themselves having to resort to what, for convenience sake, I will call 'mystification' and 'naturalisation'. That is to say, they tend to:

1) *mystify* mental processes, possible origins for their feelings and the linguistic structures they create; and/or
2) *naturalize* or *universalize* (see Eagleton 1991: 5, 56) their linguistic structures

16

or possible readers' responses to these structures.

I will argue later that these are flights from:

1) the material life on which all our existences are based,
2) the ideologies that contain our thoughts and statements,
3) various kinds of intertextual processes,
4) an acknowledgement of feedback from specific or idealized audiences. It is these limitations that I shall try to overcome in my own analyses in Chapter 4.

In other words I will not be looking at these authors from a traditional literary perspective, situating them say, in this or that literary tradition, but rather to examine their ideological assumptions and aporia. Thus, though it could be argued that both Day Lewis and Hughes occupy a position that owes some debt to the Romantics, in particular Wordsworth, Coleridge and Keats, I will be taking issue with these writers on a different territory – in relation to their current ideological positions.

1) Cecil Day Lewis

I would like to begin with Cecil Day Lewis (1944) whose text *Poetry for You, A Book for Boys and Girls on the Enjoyment of Poetry* was influential in education immediately after the war. The book was reprinted seven times in the three years after its first appearance. Clearly, it fitted a certain spirit in the post-war changes in schools. The 1944 Education Act, (the same date as the book) was intended to be a democratic advance on the old education system. Or to put it more cynically, it was the apparatus that would cope with the fact that Civil Service, managerial and professional jobs increased by 50 per cent between 1938 and 1951 (Sinfield 1989:53). The nature of the education within the grammar schools is of particular importance here: many grammar schools, in particular the prestigious ones, like my own, Watford Boys Grammar School (1962-1964), would offer a version of the Public School curriculum and ethos: Latin, Greek, prefectorial system, house system, officer training corps, rugby, not soccer, and the like. These structural and ideological changes have a bearing on how literature was taught: Francis Mulhern points out that there was a

'large-scale entry of a new social layer into the national intelligentsia' (Mulhern 1979: 318) and goes on to argue that by insisting that literary appreciation was not a class accomplishment but an individual attainment, F.R.Leavis in particular, rendered it suitable for teaching and examining. The irony here is that literature was presented as a universal culture, detached from the upper middle-class fraction that had produced and sponsored it, but it was at that very moment then used as a criterion for selection and the limited entry of middle-class and even working-class children into that 'national intelligentsia'. (I am an example of that process.)

So, *Poetry for You* with its welcoming title, informal punctuation ('don't'), slangy lexis (Whizzing', 'daft'), informal syntax and democratic tone, as here with:

> 'No, it's just untrue to say that poetry has nothing to do with ordinary men and women' (Lewis 1944: 4)

and open direct style of talking straight to the reader, as here with:

> 'When you are given a piece of toffee, or a nice dress, you don't sit about wondering what is the use of it: you put the one into your mouth, or your head into the other.' (Lewis 1944: 5)

make it very much the right book for the right time. Both my teachers and my parents recommended it to me, circa 1960. Lewis himself had impeccable credentials for the job as is evidenced by the book's cover note:

> 'C. Day Lewis was born in Ireland in 1904. As a boy he lived in London, and later was educated at Sherborne School and Wadham College, Oxford. For some years he was a schoolmaster, then gave up teaching to devote his whole time to writing. He is best known as a poet; his last book of verse, 'Word Over All', was published in 1943. He has edited two anthologies of verse, one of which, 'The Echoing Green,' is used in many schools. He has also written, under another name, several detective novels. He has done a good deal of poetry-reading for the B.B.C., and is very interested in the speaking of verse. His home is in Devonshire, but since 1941 he has been working in the Ministry of Information, helping to produce the official stories of the war.' (Lewis 1944: back cover note)

In this apparently rather innocent passage, Lewis is recommended to teachers and young readers. It seems clear that his own education within the elite, his work for the BBC and, interestingly, his work for the government are presented as presumably favourable attributes. There are certain assumptions here that, as we shall see, are relevant to other assumptions made about poetry within the book by Lewis himself. But, of course, it is also pointed out that Lewis is a poet, an anthologizer for young people and an ex-school teacher. As a composite picture it tells us that he belongs to a particular niche in society that one might call 'upper-middle class humanist'. (Incidentally, the writer of this thesis shares at least three of these attributes: educated at Wadham College, Oxford, works for the BBC and is an anthologizer for young people!) Lewis was also known by his association with Auden, Isherwood and Spender which perhaps signified a certain kind of left-wing optimism, an aspiration of a better world in which everyone and not just the elite would have access to the better things of life, including 'literature'.

I would like now to cite most of the chapter of the book in which Lewis looks at how a poem is put together. I am citing it at length, because, as will be seen, I am making some assertions that cover the whole text.

Chapter IV of *Poetry for You* from which this extract is taken is entitled 'How a Poem is Made'.

' . . . a poet may have many ideas and images, which could be the seeds of poems, but somehow they don't strike root – don't get deep enough into his imagination to fertilize it. And he can never tell which of his experiences is going to form itself into a poem, until the poem actually starts asking to be born. We might fairly apply the word 'inspiration' to this moment of the poetic process too – the moment when, with eager excitement, the poet realizes he is ready to create a poem. The best way I can describe this moment is to say that it's rather like switching on your radio to get some distant station: you move the dials, oh so delicately, there is a long silence, the instrument begins to warm up, and at last a faint voice is heard – words growing gradually more easy to hear and understand.

Where this inspiration comes from, nobody really knows. But obviously, just as you need a radio set to receive the sound waves sent out by a broadcasting station, so the poet needs a sensitive apparatus inside himself to receive the messages of inspiration. This apparatus is the poetic imagination. Everyone possesses some imagination: but the poet's has to be developed in special ways . . . You develop a muscle by exercising it. And the poet develops his imagination by exercising it.

He does this partly by writing poetry: he gets into the habit of writing poetry, and this habit is one of the things that distinguishes a real professional poet from the person who just writes a poem now and then for fun. He does it, also, by constantly playing with words, just as a conjuror absentmindedly plays with coins to keep his hand in: you can never be a poet unless you are fascinated with words – their sounds and shapes and meanings – and have them whirling about in your head all the time. Above all, the poet develops his poetic faculty through contemplation – that is to say, by looking steadily both at the world outside him and the things that happen inside him, by using all his senses to feel the wonder, the sadness and the excitement of life, and by trying all the time to grasp the mysterious pattern which underlies it. Yet, however devoted he is to his profession, however much he contemplates and practises, however skillful a craftsman in words he may become, a poet can never command inspiration. It may stay with him for months, or desert him for years. He does not know when it will come – or go. As Shelley said,

'The mind in creation is as a fading coal, which some invisible influence, like an inconstant wind, awakens to transitory brightness.'

'The flags, the roundabouts, the gala day'

Now I'm going to take you behind the scenes and show you how one of my own poems was written. I think it will help you understand what I've just been saying. Here is the poem:

Children look down upon the morning-gray
Tissue of mist that veils a valley's lap:
Their fingers itch to tear it and unwrap
The flags, the roundabouts, the gala day.
They watch the spring rise inexhaustibly-
A breathing thread out of the eddied sand,
Sufficient to their day: but half their mind
Is on the sailed and glittering estuary.
Fondly we wish their mist might never break,
Knowing it hides so much that best were hidden:

We'd chain them by the spring, lest it should broaden
For them into a quicksand and a wreck.
But they slip through our fingers like the source,
Like mist, like time that has flagged out their course.

The seed of this poem was a strong feeling I had about my own two children. It is a feeling most parents have, at one time or another – a feeling of sadness that their children must grow up, must leave their protection and go out into the dangerous and difficult world. When you are young, you sometimes resent your parents having that feeling: you want to grow up and be independent.

Now, if you look at the poem again, you'll see there are two themes, or subjects, in it – the original one, my own feeling, which comes out in the last six lines; and the children's feeling of impatience and expectation, which comes out in the first eight. These two themes are intended to balance and contrast with each other.

Before I actually start writing a poem, I often find a line of verse comes into my head – a line which gives me a clue to the theme and pattern which the poem will develop: a sort of key-line. When I sat down to begin this sonnet, such a line of verse at once came into my head. That line (it is the only one I didn't have to work for) was 'The flags, the roundabouts, the gala day.' I thought about this line, and saw that it was an image of a fete or a fair, the sort of thing a child looks forward to; obviously, it symbolized (that is, 'stood for') the grown-up world which a child is so impatient to enter. The idea of impatience then added some more lines – the first three. Here, the early-morning mist covering the valley represents the veil which the children wish to tear away, as they would tear the tissue-paper off a birthday present – the veil which shuts them off from the grown-up world. The image came out of my memory, recalled from a day several years ago when I was taking my children to school in Devonshire, and we paused at the top of a hill and saw the whole of the valley below covered with mist: I remembered thinking at the time that it looked like tissue-paper, but I'd forgotten all about the incident until I began to write this poem.

Next, I wanted a second image-sequence, as a variation on the theme expressed in the first four lines. You'll find it in lines 5 to 8 the picture of a spring bubbling up out of the earth, and children bending down to watch its 'breathing thread.' The word 'breathing' gives you a clue to the meaning of this passage: the spring represents life near its source, young life; and the children are only half satisfied with it; 'half their mind' is looking forward to the time when their life will have broadened out, as a stream broadens into an estuary, and become more important and exciting. The image of the spring, like that of the mist, came out of my memory it was a particular spring, near a country house in Ireland, which used to fascinate me as a child; I remember spending hours watching it, wondering how such a tiny thread of water managed to force its way out of the earth.

Next, the other theme had to be started – the parents' feeling about the children going out into the world. Notice that, although this theme was the original seed of the poem, it now occupies a relatively small space (lines 9 to 12): it often happens, when you are writing a poem, that you find the poem turning out quite differently from what you expected – in other words, you don't know what a poem is going to be like till you have gone some way with the composing of it; indeed, to a certain extent, a poem composes itself. Lines 9-12 say, quite simply, 'We grown-ups wish the mist of childhood might never break for our children, because when it does, they'll see the world is not such a pleasant place as they imagined. We'd like to chain them to their childhood, to save them from being hurt ("a quicksand and a wreck") as every one must sometimes be hurt by life when he grows up.' But the poem couldn't end like that, could it? After all, a parent can't really prevent his children growing up, even if it was right for him to try and do so – which it isn't. So, in the last two lines, I describe how children grow independent of their parents, slipping away from them as mist or water (the source') slips through one's fingers: they must fend for themselves, run their own race – and time has already 'flagged out their course.'

A corridor of mirrors

I wonder whether you have noticed something about those last six lines. Except for the quicksand and the wreck there are no new images in them. Even the phrase 'flagged out their course' (which, by the way, is another memory-image of mine, derived from a two-mile steeplechase I ran in as a boy of fourteen) – even this phrase echoes 'the flags' of line 4. Instead of using new images, I have repeated those

22

of the first eight lines – mist, the spring, the estuary ('lest it should broaden for them into a quicksand and a 'wreck'), the flags. In the last chapter I told you how important a part is played in poetry by repetition. It is not only words and phrases, but also images, which can be repeated. And they are repeated in this poem, so that you can see the two main themes from a number of different angles, just as you can see many different reflections of yourself if you walk down a corridor of mirrors.

Lastly, what I have told you about the sources of these particular images will help you understand how a poem grows. The seed of this poem took root in my mind. Then, without my being aware of it, it somehow attracted to itself several experiences I had had at quite different periods of my life and forgotten about. It got hold of a Devonshire mist, an Irish spring, and a steeplechase in Dorset; it added an estuary with yachts sailing on it (I still don't know where that last picture came from): and, when I began to write the poem, these four images rose out of my mind all ready to illustrate the theme . . . [in text]

The actual process of writing poetry, then, is rather like the process by which a diamond brooch is made. The poet digs into himself, as a miner digs into a hillside, to find the precious stones the themes and images of his poems. However skillful and hardworking a miner is, he will not find any diamonds unless there are some to be found there: and you won't get any poetry out of yourself unless it's there already – unless your imagination is so hot and strong that it has fused your experience into the precious stones which are the raw material of poetry, in the same way as certain chemical conditions are necessary for the making of diamonds beneath the earth's surface. You can't, in fact, write a real poem just by wishing to write one. When the diamonds have been mined, they must be selected, graded and cut before they can be used for an ornament. This process is equivalent to the work a poet has to do to make a finished poem out of the raw material his imagination yields him. And, just as the quality and size of the diamonds available to him affect the design of the brooch which the jeweller makes, so the nature and quality of our poetic material help to create the pattern of our poem.' (Lewis 1944: 34-40)

In this chapter Lewis has taken the reader through the process of putting together the poem 'Children look down upon the morning gray'. He has looked at Inspiration' and then talked about putting together the images of the poem. He has finished by trying to explain how this whole assemblage happened, or at least what it feels like to be a poet doing it.

So, in the first section, he says,

'a line of verse comes into my head' (Lewis 1944: 36)

or

'I wanted a second image-sequence' (Lewis 1944: 37)

or

'the poem couldn't end like that.' (Lewis 1944: 38)

The poem he is writing is a 'sonnet' (Lewis 1944: 36). But the problem with the passage as a whole is that there is no sense of what activity Lewis is engaged in, in a *cultural* sense. Why a sonnet? Where do sonnets come from? Who reads sonnets? What kind of culture does Lewis's own poetic voice belong to? All we can deduce from the passage is that this assembling of images *is* 'poetry' and Lewis *is* a 'poet'. Are there other kinds of poets? Can making 'poetry' be something quite different? There is something self-defining going on here. This would not matter were Lewis not in the business of saying that Lewis as poet represents 'poetry'. The implications of the cover-blurb quoted above begin to show here. This is a case of making ideology invisible.

On the matter of necessary and sufficient conditions, Lewis can *describe*:

1) using images, ('flagged out their course – derived from a two-mile steeplechase I ran in as a boy of fourteen' (Lewis 1944: 38));
2) repeating images (because it is 'important' (Lewis 1944: 38) and 'so that you can see two main themes from a number of different angles' (Lewis 1944: 39)); and,
3) even putting ideas into verse (tines 9-12 say, quite simply . . .' (Lewis 1944:38) or So, in the last two lines, I describe how . . .' (Lewis 1944: 38)).

The problem here is that these are not really *explanations*. So, we do not find here any explanation of *why* Lewis is conducting this highly specialised activity, (writing poetry), nor *how*, given this choice, this activity engages in a world of ideas, or takes part in a 'conversation' within which he is both person and poet. Indeed, one cannot find here any sense that the poem itself is part of any conversation at all (apart from with himself), or that there might be any milieu that is offering constraints and suggestions to Lewis the poet.

Then again, we do not find here anything concerning Lewis's highly specific intellectual formation that has placed him in a very particular slot in English cultural life, that might be determining many of the processes that he is describing. After all, he is not describing writing the lyrics of a popular song or the text of a comic strip. In fact, there is an irony in that though Lewis is paraded as a 'real professional poet' (Lewis 1944: 34) we do not have an idea of how this is a life-choice that goes beyond being someone who 'constantly plays with words' (Lewis 1944: 35), a life-choice which reaches right into decisions of what to write and how to write it. Being a professional poet, and coming from Lewis's particular formation within the elite, is the material base of his day-to-day existence (that is to say, it provides him with his remuneration) but we are never invited in to see how this shapes his creativity or affects the artistic decisions he makes. All we see is that he is some kind of special person who 'contemplates and practises' (Lewis 1944: 35) and, by implication, has a place within the pantheon of past greats such as Shelley (Lewis 1944: 35).

Mystification

The main way in which Lewis mystifies is through suggesting that the process of writing poetry is literally mysterious. One of the ways in which he does this is to personify 'poem':

> 'And he [the poet] can never tell which of his experiences is going to form itself into a poem, until the poem actually starts asking to be born.' (Lewis 1944: 34)

or:

> ' . . . to a certain extent, a poem composes itself (Lewis 1944: 38)

But there is also the notion in the first of these two examples that a poet can 'never' tell which of his experiences is going to become a poem. Can that really be so? By putting it like this, Lewis suggests there is something unfathomable and unreachable about how experience turns into poetry.

'Never' takes us into the unknowable as does:

'Where this inspiration comes from, nobody really knows.' (Lewis 1944: 34)

This becomes more serious, when, while talking about 'life' and poets writing about it, Lewis draws us into a web in which really everything is unknowable or at least 'mysterious':

' . . . the wonder, the sadness and the excitement of life, and by trying all the time to grasp the mysterious pattern which underlies it.' (Lewis 1944: 35)

Another area in which Lewis mystifies is where he tries to describe the arrival of images into his consciousness. These are 'a Devonshire mist, an Irish spring, and a steeplechase course in Dorset' and 'an estuary with yachts sailing on it' (Lewis 1944: 39).

He says,

' . . . these four images rose out of my mind all ready to illustrate the theme . . . ' (Lewis 1944: 39)

What he fails to grasp here is any notion that

1) these experiences,
2) the process of recalling them,
3) the process of them arising during the highly conventionalised process of writing a poem, or
4) the active selection of them as being suitable for inclusion in a poem might all be involved in a network of intertextual, cultural or ideological activity. (Needless to say, the class implications of running a 'steeplechase' and the impressive mobility of having experienced in prewar times a Devonshire mist, an Irish spring, a Dorset steeplechase and an estuary with yachts in it, are not examined.) In the following extract, we can see how the phrase 'somehow attracted' is used to cover all four of the processes mentioned above.

The seed of this poem took root in my mind. Then, without my being aware of it, it somehow attracted to itself several experiences I had

26

had at quite different periods of my life and forgotten about.' (Lewis 1944: 39)

Naturalization

Lewis engages in various kinds of literary sleight of hand as here:

> ' 'The flags, the roundabouts, the gala day.' I thought about this line, and saw that it was an image of a fete or a fair, the sort of thing a child looks forward to; obviously, it symbolized (that is, 'stood for') the grown-up world which a child is so impatient to enter.' (Lewis 1944: 36-37)

This classically ideological use of the word 'obviously' leads the reader into a rule-given game. This is where an image inevitably or certainly symbolises something else. In actual fact, we know that nothing could be further from the truth.

It is interesting to note here that Lewis, in explaining something of literary *production*, makes assumptions about a supposedly correct or inevitable literary *response*. Lewis writes according to some socially given, class-related (but not revealed) conventions. An implied reader, he suggests, will inevitably understand that certain psychological response procedures will unlock the code that he has set. But Lewis does not connect this inevitability with any person in a historical time or place, nor even, with a 'tradition'. It is merely an assumption, once again, I would suggest, emanating from the literary elite. It is, incidentally, the effortless means by which the literary elite maintains its superiority, its superior and hidden knowledge, at the very moment of seeming to offer it to 'ordinary men and women'.

Here again:

> ' . . . the early-morning mist covering the valley represents the veil' (Lewis 1944: 37)

What is revealed here by Lewis is the business of initiating the reader into a rule-given process without explaining where the rules come from

> 'The word 'breathing' gives you a clue to the meaning of this passage: the spring represents life near its source, young life' (Lewis 1944: 37).

Clearly,

1) reading poetry requires 'clues';
2) there is 'the' meaning which will only be available to you if you understand the rules; and,
3) what you may have thought was, simply a 'spring', in fact, according to some *unexplained* system, 'represents' something else that in many ways is quite unlike the source of a stream. Once again, we do not even find out here that this might be 'traditional' or conventional.

Conclusion

I think that it can be taken as read that what Lewis is doing here is done with the best of motives. He is trying to make accessible to a young audience how he put a poem together, in order to make poetry available to as many people as possible, both to read and write. However, my central argument is that by not reaching into explanations based either in the material world or that of ideology (nor even of 'tradition') he presents his readers with a fixed system that maintains itself with invisible rules. He presents himself as an owner of these rules, which, one might presume from what we know of Lewis (from the cover, say,) he acquired through his intellectual formation. And yet, mysteriously, this is never directly admitted. Similarly, though the book is crucial to the formation of an audience for poetry, (and indeed, addresses an audience very directly in its own diction), Lewis does not make any connections between his writing processes and possible or actual audiences: families, individuals or cultural groups with whom he must have been in conversation for over forty years prior to the appearance of this book.

2) Ted Hughes

I would now like to turn to C. Day Lewis's successor as Poet Laureate, Ted Hughes. His book, (1967) *Poetry in the Making, An Anthology of Poems and Programmes from 'Listening and Writing'* comes just over twenty years later than the one by Lewis. It occupies a similar niche in British education, in that it comes along in tandem with the BBC, from an adult, serious publishing house. Modestly, Hughes is not given any cover blurb, the book's link with the BBC programmes being thought sufficient to emblazon on the front, perhaps. So we know nothing here of the fact that Hughes by 1967 was a national figure (if only because of the Sylvia Plath episode), read on many if not most 'A-level English courses, and, as he reminds us in the introduction, a judge in what was then the *Daily Mirror* Children's Literary Competition. He proposes both by this and in what he says, a truly democratic principle:

> 'I assume that the latent talent for self-expression in any child is immeasurable.' (Hughes 1967: 12)

He says that the poems he includes are intended as 'models' whilst at the same time saying that:

> 'All falsities in writing – and the consequent dry-rot that spreads into the whole fabric – come from the notion that there is a stylistic ideal which exists in the abstract, like a special language, to which all men might attain. The words should be not "How to Write" but "How to try to say what you really mean" – which is part of the search for self-knowledge and perhaps, in one form or another, grace.' (Hughes 1967: 12)

So, the book rests on some important principles: absolute equality, and some kind of possible redemption through the writing of poetry. This redemption ('grace') will come about as a consequence of 'self-knowledge'. As we shall see later, when Hughes talks of saying what you mean, this becomes something deeply complex, and perhaps impossible. With a word like 'grace' he seems to be drawing on a quasi-religious tradition. Once again, it is my view that this is of limited use in offering *explanations* for literary production, no matter how suggestive it might be of the struggle to put feelings into words.

I will cite here, passages from throughout the book, relevant to the topic at hand.

> ' . . . we lived in a valley in the Pennines in West Yorkshire. My brother, who probably had more to do with this passion of mine [animals] than anyone else, was a good bit older than I was, and his one interest in life was creeping about on the hillsides with a rifle. He took me along as a retriever and I had to scramble into all kinds of places collecting magpies and owls and rabbits and weasels and rats and curlews that he shot. He could not shoot enough for me. At the same time I used to be fishing daily in the canal, with the long-handled

wire-rimmed mesh sort of net.

All that was only the beginning. When I was about eight, we moved to an industrial town in south Yorkshire. Our cat went upstairs and moped in my bedroom for a week, it hated the place so much, and my brother for the same reason left home and became a gamekeeper. But in many ways that move of ours was the best thing that ever happened to me. I soon discovered a farm in the nearby country that supplied all my needs, and soon after, a private estate, with woods and lakes.

My friends were town boys, sons of colliers and railwaymen, and with them I led one life, but all the time I was leading this other life on my own in the country. I never mixed the two lives up, except once or twice disastrously. I still have some diaries that I kept in those years: they record nothing but my catches.

Finally, as I have said, at about fifteen my life grew more complicated and my attitude to animals changed. I accused myself of disturbing their lives. I began to look at them, you see, from their point of view.

And about the same time I began to write poems. Not animal poems. It was years before I wrote what you could call an animal poem and several more years before it occurred to me that my writing poems might be partly a continuation of my earlier pursuit. Now I have no doubt. The special kind of excitement, the slightly mesemerized and quite involuntary concentration with which you make out the stirrings of a new poem in your mind, then the outline, the mass and colour and clean final form of it, the unique living reality of it in the midst of the general lifelessness, all that is too familiar to mistake. This is hunting and the poem is a new species of creature, a new specimen of life outside your own.

I have now told you very briefly what I believe to be the origins and growth of my interest in writing poetry.' (Hughes 1967:16-17)

With that postscript, Hughes sets out his stall. But to what extent should we take him at face value? There is the pleasing conceit of the idea of 'hunting' – hunting animals is like hunting for poems. He says,

'I think of poems as a sort of animal' (Hughes 1967: 15)

though later he elaborates this by saying: a is better to call it [a poem] an assembly of living parts moved by a single spirit' (Hughes 1967: 17).

As we are drawn into the delight of this metaphor, it is hard to bear in mind that Hughes is talking here about writing poems. He is also, by turning to an elongated metaphor, following directly in the tradition of C.Day Lewis in the closing section of the chapter I cited, when he talks of miners digging into hillsides for precious stones (Lewis 1944: 39). Perhaps it would be unfair to call this 'mystification' as metaphors do by their very nature offer some kind of illumination by comparison. And yet, in a passage of extended prose, there is a sense in which after the first flash of illumination, there is a problem: where, how, when and why do poems come? We know that, in actual fact, poems are not animals. They are, if nothing else, spoken, written, printed words. They are in that sense material objects embedded in the material production of sound, ink, paper, print, books, radio programmes, newspapers and so on (Voloshinov 1986: 11). Human beings, like Ted Hughes, who have had to earn a living, produce poems within this system.

But Hughes says that he is offering a description on the 'origins' of his 'interest' in poetry and its 'growth'. He has done this by setting up the metaphor, describing his life with his brother and interest in animals. Something is missing here. Thousands of young lads have, over the years, lived in rural locations, hunting animals with their older brothers and fathers. Some of them, like Ted Hughes, have even gone to grammar schools but, as we know, very few of them have written world-famous poems.

For a start we might ask, who are Hughes's parents? What exact milieu does Hughes come from? He tells us he lived in a 'valley in the Pennines' but as a farmer's son? Or as the son of a rural professional, like a doctor or vet or lawyer or teacher? Or is he, like John Clare, an auto-didact? By leaving this kind of information out, there is something cunning going on here that does indeed suggest something Clare-like. In fact, Hughes's father was an ex-carpenter turned newsagent-tobacconist, that is to say, someone we could describe perhaps as an artisan rising or aspiring to petit bourgeois status. However, Hughes presents himself as the rural boy immersed in animal life, not quite as pastoral idyll, but more as part of a 'natural' kill-or-be-killed, down-to-earth tradition. There is a Romantic implication that perhaps poems simply spring 'naturally' from this environment.

Then again, what of school? He tells us of distinctly working-class friends – which begs the question – why is he so precise about their class origins (sons of 'colliers' and 'railwaymen') but not his own? He does not make clear why there is a cultural clash. There are fascinating glimpses here of important cross-currents, a real struggle at adolescent self-definition, but nothing that offers explanations. The rush to complete the elongated metaphor of hunting seems to exclude these more mundane considerations. After all, we might ask, where did he meet 'poems'? Not in the wild presumably. On his parents' shelves? In the school library? In the mouth of an influential teacher? And what poems were they? For the listener and reader of these *Listening and Writing* programmes, whether as teacher or pupil, these are legitimate questions. Otherwise all one is left with is the notion that you can go out hunting for poems and you will find them. This, of course, ties in with Hughes's statement in the introduction concerning every child's 'latent talent for self-expression'. It is almost as if he is saying, 'They won't need to know all that stuff about reading lots of poetry, the classical and university education – it will put them off. I will suggest that writing poetry is difficult and exciting but above all linked to nature, if only savagely, – like hunting.' Is there also here an implication that children are near to this state, as he was, acting as actual or fantasy-driven hunters, wanting to be out there in the wild hunting down animals? The notion of child as savage runs very deep in our culture (see Cunningham 1991: 97-101).

So, just as Hughes *seems* to be offering us cultural and class explanations of where he comes from and how this leads to him becoming a writer of poems, he does precisely the opposite. He conceals – or it is hidden. What we have instead is a tease, a set of suggestions that may or may not be accurate but which leave us with all kinds of culturally resonant feelings about nature and the wild, difficult relationships with working-class boys, and something strangely exciting about the writing of poetry.

Quite why it is that Hughes and the BBC have thought that the best place to start with children and poetry is animals, is not revealed here. The whole ideology surrounding children and animals is a peculiar and complex one. This interest (is it obsession?) has the ideological advantage of offering up a classless dramatis personae on to which one can project all kinds of fantasies: omnipotence, fear, domination, loving, idealised family life and, if necessary, alternative class systems, as with, say, Babar the Elephant (see for example: de Brunhoff's *Babar the King* (1936)). How Hughes translated his experiences into 'animal poetry', or how and why he placed himself both within and in opposition to this tradition is not revealed here.

Then, we might look for some suggestion of audience. Just as we see the brother as a foil, companion and game-keeper perhaps we could have had a glimpse somewhere here of people witnessing Hughes the hunter, Hughes the talker, Hughes the tentative poet – all as possible explanations of what he himself calls 'the origins and growth of my interest in writing poetry.'

Now let's move on to the writing-process itself:

'An animal I never succeeded in keeping alive is the fox. I was always frustrated: twice by a farmer, who killed cubs I had caught before I could get to them, and once by a poultry keeper who freed my cub while his dog waited. Years after those events I was sitting up late one snowy night in dreary lodgings in London. I had written nothing for a year or so but that night I got the idea I might write something and I wrote in a few minutes the following poem: the first 'animal' poem I ever wrote. Here it is – The Thought-Fox.

I imagine this midnight moment's forest:
Something else is alive
Beside the clock's loneliness
And this blank page where my fingers move,

Through the window I see no star:
Something more near
Though deeper within darkness
Is entering the loneliness:

Cold, delicately as the dark snow,
A fox's nose touches twig, leaf;
Two eyes serve a movement, that now
And again now, and now, and now

Sets neat prints into the snow
Between trees, and warily a lame
Shadow lags by stump and in hollow
Of a body that is bold to come

Across clearings, an eye,
A widening deepening greeness,
Brilliantly, concentratedly,
Coming about its own business

Till, with a sudden sharp hot stink of fox
It enters the dark hole of the head.

The window is starless still; the clock ticks, The page is printed.

This poem does not have anything you could easily call a meaning. It is about a fox, obviously enough, but a fox that is both a fox and not a fox. What sort of fox is it that can step right into my head where presumably it still sits . . . smiling to itself when the dogs bark. It is both a fox and a spirit. It is a real fox; as I read the poem I see it move, I see it setting its prints, I see its shadow going over the irregular surface of the snow. The words show me all this, bringing it nearer and nearer. It is very real to me. The words have made a body for it and given it somewhere to walk.

   If, at the time of writing this poem, I had found livelier words, words that could give me much more vividly its movements, the twitch and craning of its ears, the slight tremor of its hanging tongue and its breath making little clouds, its teeth bared in the cold, the snow-crumbs dropping from its pads as it lifts each one in turn, if I could have got the words for all this, the fox would probably be even more real and alive to me now, than it is as I read the poem. Still, it is there as it is. If I had not caught the real fox there in the words I would never have saved the poem. I would have thrown it into the waste-paper basket as I have thrown so many other hunts that did not get what I was after. As it is, every time I read the poem the fox comes up again out of the darkness and steps into my head. And I suppose that long after I am gone, as long as a copy of the poem exists, every time anyone reads it the fox will get up somewhere out in the darkness and come walking towards them.' (Hughes 1967: 19-20)

In the passage preceding the citation of the poem, Hughes captures two fields: his relation to foxes and sitting in his lodgings. Here he is at his most concrete: farmers and poultry-keepers who kill foxes and 'dreary' 'London' lodgings. But also he adds in the feeling of frustration of not writing. In fact, the whole sequence, this passage, the poem and the passage that follows it, is a kind of commentary on the method, process, purpose and effect of writing itself. Events take place in Hughes's past; events take place in the present of writing that impinge on the writing process; he writes a poem that (amongst other things) reflects on how past images impinge on the present; he gives us a piece of writing that both conjures up the past events but also reflects on these matters; he writes a commentary that dissects some of all this.

Perhaps it is churlish to say it, but there is still quite a lot missing. Why should someone sitting in dreary lodgings late at night want to do that strange and peculiar thing: write a poem? Why should it be one that comes out in quatrains with an implied and actual rhyme system? Why should Hughes be setting up a situation of the *lone* writer and the *lone* fox? Both humans and foxes are social creatures and yet both occupy here a 'loneliness' (line 8) and both are 'Coming about its own business' (line 20). There is nothing inevitable about a fox, a man, and the writing of a poem which should dictate that aloneness is the matter in hand. However, it does happen that the mainstream of 'serious' poetry since the Metaphysical poets has occupied this territory. It is not so much that it is 'wrong' or misguided but that there are ideological implications here, the most obvious one being the implication that human beings are stuck in a kind of lonely separation from each other. As we shall see later this fits in with Hughes's words on experience in his concluding chapter. So, though the ideological implications are not spelt out here, later in the book connections are made.

In the following passage, Hughes addresses the problem of what it means to put thoughts into words and into poems:

'At school I was plagued by the idea that I really had much better thoughts than I could ever get into words. It was not that I could not find the words, or that the thoughts were too deep or too complicated for words. It was simply that when I tried to speak or write down the thoughts, those thoughts had vanished. All I had was a numb blank feeling, just as if somebody had asked me the name of Julius Caesar's eldest son, or said '7,283 times 6,956 quick. Think, think, think.' Now for one reason or another I became very interested in those thoughts of mine I could never catch. Sometimes they were hardly what you could call a thought – they were a dim sort of feeling about something. They did not fit into any particular subject – history or arithmetic or anything of that sort, except perhaps English. I had the idea, which gradually grew on me, that these were the right sort of thoughts for essays, and yet probably not even essays. But for the most part they were useless to me because I could never get hold of them. Maybe when I was writing an essay I got the tail end of one, but that was not very satisfying.

Now maybe you can see what was happening. I was thinking all right, and even having thoughts that seemed interesting to me, but I could not keep hold of the thoughts, or fish them up when I wanted them. I would think this fact was something peculiar to me, and of interest to nobody else, if I did not know that most people have the same trouble. What thoughts they have are fleeting thoughts – just a flash of it, then gone – or something, they just cannot dig those ideas up when they are wanted. Their minds, in fact, seem out of their reach. That is a curious thing to say, but it is quite true.

There is the inner life, which is the world of final reality, the world of memory, emotion, imagination, intelligence, and natural common sense, and which goes on all the time, consciously or unconsciously, like the heart beat. There is also the thinking process by which we break into that inner life and capture answers and evidence to support the answers out of it. That process of raid, or persuasion, or ambush, or dogged hunting, or surrender, is the kind of thinking we have to learn and if we do not somehow learn it, then our minds lie in us like the fish in the pond of a man who cannot fish.

Now you see the kind of thinking I am talking about. Perhaps I ought not to call it thinking at all – it is just that we tend to call everything that goes on in our heads thinking. I am talking about whatever kind of trick or skill it is that enables us to catch those elusive or shadowy thoughts, and collect them together, and hold them still so we can get a really good look at them.' (Hughes 1967: 57-58)

Once again this is a deeply *suggestive* passage but has its problems. He says,

'There is the inner life, which is the world of final reality, the world of memory, emotion, imagination, intelligence, and natural common sense, and which goes on all the time, consciously or unconsciously, like the heart beat.' (Hughes 1967: 57)

Now this strikes me as a remarkable claim: that the 'inner life' is 'the world of final reality'. The philosopher John Searle has asked what is in effect the opposite question: is there a reality out there that can go on without us knowing about it or taking part in it?

'. . . a fact is language independent if that very fact requires no linguistic elements for its existence.' (Searle 1995: 61)

The answer has to be yes, or we would not be able to operate as we do, understanding and using gravity or avoiding danger. Hughes, though, is suggesting that it is inside us where there is a final repository of everything. It is, in the way he has phrased it, a very individual thing: 'an inner life'. And it does not appear to have elements that are shared or constructed in or by social intercourse. Then in order to make contact with this 'inner life' we, individually, separated off from each other, rather like an angler (as opposed to a fishing crew trawling!) probe it. Once again, though the image is pretty, this has to be fallacious. Our probings of consciousness, if indeed that is what Hughes is referring to, are highly socialised activities, conditioned and constrained by such structures as the institutions of religion, psychology, philosophy, psychotherapy and the like. Indeed, if the image is of an angler then we need to think of him as dressed in culturally fixed angler's clothes and he has bought his rod, bait and tackle in an angler's shop. The angler fishes in socially designated and approved places and ways and is, as I have suggested, a 'he' not a 'she'. Once again, Hughes's image is of a lone consciousness. It has now become massive and supreme, divided off from its environment and social situation.

He then finishes the sequence with the fall-back position of this kind of writing – the use of words like 'elusive' and 'shadowy'. Just as Hughes invites his young listeners to go fishing for concrete experiences he seems to be saying that the process of doing it is beyond description. There is something teasing about this and, in the end, mystifying. It is almost as if Hughes is stuck with the problem of saying that everyone can be creative but only if we recognize that it is a mystical process. I can sense here a kind of claw-back: 'yes, everyone can be creative, but surely there must be something special about me, Ted Hughes?' We get a hint of this when he says:

'There are no words to capture the infinite depth of crowiness in the crow's flight.' (Hughes 1967: 119)

and:

' . . . words tend to shut out the simplest things we wish to say. In a way, words are continually trying to displace our experience. And in so far as they are stronger than the raw life of our experience, and full of themselves and all the dictionaries they have digested, they do displace it.' (Hughes 1967: 120) and:

> 'In our brains there are many mansions, and most of the doors are locked, with the keys inside.' (Hughes 1967: 121)

What is going on here? Hughes is saying that all this work to talk, write, and make poetry is in a way pointless. It cannot do what it claims to do: describe, and, moreover, it does something quite pernicious – it suggests that language might be a substitute for experience. This is really a bit much for a poet to be saying. At the very moment of making a living out of pinning down experience in new and interesting ways, he is saying that it is dangerous and impossible stuff.

He elaborates this. First he offers a humanistic model of language:

> ' . . . the events that are developing in us all the time, as our private history and our personal make-up and hour by hour biological changes and our present immediate circumstances and all that we know, in fact, struggle together, trying to make sense of themselves in our single life, trying to work out exactly what is going on in and around us, and exactly what we are or could be, what we ought and ought not to do, and what exactly did happen in those situations which though we lived through them long since still go on inside us as if time could only make things fresher.' (Hughes 1967: 123)

And then takes it away by saying:

> 'And all this is our experience. It is the final facts, as they are registered on this particular human measuring instrument. I have tried to suggest how infinitely beyond our ordinary notions of what we know our real knowledge, the real facts for us, really is. And to live removed from this inner universe of experience is also to live removed from ourself, banished from ourself and our real life.' (Hughes 1967: 123-124)

Here then we meet Hughes and twentieth-century anomie. Man alienated from himself. Though this is clearly a philosophy that underpins much of his poetry, (see 'The Thought-Fox' earlier) it is intellectually untenable. We are not 'banished from our real life'. Our real life is where we live, working, eating, sleeping, reproducing. We may feel alienated from these processes because as

Marx pointed out, we do not own them (Marx 1970a) or we are deprived of the fruits of our own labours. But the fact remains that we cannot live unless we participate in material existence, even if the way we participate is largely fixed for us.

So what Hughes offers is a lonely person, for whom words will not do the job we think they do, someone unable even to reach into himself. My contention here is that if you offer a model of a lone person (and a lone fox!) then it is no coincidence that the image of language use and consciousness you propose will be one in which you are banished from yourself. In fact, you have banished yourself from other people.

Interestingly enough, because Hughes must be ambivalent about the idea of saying that words are incapable, he finishes on a more optimistic, albeit mystical and metaphorical note:

'The struggle truly to possess his own experience, in other words to regain his genuine self, has been man's principal occupation, wherever he could find leisure for it, ever since he first grew his enormous surplus of brain. Men have invented religion to do this for others. But to do it for themselves, they have invented art, music, painting, dancing, sculpture, and the activity that includes all these, which is poetry.

Because it is occasionally possible, just for brief moments, to find the words that will unlock the doors of all those many mansions inside the head and express something – perhaps not much, just something – of the crush of information that presses in on us from the way a crow flies over and the way a man walks and the look of a street and from what we did one day a dozen years ago. Words that will express something of the deep complexity that makes us precisely the way we are, from the momentary effect of the barometer to the force that created men distinct from trees. Something of the inaudible music that moves us along in our bodies from moment to moment like water in a river. Something of the spirit of the snowflake in the water of the river. Something of the duplicity and the relativity and the merely fleeting quality of all this. Something of the almighty importance of it and something of the utter meaninglessness. And when words can manage something of this, and manage it in a moment of time, and in that same moment make out of it all the vital signature of a human being – not of an atom, or of a geometrical diagram, or of a heap of lenses – but a human being, we call it poetry.' (Hughes 1967: 124)

This is a kind of poet's manifesto, and offers much more than was allowed in Hughes's more pessimistic utterances. There are more signs of seeing human beings as social and poetry itself as a social phenomenon. There is even a classic concession to materialism which sees that poetry is linked to the biology of enough brain and the leisure allowed by freedom from subsistence. We see poetry as something 'invented' and not, say, floating down from heaven. These are, though, not much more than suggestions, and, to a certain extent contradict the thrust of much that has preceded it.

3) Constance Levy

I want now to turn to two books: Jeffrey S. Copeland (1993) *Speaking of Poets, Interviews with Poets who write for Children and Young Adults* and Jeffrey S. Copeland and Vicky L. Copeland (1994) *Speaking of Poets 2. More Interviews with Poets Who Write for Children and Young Adults*. These include interviews with many of the eminent American poets writing for young people over the last thirty years, people such as Arnold Adoff, Lilian Moore, Aileen Fisher, Karla Kuskin, Mary Ann Hoberman, Myra Cohn Livingston, Gary Soto, Eloise Greenfield, William Cole, Eve Merriam, Paul Fleischmann and Maxine Kumin. In the introduction to the first volume Copeland (J.S.) writes:

> 'We are now in an era in which poets understand a great deal more about the process of literary response, the process by which the children interact with their poetry. It is an era in which the study of children's poetry preference, a study still in its infancy, has given the poets the power to see within the psyche of the reader. It is an era in which poets speak to their readers not only through the images and ideas in a poem but also through extended notes, dialogues, and comments about how they view the nature of poetry and the wonders of childhood.' (Copeland 1993: xi)

Apart from the slightly gushing tone ('wonders of childhood') the serious point being made here is that many of the poets working in and around children and young people may well be teachers and ex-teachers, in contact with fellow teachers or what the Americans call teacher-educators. The institution of children's literature in North America is very much intermingled with big teachers' conferences and locally sponsored tours, conferences and workshops. This means that many of the writers represented in the book are in contact not only with children in schools but also many of the ideas around reader-response theory and child psychology. It is this kind of awareness to which Copeland is referring.

It should also be pointed out here that the whole tradition of what might be regarded as suitable in the way of poetry in schools in the USA shows some marked differences from the British approach. Along the axis of formal-informal, using markers such as: adherence (or not) to fixed poetic forms; use of colloquial language; inclusion/exclusion of day-to-day lived experience; inclusion/exclusion of a personal confessional tone, then the American approach to poetry in schools has tended to allow and encourage the informal. This is exemplified by the revered position held by a poet such as Carl Sandburg (1878-1967), whose slangy, free verse poems talked about skyscrapers, road-workers, jazz, cars, telephone exchanges and often reproduced proverbs, jokes, dialogues and the like (Sandburg 1950).

There is a wide range of responses to the Copelands' questioning but the questions themselves reveal an awareness of what produces a poet for young people. Here is the basic pattern of some kind of questionnaire (not reproduced in either book) which I have deduced from the articles and which seems to provide the framework for the poets' articles:

1) The poet's childhood and family background.
2) A particular spark that started the poet off.
3) Major influences on the poet.
4) How the poet's publishing career began.
5) How the poet wrote a specific poem.
6) What are the physical conditions of the poet's writing.
7) Particular features of the poet's writing such as 'imagery' or 'alliteration'.
8) Particular themes in the poet's writing.
9) Plans for the future.
10) Suggestions for young writers.
11) Special message for the poet's readers or special advice for people who want to introduce the poet's work to young readers.

There are various assumptions here that are worth mentioning:

1) Childhood and family background are seen as a first priority in a description of a children's poet, but later work (apart from professional writing) crops up only incidentally. However, the professional life as a writer is seen as significant.

41

2) The question of literary influences is seen as important – no poet is seen is separate from literary traditions.
3) Somewhere in the interview writers are invited to describe their relationships with their audiences.

These three areas of concern make it likely (though not certain) that various key elements behind literary production are included. There is a very good chance that writers will have to consider where they are coming from in a cultural and/or material sense. And indeed many of them

1) take on board in some way or another that they exist in an intertextual world and
2) consider how in some way or another they relate to their audience.

That said, looking across the whole body of interviews the question does not determine that the connections are made all the way from the implied field of any specific question through to aspects of poetic composition. Some of the poets seem able to keep each of the fields sealed off from each other: their childhood experience, say, seeming to have little to do with their predisposition to read a certain kind of author.

I want to take a closer look at one poet in particular: chosen as she is the one who answers the questions most thoroughly and who makes the most connections between the fields. She is Constance Levy, who at the time of the interview, 1994, had published two books of poetry for young people: (1991) *I'm Going to Pet a Worm Today and Other Poems* (New York: McElderry/Macmillan) and (1994) *A Tree Place and Other Poems* (New York: McElderry/Macmillan). I should point out immediately that Levy's interview/article is nowhere near as grandiose as either Day Lewis's or Hughes's books. It is short, down-to-earth and without any sense that final words or summatory judgments are being given. The tone is enthusiastic rather than pontificatory.

Here are some of my observations on the interview with Constance Levy (Copeland and Copeland 1994: 127-139):

1) Background

We gather that Levy comes from a modest family, daughter of self-educated, European immigrants:

'I grew up in St Louis, Missouri, in a three-story, six-family apartment with my parents, older sister, maternal grandmother, and my mother's brother and sister, my favorite uncle and aunt.' (Copeland and Copeland 1994: 127)

and:

'My parents had both immigrated to this country as children around the turn of the century. My mother arrived from Russia when she was seven and my father at age fourteen from Lithuania. Neither of them was able to attend high school because they had to go to work, a necessity in those days. So, beyond elementary school they were self-educated. My father was an avid reader of newspapers and magazines, and my mother was a lover of poetry. She remembered poems she had learned in school and frequently recited them for me. I really loved listening; she recalled them with such pleasure, and the music of her words introduced me to another dimension of language. I am convinced that my love of poetry began there.' (Copeland and Copeland 1994: 127-128)

She locates her interest in poetry as deriving from her mother but also sees her father providing a particular kind of urban input derived from her family's socioeconomic role in a particular place and time.

'My father operated a men's clothing store across the Mississippi River in East St. Louis, Illinois. At that time East St. Louis was a bustling town where farmers would bring their livestock to the stockyards. His store was near these stockyards. He worked long hours, but on Sundays he always found interesting places to take us in St. Louis. The zoo was one of his favorites. We knew every inch of the zoo and much of surrounding Forest Park.' (Copeland and Copeland 1994: 128)

But the nuclear family was in touch with an extended family which was strong on oral culture:

'Aunts and uncles and cousins visited us often. One uncle played the piano for sing-alongs, and everyone talked and joked and enjoyed each other's company. For me, the best company was that of people who could make you laugh. The way you say things to make something humorous has always fascinated me. I didn't realize it then, but I know now that there is a close relationship between jokes and poetry, the choice of the right words for sound as well as meaning, the timing, the rhythm, and the effective punch line. Somehow I believe now that my feeling for the art of words found a lot of nourishment back then with the family conversations and joking, and maybe we should add Jack Benny and Fred Allen on the radio.' (Copeland and Copeland 1994: 128)

Missing here, perhaps as part of a certain coyness, is a willingness to say that this background is Jewish – I would guess from

1) the name 'Levy' (albeit perhaps her husband's),
2) the countries of origin of her parents and
3) the family's trade in the garment industry. This means that the self-education, the humour and the oral culture are not fully explained.

Quite clearly, the background was strong on positive feelings, affirming parenting which has left Levy with strong and vivid memories of small pleasurable actions in her childhood:

'When I was very small I was always digging holes in the ground. I really thought I could reach China if I dug deeply enough. I wasn't sure, but just maybe . . . You find interesting things when you dig, not just worms and rocks. I found arrowheads often, sometimes even the prized flint arrowheads. I also remember playing with ants a lot and letting them crawl over my hands. I liked the tickle, a lingering sensation even in memory.' (Copeland and Copeland 1994: 129)

She then makes a direct link between these memories and what she wants to celebrate in her poetry:

'I also loved big expanses of grass like those we found in Forest Park. We would run out in a field and twirl around until we were too dizzy to stand. If there was a nice, soft-looking green hill, we rolled down like logs. I can still feel the softness and the scratchiness and smell the earth and the greeness. I'm just now working on a poem about that. When I see such a hill now I still get the urge.' (Copeland and Copeland 1994: 129)

She turns this into an ideological and pedagogical point:

Parents and teachers need to remember what it feels like to be a child. Poets need to do this, too; they need this memory to capture childhood in the lines.' (Copeland and Copeland 1994: 130)

There is some way in which Levy seems to see an unbroken continuity between her childhood and her present, during which she has always been writing poems. The source of this is made clear (given the space) as coming from the self-educated background of a literate lower middle-class immigrant family full of communal oral culture. We can assume that this background was full of ambition for its children but within this interview this is not revealed as stressful or oppressive.

It is difficult to see from the interview the exact links and connections between wanting to write poetry, writing poetry that celebrates childhood, and producing poetry that is intended for a child audience. We can presume from her mentioning of herself as an ex-reading specialist that much of her life she has been a teacher, but this evolution is not explored, nor are these crucial links with the poetry.

2) Influence

Though Levy does not express this as intertextual awareness . . .

'I remember Christina Rossetti's 'Who Has Seen the Wind?' and Robert Louis Stevenson's 'The Swing' most of all. My swing was in the schoolyard, but Stevenson's let me see rivers and cattle and countryside through his eyes.' (Copeland and Copeland 1994: 130-131)

. . . she makes the important observation that:

'I think we are drawn to writers that we share something with, those who write the way we would like to write, those who see the world in a similar light, or who simply delight us. And maybe it is also because they reassure us that we are on the right track.' (Copeland and Copeland 1994: 131)

There is a sense here that to write with certain kinds of themes and with certain kinds of forms is to join a certain kind of mini-culture, where it is possible to have intimate 'conversations' with other writers dead or alive. Later, she talks about other kinds of real conversations with children and teachers – the combination of all these providing the crucial feedback systems that sustain specific kinds of writing. This emerges much more clearly here than with either C. Day Lewis or Ted Hughes.

3) Writing Situation

Levy describes the situations that lie behind the writing of two poems Dawn Watch' and 'Rah, Rah Peas!' In the first case, she is graphic about the actual material conditions of the sunrise but is unable or unwilling to make connections between the raw experience, her cultural interest in such a phenomenon, her convention-bound interest in turning this into a poem, and the intertextual threads that help produce the specific diction of the poem itself.

'I was taking a walk one morning before the sun had come up. Sometimes early in the morning there is a seepage of light that comes around the horizon. The sun isn't up yet, but there is a certain light that comes up. Well, this particular morning I looked up into the sky suddenly and realized there was a line of demarcation, almost a straight line, directly above me. It was still night on one side of this line with the moon still shining and the stars still twinkling. On the other side there was a yellowish light. There were no stars or other signs of night on this side of the line. I was very excited about this because I was walking right down the middle. I put one arm out and it was in the night. I put the other arm out and it was in day. I just walked a while that way. I was very excited about this and started thinking of the poem as I was walking home. It was very frustrating because I had to keep saying lines over and over as I walked home so I wouldn't forget them. When I got home I jotted down a few words and lines. And, as I always do, I came back to it later, worked it over and over, and eventually finished it.' (Copeland and Copeland 1994: 134)

However, in the second example, 'Rah, Rah Peas!', some of this becomes a little clearer:

> 'In contrast to this was the writing of 'Rah, Rah Peas!' I wrote this one because I really had to tell how I felt about raw peas. To this day, I love eating fresh, raw green peas right out of the pod. Many children don't even know where peas come from. I found that out while sharing poetry with children in the schools. You learn so much them. Well, when I would tell children how much I love green peas, some would say, 'Aw, peas!' I remember saying, 'Don't say, "Aw, peas." Try some raw peas!' I knew right away this was a line I could use. I started working on this poem, and each time I came back to it I realized it was starting to sound like a cheer. I decided that was what the poem wanted to be, so I went along. Now when I do the poem in schools with children or in workshops with teachers, we do it as a cheer. We all stand up and do cheerleader movements while shouting, 'Don't say, "Aw, peas!" Try some raw peas!' At the very end, after we say the last line, we throw our arms out and say, 'Hooray!' and clap. Usually they want to do it over and over, and they have had marvelous times – so have I! It's good exercise too!' (Copeland and Copeland 1994: 134)

Levy situates the writing of the poem very firmly in a feedback situation with her audience in a twofold way: 1) in that she observes children not really knowing the biology of peas 2) a verbal structure or mannerism produced by the children. It is not clear from Levy exactly why this triggers the response: 'write a poem' unless we piece it together from all that has preceded this moment in the interview.

However, there is a clear presentation of the intertextual oral culture that she takes part in to produce her 'cheer'. This means that her poem immediately becomes a form recognizable to the children and in which they know how to participate.

4) Her Present Professional Conditions and Considerations

Later in the interview we see that Levy is 'a reading specialist' who has made a decision to de-professionalise herself, and re-invent herself as a peripatetic creative artist.

'I became certified as a reading specialist, but I decided that rather than teaching full time I would be more effective by becoming a visiting writer in the schools for the Missouri Arts Council. I found as I went into the schools to read poems and share ideas with them that children would come to me with little pieces of paper with poems on them that they had written while I was reading and talking with them. That's when I realized children really can write poems very easily when they are inspired by hearing poems read aloud. They all enjoyed listening. They seemed to have been starved for lack of it and wanted to hear their own favorites over and over. Teachers who bring poetry into their classrooms become as enthusiastic about it as I am. They find children are writing things that are beyond what they had expected of them.' (Copeland and Copeland 1994: 139)

Interestingly, she says that this makes her 'more effective'. It is clear that she does not intend this simply to signify so-called 'reading skills' but that she is able to create situations in which the children themselves can join in these poetry-conversations as participants. There is a strong implication here of classic democratic principles that are often expressed in America in a 'you-can-do-it' kind of way. One can hear in this passage the re-interpretation of the American constitution that Dewey and other classic liberals used to try and liberalize American early childhood education (see Dewey 1902: 22) notwithstanding Karier's criticisms of Dewey's conversion to education serving capital (Karier 1976: 90-97).

5) Conclusion

In an unassuming, jargon-free exposition Levy takes us into some key areas of literary production. She avoids mystification, and though she is inclined to homogenize differentiated children into one idealized child, she mostly avoids naturalization too. However, her creativity is grounded in material life and events, along with some kinds of intertextual and feedback activity. These approaches offer some clear pointers of how I can proceed in the examination of my own work.

There is a mysterious lacuna around her immigrant background but it is not clear how significant this is. And, perhaps as a consequence of the interview format, some crucial connections between the fields are not made. However, in a down-to-earth way Levy and her interviewers provide some useful explanations for literary production.

Chapter 2

IN THIS CHAPTER I WOULD LIKE to show the theoretical basis I will be using when approaching my own work. What I am looking for are essentially some explanations for, and insights into the genesis of my poems. To do this, I will be trying to deal with such questions as:

1) how might we distinguish between existence and expression?
2) how is this matter affected by the social, literary and ideological environment?
3) how does the question of audience become relevant, whether speaking of actual or imagined audiences of the work or, more specifically, in relation to how I read my own work?

To explore this territory I will be drawing on work that has looked at:
1) Materialism
2) Intertextuality and questions of discourse.
3) Reception and response theory.
4) Ideology
5) The self

1) Materialism

i) Some first principles

The problem around materialism is one that has divided the post-modern world. In essence the question is whether we can accept that there is a material world that exists independently of human existence or whether what we perceive is constructed by our consciousness and/or by the texts (Frow 1990;

Shotter 1993) and/or discourses that we create. The immediate problem for me both as writer and self-critic is to delineate a material actuality in which I have lived and am still living and to show that this has in some very complex ways affected what and how I write. In this thesis I will wish to assert that when I refer to some 'stairs' in a poem these were once real material stairs that human beings as material beings trod upon but, *of which*, as conscious beings, we can make many diverse images, constructs and symbols. I use the word 'assert' in the previous sentence because anything that a materialist takes as 'proof' of the material world, can be turned by a post-modernist into a 'text' in itself. Using the term 'textualism' to describe the theoretical practice of suggesting that everything is in the final analysis a text, Callinicos puts it like this:

> 'Textualism . . . denies us the possibility of ever escaping the discursive. Ii n' y a pas de hors-texte as Derrida famously put it.' (Callinicos 1985: 86)

My assertion, 'reality exists', comes on what might be called the 'agreement principle'. That is to say, all human beings behave as if gravity existed. All human beings accept that they need food, water and shelter otherwise their bodies will not survive in their present form. We are in de facto agreement.

The philosopher Roy Bhaskar (1989), who has taken up cudgels with the post-modernists in *Reclaiming Reality, A Critical Introduction to Contemporary Philosophy*, points out that though social practices might be dependent on concepts it does not follow that this 'exhausts' their existence. Social practices . . .

> ' . . . always have a material dimension. This is an important consideration, as reflection on the prevalence and impact of the phenomena of hunger, homelessness and war upon so much of human history shows.' (Bhaskar 1989: 4)

He puts it more wittily later on:

> 'The concept 'dog' cannot bark but real dogs do . . . and would do without their concept.' (Bhaskar 1989: 45)

Bhaskar is a Marxist and is joined by a group working in Washington and one of them, Teresa L. Ebert slims the argument down to an aphorism:

> 'The fact that we understand reality through language does not mean reality is made by language.' (Ebert 1995: 117)

and, drawing on Marx, adds:

> '... issues about the 'nature of individuals' – gender, sexuality, pleasure, desire, needs – cannot be separated from the conditions producing individuals: not just the discursive and ideological conditions but most important the material conditions, the relations of production, which shape discourses and ideologies.' (Ebert 1995: 127-128)

So Ebert extends the argument into the question of 'the conditions producing individuals' which leads her to the key Marxist idea of 'the relations of production' which I will consider below. She is saying that 'discourses' do not float free of how we organise ourselves into producing the things we, as the human race, need and survive by. Callinicos in another attempt to nail the problem points out that Marxism denies that 'discourses are autonomous' . . .

> '... this means: first, our talk has extra-discursive referents; secondly, among these referents are the social practices partially constitutive of discourse.' (Callinicos 1985: 87)

So, not only is 'discourse' 'shaped by' what goes on in material existence, Callinicos is saying that discourse is partially made up of material existence. I take this as suggesting that our oral and written interchanges cannot escape from bearing the traces of our socioeconomic existence.

It is assertions like these, that 'post-Marxists' and indeed anti-Marxists find hard to swallow. For some (see Bennett 1990; Jackson 1994) it is inevitably and finally some kind of determinism. Others, like Christopher Norris (1981), make the claim that as language is the only means by which reality can be described, then language is all we know. The ultimate denial of reality as a referent comes from 1) De Man, who famously wrote:

> '. . . the bases for historical knowledge are not empirical facts but written texts, even if these texts masquerade in the guise of wars or revolutions' (De Man 1983: 165)

and 2) Hayden White, who when referring to the 'intuitions' of Hitler and Mussolini wrote:

'One must face the fact [(!) MR] that when it comes to apprehending the historical record, there are no grounds to be found in the historical record itself for preferring one way of construing its meaning over another.' (White 1987: 74)

In other words, according to de Man and White there are no reliable or realist referents for meaning, a position that war victims, holocaust survivors and their relatives, for example, find impossible to tolerate. It is precisely these positions taken up by de Man and White with which this thesis takes issue.

Put in a Saussurian way, meaning is supposedly not to be found in the relation between words and objects but between words (signifiers) themselves, in their differences. This in turn has led to Lacan's theories and an explosion of ideas around the alleged failure of language to refer, illuminate and define. Instead, all one can find is a lack, an absence and inevitable imprecision (Eagleton 1983: 166-169).

These theories not only eliminate the material, they also excise the social, the fact that 'language' is in reality always 'language-in-use', and 'language-in-use-in-specific-historical-circumstances'. This means, as Bakhtin observed, that language is

'populated – overpopulated – with the intentions of others.' (Bakhtin 1981: 294)

Imprecision or failure of understanding between people derives from the fact that words and sentences are *sites of contest* for meaning between individuals participating in social existence, thus the amazing toings and froings over a word like 'nigger' or 'nigga' in the mouths of say a white supremacist policeman in 1965 and a rapper in 1990.

Though there is no room given to 'textualism' in this study, a determinist model of language is rejected too. That is to say, it is not claimed here that social circumstances simply determine, or produce a form of language. Language-in-use arcs back on the social circumstances that produce it. Marx was aware of this when arguing with the crude materialists of his day. In the *Theses on Feuerbach* he put it like this:

'Thesis 3 The materialist doctrine about change of circumstances and education' [i.e. those materialists in Marx's time who were saying that the material world simply determines all existence] 'forgets that circumstances are changed by men and the educator himself must be educated.' (Marx 1965: 665-667)

In other words Marx recognised a dialectic in which we are shaped by material reality but we ourselves also shape circumstances. This is perhaps most clear when looking at a landscape and the art connected with it. Liberal critics, unwittingly behaving like vulgar Marxists, will frequently describe artists and writers as being 'shaped' by a certain landscape – a description that overlooks three facts:

1) landscapes are purely physical environments and cannot of themselves 'shape' consciousness. It is only in the interaction of the writer's consciousness with the landscape that effects manifest themselves;
2) almost every landscape on earth has been materially shaped and affected by human activity, (as evidenced, say, by the pollution found even in the Antarctic) and
3) in re-imaging and picturing that landscape artists and writers affect how that landscape is materially treated – as shown by tourism and, say, the phenomenon of 'Bronte country'.

It was in the collection of essays known as *The German Ideology* that Marx made his most extended arguments on this matter:

'..at each stage [of history] there is found a material result: a sum of productive forces, a historically created relation of individuals to nature and to one another, which is handed down to each generation from its predecessor; a mass of productive forces, capital funds and conditions, which, on the one hand, is indeed modified by the new generation, but also on the other prescribes for it its conditions of life and gives it a definite development, a special character. It shows that circumstances make men [sic] just as much as men make circumstances.' (Marx 1965: 50-51)

This, in brief, is the essential position that I am adopting in this study. As a notion it has been rephrased many times since, sometimes by Marx himself, often by people calling themselves Marxists who have crudely ignored the phrase 'as much as men make circumstances'. What is crucial here is that Marx is claiming that there is a basic material situation within which we must act and which we cannot ignore. It is specific in time and place and has a particular character. The overriding influence on that character is here encapsulated by the phrase 'a mass of productive forces'. From what we know of Marxist thought this is a shorthand phrase to mean, in effect, the following:

1) the stage of development in technology and the particular form of social organisation that delivers the making, distributing and servicing of everything we need in order to survive, flourish and procreate;
2) the specific ways in which human beings are organised and ruled in order to make, produce and service.

These two ideas Marx described as the 'forces of production' and the 'relations of production' (Marx and Engels 1965: 27-87). So the fully fleshed out Marxist view of the material world cannot be restricted to observations on the nature of objects: rocks, forks, walls and the like. Marx and Marxism moved materialism on from there. It encompasses the notion that human beings are acting on materials, engaged in material processes as part of the essential efforts to feed and clothe themselves and provide the conditions for procreation. In order to engage in these processes human beings put themselves into various different social forms ('modes of production') and these too are part of the material world. Moreover, Marx was at pains to point out that in engaging in these processes, human beings change:

> 'Labour is in the first place , a process in which both man and Nature participate, and in which man of his own accord starts, regulates and controls the material re-actions between himself and Nature. He opposes himself to Nature as one of her own forces, setting in motion arms and legs, head and hands, the natural forces of his body, in order to appropriate Nature's productions in a form adapted to his own wants. By thus acting on the external world and changing it, he at the same time changes his own nature.' (Marx 1954: 173-4)

In passing, I will make the observation here that the last statement in this citation, located as it is in human labour, is at the heart of my understanding of how it is that as we write we change ourselves. However, all of us are situated around the act of labour in a variety of positions: selling labour, buying labour, profiting from the fruits of labour through rent and interest payments and dividends, controlling labour, supervising labour, training labour for the labour market and so on. The key matter for an individual and, in my case, for a writer, is where in the 'mode of production' do I sit ? By way of answering that question in this study I will be looking at the particular social formation and the particular moment in history I was born into, grew up in and now work in. Balibar and Macherey suggest the writer is active (an 'agent') but constrained by 'conditions' in which 'he' lives, 'contradictions' in the way society runs, and the ideological milieu:

> ' . . . the writer . . . is a material agent, an intermediary inserted in a particular place, in conditions he has not created, in submission to the contradictions which by definition he cannot control, through a particular social division of labour, characteristic of the ideological superstructure of bourgeois society, which individuates him.' (Balibar and Macherey 1992: 49)

I will say here that the question of 'contradiction' is an elaborate one, but signifies the idea from Marx that at any given time, a society based on profit and not human need will set up contradictions that work their way through to our individual existence. So, as an example of a Marxist 'contradiction', it can be seen that we are guided in our upbringing and through the consumer society to acquire personal wealth, be *individualistic*, – 'look after your own' – and yet the production and distribution of all goods and services is *co-operative*. Contradictions and conflicts emerge in society at large when the only way that people can provide for themselves as *individuals* is for them to act *collectively* against production and distribution. Or again, a huge amount of time and effort is put into pleading with us to desire: to desire a massive amount of goods, consumables and leisure services but most people do not have the time or the money to *acquire* or enjoy them. Or again, there is the free movement of capital but not the free movement of labour (immigration laws); the free movement of capital but not the free movement of ideas (as with the use of the libel laws and the lack of a freedom of information act) and so on.

To continue with the broad question of materialism, Bhaskar puts a slightly different tilt on it by suggesting that a 'person's individuality' is made up (constituted) by where they have been (and continue to be) situated socially.

'In other words, what they are is mainly a product of what they have done or what has been done to them in the particular social relations into which they were born and in which they have lived. What they do or have done to them must be understood in terms of their historically and socially conditioned capacities, powers, liabilities and tendencies.' (Bhaskar 1989: 7)

I will be exploring this area of 'historically and socially conditioned capacities, powers, liabilities and tendencies' as understood in the materialist context described here, in the next chapter and in relation to individual poems in Chapter 4.

I. Materialism (continued)

ii) Materiality of language and writing

Though, as I have said, it has been fashionable to see language as the means by which we construct reality (e.g. Shotter 1993), the Marxist view is that language arises and develops in specific milieus, within specific historic modes of production. Language as a product of human beings' consciousness has the capacity to be part of the ways in which human beings influence each other. However, 'language' does not have the power to affect consciousness on its own. It is language-in-use, within the specific social formations that human beings make, that has that power.

The first person to explore this coherently was V.N. Voloshinov. His starting point was to make clear that language itself has a material aspect. This has particular significance when talking of consciousness and its expression in language.

'Every phenomenon functioning as an ideological sign has some kind of material embodiment, whether in sound, physical mass, color, movements of the body, or the like . . .

. . . *consciousness itself can arise and become a viable fact only in the material embodiment of signs.*' (Voloshinov 1986: 11)

(original italics and in all citations that follow)

'1. *Ideology may not be divorced from the material reality of sign* (i.e. by locating it in the 'consciousness' or other vague and elusive regions);
2. *The sign may not be divorced from the concrete forms of social intercourse* (seeing that the sign is part of organised social intercourse and cannot exist, as such, outside it, reverting to a mere physical artifact);
3. *Communication and the forms of communication may not be divorced from the material basis.*' (Voloshinov 1986: 21)

Here is a strenuously asserted anti-idealist view of consciousness, ideology, communication and language – not as is usual from the basis that these 'superstructural' features are 'produced' by the 'economic base' – but that consciousness and the like can only be perceived (become a viable fact') in material forms.

Voioshinov does not then go on to explore what follows from this: namely that if these forms are material, then they themselves are inseparable from material production. Thus: the materialist view of, say voice production, is that among the determinants of tone, timbre, volume, effort and pitch of a speaker/ performer like myself are his or her social conditions, his or her position (and that of his or her parents) in the mode of production. The same applies in part to writers. The forms of the book, the newspaper, the pamphlet, the script are material forms that owe their origins, specific shape and their persistence to stages in development in society – developments in education, a certain class's wealth and available leisure-time and the like. My own gestures and facial expressions as a performer of my own poems in schools are material signs that bear witness to aspects of class which in turn originate in specific positions in relation to the mode of production in a historical time and place.

However, just as language in its distribution by mouth or print is material, so it has been argued that writers are enclosed within a semi-autonomous economic world that is itself one of the determinants on writing. Pierre Bourdieu has called this: 'the field of cultural production' which he claims has its own material dynamic:

1. Materialism (continued)

iii) Material conditions of writers

'Given that works of art exist as symbolic objects only if they are known and recognized, that is, socially instituted as works of art and received by spectators capable of knowing and recognising them as such, the sociology of art and literature has to take as its object not only the material production but also the symbolic production of the work i.e. the production of the value of the work or, which amounts to the same thing, of belief in the value of the work. It therefore has to consider as contributing to production not only the direct producers of the work in its materiality (artist, writer, etc.) but also the producers of the meaning and value of the work – critics, publishers, gallery directors and the whole set of agents whose combined efforts produce consumers capable of knowing and recognising the work of art as such, in particular teachers (but also families, etc.). So it has to take into account not only, as the social history of art usually does, the social conditions of the production of artists, art critics, dealer, patrons, etc., as revealed by indices such as social origin, education or qualifications, but also the social conditions of the production of a set of objects socially constituted as works of art, i.e. the conditions of production of the field of social agents (e.g., museums, galleries, academies, etc.) which help to define and produce the value of works of art. In short, it is a question of understanding works of art as a manifestation of the field as a whole, in which all the powers of the field, and all the determinisms inherent in its structure and functioning, are concentrated.' (Bourdieu 1993: 37)

So cultural production, according to Bourdieu, is not simply, say, the act of a writer writing and publishing a book. There is

1) the material production of the writer through his or her formation – 'the social conditions of the production of artists' and
2) the material production of value of artists through the formation of critics, audience and buyers. In late industrial societies this activity is usually located in academic and educational institutions.

No writer, myself included, can live or write at a point separate from these activities. The second of the categories (2) creates tastes and audiences and, in a highly material way, determines popularity, salability and thus the writer's living standards. In fact, every writer is in tension with these 'social agents' – whether to court, ignore or antagonise them. This tension reaches right into the heart of every piece of writing, every use of language, every code or convention absorbed, celebrated or defied. In my particular case, my relation to the institution of 'poetry' and, more specifically, 'poetry for children' and 'poetry in schools' is difficult and problematic. But whatever it is, it is inseparable from Bourdieu's 'set of agents'.

Bourdieu argues that every artist and every member of an audience for a particular work of art, occupies a 'habitus'. This is a term to express the idea that as makers and receptors of art we are schooled into a consciousness enabling us to create and/or understand and 'appreciate' any given work of art. The schooling for 'high art' is itself historically and materially created in (usually) educational institutions that themselves owe their origins and character to a particular stage of development in society:

> '. . . we must . . . ask, not how a writer comes to be what he is, in a sort of genetic psycho-sociology, but rather how the position or 'post' he occupies – that of a writer of a particular type – became constituted. It is only then that we can ask of the knowledge of particular social conditions of the production of what I have termed his habitus permits us to understand that he has succeeded in occupying this position, if only by transforming it.' (Bourdieu 1993: 162)

This is an attempt to demystify the genesis of the writer, turning away from purely psychological explanations and directing our attention to constituting and sustaining environments. In fact, in this study I take my cue from Bourdieu's statement and one by Giroux, who delineated a habitus as:

> 'the subjective dispositions which reflect a class-based social grammar of taste, knowledge, and behaviour inscribed permanently in the "body schema and the schemes of thought" of each developing person' (Giroux 1983: 84)

in order to avoid becoming sucked into purely psychological and psychoanalytic speculation. And following Bourdieu I can say that I have come to occupy a certain 'position', as he puts it, within 'poetry'. It is a sub-field, 'poetry for children'. I will be looking more closely at this in the next chapter but suffice it to say for the time being: I find myself (part intentionally, part not) as some kind of breaker of rules. In fact, over twenty years of writing, some have argued that I have done just as Bourdieu describes: I 'occupy' a habitus through my own formation and a materially and socially conditioned set of readers and educators have enabled me to have an audience. Sometimes this was and still is fiercely opposed but having become established within the cultural field I have contributed to a movement that has 'transformed' the cultural identity of 'poetry for children'. There is not time here to dwell on the specific historical and socioeconomic conditions of schools, teachers and educators and, of course, children who have enabled all this to take place but I will observe here (and below) that they are ever-present as material determinants of my writing.

I. Materialism (continued)

iv) Relation of literature to society

Finally, for us to see the wider situation we have to look at writing in society. I have already described some of the ways in which 'society' makes itself felt on writers and writing. A more global picture is required. Marx and Engels (1976), Trotsky (1960, 1970), and many Marxists since have grappled with the relation of the arts to society (e.g., Lifshitz 1933; Caudwell 1937; Thomson 1941; Finkelstein 1947; Demetz 1959; Fischer 1959; Lukacs 1970; Brecht 1964; Benjamin 1970; Anion 1970; Eagleton 1976a, 1976b; Laing 1978; Bennett 1979; Slaughter 1980; Lindsay 1981). Marx and Engels worked from a broad and rough analogy or metaphor usually described as the 'base and superstructure'. Quite how this metaphor should be interpreted has been the subject of debate ever since (see e.g., Williams 1973, 1977; Harman 1986; Barker, Callinicos and Hallas 1987; Jakubowski 1990 and most of the writers cited above on Marxism and the arts). Perhaps one of the more productive ways to look at the problem is to consider the whole metaphor as referring quite closely to the structure of a building. The base is then the foundations and the superstructure is the upper part of the building above it. We can say that the upper part cannot exist without the foundation being in place, whilst at the same time, whatever happens in the upper part of the building will be felt in the lower. In this way, we can say that the building would never have been built without its foundation whilst the whole cannot be understood without there being an upper and lower part.

This lower part (the base) is 'economic activity', understood to mean a process involving both the forces and the relations of production. The superstructure we can take to mean ideological, religious, legal and artistic activity. To avoid confusion 'superstructure' has to refer to these activities in terms of their ideas and not in terms of their own economic structures which, as Williams (1977) pointed out, can be seen as part of the 'base' as in the film and TV 'industry'.

There is an immense importance for Marxists to deal with the matter of 'correspondence' or 'reflection' (see Harman 1986). That is to say, Marx and Engels themselves were keen to point out that we should not understand the metaphor to mean that the superstructure simply reflects or corresponds to the base or that it is totally determined by it (Engels to Bloch 21.9.1890). In other words art or law or religion does not simply mirror the mode of production's current situation but that the two can be out of phase with each other, as if, say, a renovation had been done on the upper building which imposed strains on the foundations (or vice versa). Though the dominant ideas of a society are there to keep the system going, they are sometimes 'out of sync' with sudden shifts in the base. So it was that the old dominant ideas of 'women can't do heavy work' had to be dropped when the system sent its men off to kill each other in the Second World War but was then readopted when the survivors came home; the ideas around the old phrase 'the Devil finds mischief for idle hands' had to be adapted to fit mass unemployment, and the concept of the 'leisure industry' was invented.

To increase the complexity, one also has to come to terms with ways in which the whole structure reveals contradictions in the system: contradictions between, say, a state religion preaching 'love thy neighbour' (superstructure) and a business *practice* of 'exploit your neighbour' (base); the contradiction between an 'overproduction of food' (forces of production in the base) and a starving population without the means to buy the food (as a consequence of the relations of production in the base). It is in some of these contradictions and ways in which the parts are not in phase with each other that we see the source of change in society (Harman 1986).

To illustrate the matter in a more personal way: broadly speaking, I have grown up in a late (and at times very tired) capitalist country with a very specific post-imperialist formation. Because of gains made by trade unions and then social democrats within this wealthy society, there has grown up a highly developed form of state education. It is impossible to look at aspects of post 1970s children's literature, including my own flourishing within it, without seeing ways in which such material facts as the need for British capitalism to produce a literate working class, have affected what literature is produced for children, how it is produced and how it is written and illustrated (see some excellent examples that celebrate and negotiate urban and working class life e.g., Westall's *The Machine-Gunners* (1975), the Ahlbergs' *Peepo!* (1981), Hughes' *Affie Gets in First* (1982), Swindells' *Stone Cold* (1993)).

Meanwhile in this period, certain superstructural interventions have had profound effects throughout the system, both on consciousness and the economic base. Clearly, the particular British, (or is it English?) intervention made by the phenomenon we call 'Thatcherism' could not have gone on *without* the economic situation being what it was, but at the same time important ideological decisions (superstructure) were made, for instance, in the field of education that returned the problem to the economic base, e.g. the system demanding youngsters to be trained in new technologies without providing resources to do it. So it was that 'spelling' became a more important (and cheaper) objective for those in power than what the system really needs, which is word-processing.

The functionaries required to implement these superstructural policies were teachers, having their pay frozen (because of constraints within the base) whilst supporting each other in collective work (thereby revealing a contradiction in the base between the individualism of private ownership and the collective nature of late capitalist labour). Furthermore, teachers started to see the ways in which they were being asked to carry out policies that were in conflict with the interests they learn to value in their collective activities – as with activity against education cuts. They resisted. On a personal note, I observe that I might arrive in a school to perform my work – an activity paid for out of the education budget – while these matters are in the air.

It is important to point out, however, that part of the power of the metaphor 'base and superstructure' rests on its offering us the possibility of conceiving of it as an *asymmetrical duality*, an interconnectedness weighted towards the constraints imposed by necessity (survival and the organisation necessary to achieve it – base activity). It is a strong rebuttal to the 'common sense' notions that we carry with us that our consciousness, our attitudes and our emotional life could or might exist in a bubble, detached from our 'social existence' (see Marx 1970: 20-21 and below), a major part of which is taken up with the material business of occupying a position in the 'relations of production' which we have to do, at the respective level of development of the 'forces of production' of our epoch.

Voloshinov used some of these ideas in the late 1920s and 30s when looking at the specific part of human activity that concerns us here – language, reading and writing:

In order for any item, from whatever domain of reality it may come, to enter the social purview of the group and elicit ideological semiotic reaction it must be associated with the vital socioeconomic prerequisites of the particular group's existence; it must somehow, even if only obliquely, make contact with the bases of the group's material life.' (Voloshinov 1986: 22)

The material existence of an audience's life must share some common ground with the referents of any given text. This is what enables an audience to 'respond' have an 'ideological semiotic reaction'. In fact, Voloshinov argues, this moment of response is itself located in the material world. There are specific material 'circumstances' for each and every moment of communication. These affect what is available, what is responded to and indeed how it is responded to. Moreover, the specific material conditions of communication are themselves part of a wider picture: the historical and socioeconomic conditions of the day:

'Utterance as such is wholly a product of social interaction, both of the immediate sort as determined by the circumstances of the discourse, and of the more general kind, as determined by the whole aggregate of conditions under which any given community of speakers operates.' (Voloshinov 1986: 93)

Finally, dubbing this approach as 'a sociological history of literature', Voloshinov and his colleagues tried to set all this in the wider context thus:

' . . . a sociological history of literature . . . studies: 'the concrete life of a work or art in the unity of the developing literary milieu; the literary milieu within the process of generation of the ideological milieu with which it is encompassed; and, finally, the ideological milieu in the process of generation of the socioeconomic milieu with which it is permeated': (Titunik 1986 in Voloshinov 1986: 181 citing Medvedev 1934: 42)

This contextualising is what I will be attempting in the chapter that follows.

I will conclude with the famous and schematic statement of Marx that provided the springboard for much of what has been written on this matter.

'In the social production of their existence, men inevitably enter into definite relations, which are independent of their will, namely relations of production appropriate to a given state in the development of their material forces of production. The totality of these relations of production constitutes the economic structure of society, the real foundation, [i.e. the 'base' MR] on which arises a legal and political superstructure and to which correspond definite forms of social consciousness. The mode of production of material life conditions the general process of social, political and intellectual life. It is not the consciousness of men that determines their existence [he said, anticipating the post-modernists! MR] but their social existence that determines their consciousness.' (Marx 1970b: 20-21)

Later in the same passage Marx distinguishes between a transformation in the 'economic conditions of production' (like, say the industrial revolution) and the

' . . . legal, political, religious, artistic or philosophic − in short, ideological forms in which men [sic] become conscious of this conflict and fight it out.' (Marx 1970b: 21)

This is precisely how I see my own artistic activity, working through artistic forms that belong to a specific time and place in history and which reveal contradictions and conflicts. When people take up the role of audiences of artistic forms this is one of the ways in which they might become conscious of material contradictions and conflicts in society as a whole.

2) Intertextuality

I have already touched on this matter when citing Callinicos challenging the 'textualism' of certain post-structuralists. But it would be foolish to throw the baby out with the bath-water. It will not be claimed here that my texts or any texts are *simply* and *only* manifestations or reflections of a material reality. The term 'Intertextuality', if limited in ways I shall suggest, should prove useful when I come to look at specific poems.

It is clear that writers inhabit the world but within that world, (and always within that world) they also inhabit a world of texts. Following Voloshinov we would recognize these texts as having a material reality as pages, print and books, a fact which impinges greatly on how those texts are inserted into people's lives. However, at this stage of the argument we can look at how the ideational import of texts relate to each other. This leads us to the problematic term 'intertextuality'.

Here are some prefatory thoughts: it is clear from the previous section on materialism, that I would reject any notion that might suggest that ideas, disembodied from the lived lives of real human beings, or indeed detached from the material world of the circulation of those physical objects we call texts, can simply influence each other or determine each other. So, though we might say loosely, that *Leaves of Grass* (Whitman 1891-2) is 'influenced' by the 'King James Bible' (1611), it is clear that Walt Whitman's reading or knowing of that Bible, took place within, and was affected by *the specific historic circumstances of nineteenth century liberal America.* There is no point where the words of that Bible floated free of language-in-use-by-real-human-beings-in-their-specific-place-and-time. (I have hyphenated the phrase in order to convey the idea that it is one unified concept)

In their introduction to *Intertextuality: theories and practices* Michael Worton and Judith Still (1990) recognise this when they say:

The dominant relations of production and the sociopolitical context – which could be included within a broad definition of text are of course a major force influencing every aspect of a text.' (Worton and Still 1990: 1)

The problem here, acknowledged but blurred by Worton and Still, is that if the 'dominant relations of production' (e.g. capitalism) are regarded as a 'text' then the word 'text' comes to refer to everything. There is no distinction made between the material world and the views of it; between thing and idea. This is not to deny that an understanding of the material world is mediated through words.

However, later they say:

'Kristeva has argued that every text is under the jurisdiction of other discourses.' (Worton and Still 1990: 9)

This is both deterministic and reificatory. It cannot be texts or even 'discourses' that control and determine another text. Texts are inanimate objects that can only be animated by consciousness and human activity which in turn arise out of 'social existence'. It is human behaviour that sets up ground rules and patterns and even then, the producers of new texts have it within their power to alter, change, subvert whatever discourse they find themselves within. Otherwise there would never be change (see Marx above on labour).

But then searching about in these ambiguities and difficulties Worton and Still cite Kristeva on Bakhtin:

> ' . . . the "literary word" . . . [is] *an intersection of textual surfaces* rather than a *point* (a fixed meaning) . . . [it is] a dialogue among several writings: that of the writer, the addressee (or the character) and the contemporary or earlier cultural context.' (Worton and Still 1990: 16 citing Kristeva 1986: 36)

This is a much more coherent formula whereby we can see that the setting down of a text is an inevitable part of a conversation with other texts. A writer, simply by using words, cannot escape from using already-used signs, signs imbued with historical meaning, social connotation. But more than this, a writer joins the world conversation that modifies the already-used and indeed converses with that already-used. This does not simply take place at the level of word but also of phrase, sentence, verse, paragraph, total literary unit, or for that matter, at any linguistic level one might care to distinguish. Once again, in loose shorthand one might say that one novel is 'in conversation' with another, but we always have to bear in mind that it is first the socio-historically positioned writer writing who is having that conversation, and thereafter the socio-historically positioned readers manipulating conversations with their lives and the texts that they know.

There is a danger in this model, however, to see the 'already-used' as total pre-determinants. Worton and Still cite Barthes from *Writing Degree Zero*:

> ' . . . it is impossible to develop [my selected mode of writing] within duration without gradually becoming prisoner of someone else's words and even of my own.' (Worton and Still 1990: 19 citing Barthes 1984: 23)

On which they comment:

> This is intertextuality in the sense that a text may appear to be the spontaneous and transparent expression of a writer's intentions but must necessarily contain elements of other texts.' (Worton and Still 1990: 19)

Whereas Barthes is being histrionically deterministic, Worton and Still are much more neutral – the only inevitability for them being the fact that the residue of other texts will be present.

In the same work, John Frow ('Intertextuality and Ontology' (Frow 1990: 45-55)) states:

> Texts are made out of cultural and ideological norms; out of the conventions of genre; out of styles and idioms embedded in the language; out of connotations and collocative sets; out of cliches, formulae, or proverbs; and out of other texts.' (Frow 1990: 45)

which is interesting but no revelation. Then citing Jenny:

> 'Genre archetypes, however abstract, still constitute textual structures.' (Frow 1990: 45)

This takes the argument further: we should see such forms as 'poem' or 'newspaper editorial' as texts themselves, perhaps as some kind of shadowy blueprint.

Frow expresses this as:

> 'The process of intertextual reference is governed by the rules of the discursive formation within which it occurs.' (Frow 1990: 46)

'Rules' and 'governed' seem rather strong terms here, particularly in a literary world less and less dominated by an Academy's 'rules'. Perhaps 'conventions' would be a more useful term. Later he uses the phrase 'cultural codes'. This crops up when looking at what might be appropriate critical activity in the field of intertextuality.

> ' . . . detailed scholarly information is less important than the ability to reconstruct the cultural codes which are realised (and contested) in texts.' (Flow 1990: 46)

This seems particularly relevant to my work in this thesis. Part of what I am doing here is identifying those texts I am consciously and unconsciously in conversation with. I am trying to identify why that might be, what it was in my formation that led me to those texts, but I am also looking at what cultural codes, and what conventions I am operating with, or conversely, contesting. Frow summarises this activity as

'... the work performed upon intertextual material and its functional integration in the later text.' (Frow 1990: 46)

This is pleasingly dialectic. The writer works with and on previous textual material.

However, Frow then takes us into the realm of the immaterial:

'Insofar as the 'real' signified by literary (or any other) texts is a moment of a signifying process, and indeed is only ever available to knowledge within and by means of a system of representations, it has the form not of a final referent but of a link in an endless chain of semiosis . . . In this sense the 'reality' both of the 'natural' and the social worlds is text-like' (Frow 1990: 47)

Here, he strays beyond what I will be accepting in this thesis as 'intertextuality' and taken us back into Callinicos's 'textualist' swamp. We can ask: if all we have is an 'endless chain of semiosis' how is it that we are able to apply scientific principles in manufacture and transport ? To say that the referent never quite catches reality and that reality is only available to us through representation does not mean that there is no reality and there is only text, and/or endless chains of incapable words.

'. . . it is the physical sciences' success in providing knowledge of the structure of reality which makes possible technological control of nature. The gargantuan apparatus of intervention into the physical world that is such a dominant characteristic of modernity would be inconceivable unless, as a matter of fact, theoretically driven scientific research had come up with a series of fairly close approximations to the truth of the physical world.' (Callinicos 1995: 185)

Then Frow makes the claim that

'Economic practice . . . is to be thought of as discursive.' (Frow 1990: 52)

If this were the case, 'economic practice' itself would be non-economic and therefore pointless. Why would we make and produce *things*? There may well be 'discourses' in and around economic practice, discourses used by participants and observers mediating existence, but this is not the whole story. Economic practice is what humans have to do to survive and reproduce themselves. I (and the rest of the human race) am not able to talk and write (or indeed discuss 'economic practice' and 'discourse' !) until I have engaged in economic material activity to ensure that I am fed, watered and have shelter i.e. participated in 'economic practice'.

Having made this claim, supposedly derived from Foucault, Frow, who elsewhere has written Marxist analyses (1986), now becomes uneasy:

'. . . [an] extension of the concepts of text and discourse to the field of the social ultimately begs the question of what it is that conditions the textual – that is, the question of the conditions of existence of textuality.' (Frow 1990: 53)

Quite! And again:

'There is the need to be constantly suspicious about the extent to which broad domains of social being can thus be incorporated within the single conceptual domain of textuality . . . ' (Frow 1990: 54)

I have quoted this argument at length because it is precisely at this point that the post-modernists argue with the materialists and Marxists. Interestingly, even as Frow extends intertextuality into total existence, he wavers and spots the impossibility. In other words, as I am claiming here, for the term intertextuality' to be useful, it must be limited in its application – it cannot apply to everything.

In 'Compulsory reader response: the intertextual drive' (Worton and Still 1990: 56-78) Michael Riffaterre links both with Bourdieu's ideas I have mentioned earlier as well as some of the response and reception theory that I am exploring in the next section. He writes:

'An intertext is one or more texts which the reader must know in order to understand a work of literature in terms of its overall significance (as opposed to the discrete meanings of its successive words, phrases and sentences).' (Riffaterre 1990: 56)

Perhaps this is a little incautious: no one knows the 'overall significance' of a text but he adds:

> '... intertextuality enables the text to represent, at one and the same time, the following pairs of opposites (within each of which the first item corresponds to the intertext): convention and departures from it, tradition and novelty, sociolect and idiolect, the already said and its negation or transformation.' (Riffaterre 1990: 76)

This more modest use of 'intertextuality' seems much more valid and again we arrive at a sense of conversation. In reading this I become only too aware that my own work is in conversation with (amongst other things) other poetry, and indeed a whole range of discourses around schooling, home etiquette and parenting.

By way of an appendix to this section I would like to summarise a schema conceived by Genette. Even if I do not adopt Genette's exact terminology elsewhere in this thesis, his outline can be taken as the blueprint that I will be using in later sections when I am looking at the relation between a given poem and 'other texts'. It will also be noted that Genette has limited the idea of intertextuality and not suggested it is 'everything'. (I have translated, summarised and illustrated Genette's text for this thesis.)

Genette describes five types of transtextual relations' i.e. any ways in which one text is linked to another – explicitly or implicitly.

1) 'Intertextuality' a relation of co-presence between 2 or several texts; the effective presence of one text in another e.g., citation, plagiarism, allusion.

2) 'Paratextuality' e.g., title, sub-title, preface, notes, illustrations,

3) 'Metatextuality', the relation (or commentary) which unites one text with another of which it speaks without necessarily quoting it or referring to it explicitly.

4) 'Hypertextuality', all relations uniting typotext' (text A) with 'hypertext' (text B) e.g., parody, imitation, translation, versification, 'transmetrification' (changing metre of a poem); 'transtylisation' (changing style), cutting, expanding, summary, abridgement, 'transmotivation' (transferring of a motive from one character to another), 'transvalorisation' (transferring or changing the power of a protagonist to attract sympathy or not), 'devalorisation' (e.g. Shakespeare increasing Macbeth's villainy from his source material)

5) 'Architextuality' – the relation of the text with the unwritten texts of genres

and their constraints. (derived from Genette 1982: 7-14)

This strikes me as an elegant way of breaking some intertextual processes down into quite different elements. So it is clear that if I produce a parody, as I have done in the creative work for this thesis, then this intertextual process is different from, say a barely conscious 'co-presence' of, say A.A. Milne, or again, different from, the process of working within a genre (Genette's 'architextuality').

Lumping all these different processes as intertextual might be generally speaking accurate, but it is also crude. Genette overcomes this crudeness.

3) Some Notes on Reading, Response, Reception and Meaning

The purpose of this section is to offer a model for the reading process. This is in effect the base line from which both I, as the reading writer, and any actual audience has to travel. When in Chapter 4 I am talking about: 1)specific acts of alteration of texts or 2)more general absorption of actual or imagined readers' attitudes, the base-line is a notion in my head of reading-process. My understanding of that process, is what I shall now try to describe.

The starting point for this section is a comment from Macherey:

'We might say that the author is the first reader of his own work; he first gives himself the surprises that he will hand on to us . . . ' (Macherey 1978: 48)

This serves to remind us that writers, even as they write, read. In this thesis I am trying to:

1) reconstruct that particular moment of writing-reading-writing and
2) thereafter with specific poems make connections between i) my reading of my work and ii) my (re)writing of it.

It could be said that it is virtually impossible to think of the act of writing as separate from the reading process. As each word and phrase goes down on to the page the writer reads what is written, and then considers its significance and potential impact on an imagined or internalised audience. What distinguishes these writing-readers from the ordinary reader is that they can (and do) change the text they read: experiment with one potential impact and exchange it for another. I have grown to understand that what takes place is a *feedback process* where an idea:

1) is concretised into text which is then in turn
2) tested for *potential* impact on an imagined or idealised reader (s) and then
3) kept, changed or scrapped as the writer thinks fit. After this fluid process (that may take seconds, minutes or even years), there is usually some eventual stability and we have a text for other readers to read.

I would like to begin with a schema, a basic summary of how I picture the reading-process. The schema derives from various sources: e.g., Culler (1975), Rosenblatt (1978, 1985), Iser (1978), Corcoran and Evans (1978), Fish (1980), Freund (1987), Benton et al (1988) Eco (1992).

1) A culturally specific matching of material marks on a page (letters on a computer screen, etc.) with the meaningful units of language, words, phrases, sentences, passages, and whole works.
2) The employment of previous reading, listening, writing and speech experiences ('repertoires' (Iser) 'competence' (Culler)) in order to: coalesce and realise sensations, emotions, ideas around these meaningful language units; to recognize a writer's and/or a text's conventions and strategies; to allow oneself to 'play' according to the writer's and/or text's suggestions.
3) The employment of life experiences (situation and participation in the historical process) in order firstly to enable one to participate in this process of reading but also to contribute in many different ways to this coalescing and realising of sensations, emotions and ideas.
4) The employment of a mixture of both the previous two elements (2 and 3): namely in a process whereby the life experience of reading experiences is used. This is the means by which one text is prioritised over another; texts are variously legitimised, validated, exiled, effaced and so on.
5) A constant interplay between the language experiences and life experiences which, though it goes on in every sensate individual, is paradoxically an utterly social act. It is social because language is born out of social activity (speech and communication of all kinds) whilst at the same time, the individual is both created by and creates him or herself within social interactions too.
6) In the specific case of the writing-reader: an active projection into what are imagined and/or internalised responses of other readers. The source of these imagined readers may be various e.g., i) the differentiated memory of previous

kinds of reading that the writer him or herself did, ii) the memory of how other readers have responded to the writer's work iii)the memory of what professional readers (critics) have said about their own or other's work, iv) the immediate input of the readers who are the first, second (and subsequent) readers of the putative text before it is stabilised (if indeed it is).

It cannot be emphasised more that this schema is not intended to be a sequence. It is only an attempt to withdraw various elements from what is a complex, fluid process in which all these elements interact and interfuse.

I would now like to illustrate and refine the schema with come comments from various theorists in the field. Historically, it is usual to trace the evolution of this subject from I.A. Richards (1924,1929), to Louise Rosenblatt (1937, 1978), Holland (1968) and then perhaps to Culler (1975), Iser (1978) and Fish (1980). However, following the ideological bent of this thesis, I thought that it would be more appropriate to begin with where we left off with Voloshinov (cited here again):

'In order for any item, from whatever domain of reality it may come, to enter the social purview of the group and elicit ideological semiotic reaction it must be associated with the vital socioeconomic prerequisites of the particular group's existence; it must somehow, even if only obliquely, make contact with the bases of the group's material life.' (Voloshinov 1986: 22)

Voloshinov is primarily talking here about writing and speech but reminds us with the phrase 'ideological semiotic reaction' that reading is a response to signs and that for that process to happen, connections must be made with where and how the reader actually exists, i.e. from within the 'socioeconomic prerequisites' of a social group. In crude terms, if I am to tell the joke: 'Did I tell you the one about butter? And you say, no, and I say, I won't tell it – you might spread it . . . ' then for you to 'get' the joke you have to live in the particular socioeconomic formation that knows of butter and that butter *spreads* as opposed to, say, 'runs' like ghee, or for that matter jumps about like a dog. But Voloshinov also reminds us that these are not purely individual characteristics of readers, they are social, shared responses. He goes on to say that:

'The *word is oriented toward an addressee*, toward *who* [sic] that addressee might be: a fellow-member or not of the same social group, of higher or lower standing (the addressee's hierarchical status), someone connected with the speaker by close social ties (father, brother, husband, and so on) or not. There can be no such thing as an abstract addressee, a man unto himself, so to speak. With such a person, we would indeed have no language in common, literally and figuratively . . . ' (Voloshinov 1986: 85-86)

which reminds us that writing (as only one kind of 'utterance') is inseparable from actual readers. But then he points out that readers and writers ('addressers' and 'addressees') are not simply discrete individuals.

'Each person's inner world and thought has its stabilised *social audience* that comprises the environment in which reasons, motives, values and so on are fashioned . . . ? (Voloshinov 1986: 86)

In other words, and in the case of readers, a reader's psyche has within it (or perhaps it is all of it) a socially formed basis. When the reader makes judgments and evaluates what has been read, it comes from what Voloshinov identifies as a 'stabilised social audience' that has been internalised.

He goes on to make the point that we cannot really think of texts or parts of texts as simply either something that is written or something that is read. It can only be understood as an entity that is both written and read at the same time and contains within it aspects of both the producer and the receiver:

'Orientation of the word toward the addressee has an extremely high significance. In point of fact, *word is a two-sided act*. It is determined equally by *whose* word it is and *for whom* it is meant. As word, it is *precisely the product of the reciprocal relationship between speaker and listener, addresser and addressee*.' (Voloshinov 1986: 86)

When a writer comes to write, he or she anticipates reactions and engages in some kind of dialogue with previous utterances (texts) and previous audience responses:

'A book . . . is calculated for active perception . . . a verbal performance of this kind also inevitably orients itself with respect to previous performances in the same sphere, both those by the same author and those by other authors . . . Thus, the printed verbal performance engages, as it were, in ideological colloquy of large scale: it responds to something, objects to something, affirms something, anticipates possible responses and objections, seeks support, and so on.' (Voloshinov 1986: 95)

So here Voloshinov shifts his attention a little more towards the reader (addressee) as someone with whom the author engages in a kind of dialogue. But we might also say that a reader follows some of the processes that Voloshinov describes here: responding, objecting, affirming, anticipating, objecting and seeking support. So the part of reading that we might call 'understanding' or 'meaning' comes about as a consequence of a kind of dialogue:

> 'Meaning is the *effect of interaction between speaker and listener produced via the material of a particular sound complex.*' (Voloshinov 1986: 102-3)

Or to rephrase it for our purposes: meaning is the effect of interaction between writer and imagined or actual audiences produced via the material of the printed page or computer screen etc. The virtue of Voloshinov's approach is that

1) he situates all texts in a social context – i.e. they are written for an audience and
2) meaning derives from this process.

In general terms he also makes clear that that 'social context' is not some kind of neutral soup. It is peopled by socioeconomic groups and individuals in places within those groups.

Randall Johnson expresses the idea like this:

> If cultural works are produced in objective historical situations and institutional frameworks by agents using different strategies and following different trajectories in the field, the reception of such works, regardless of the level of that reception, also takes place in specific historically constituted situations. Works have significance for certain groups and individuals based on their own objective position, cultural needs and capacities for analysis or symbolic appropriation.' (Johnson in Bourdieu 1993: 20)

and John Hill

> We would want to argue that readership must be understood in terms of broader patterns of socio-cultural consumption whereby texts are read both 'aesthetically' in terms of codes specifically 'artistic', and 'socially', in relation to the broader contours of life-experience engendered via class, race, sex and nation . . . ' (Hill in Barrett, Corrigan, Kuhn and Wolff, 1979:122)

and Tony Bennett:

> ' . . . [the way in which] the text produces its effects consists not of naked subjectivities but of individuals interpellated into particular subject positions within a variety of different – and sometimes contradictory – ideological formations. This further entails recognising that such positions vary in accordance with considerations of race, class and gender and, concerning their insertion within the system of intertextual relations, on the degree to which, within the educational apparatus, the institution of Literature has borne upon their ideological formation, upon their positioning as readers.' (Bennett in Mulhern 1992: 208)

So, three writers here situate reading and meaning in the social – an important departure from the 'common sense' view of reading as a lonely individual act. These kinds of statements are also different from what is usually understood to be the 'reader-response' school and its applied use in education. This group often tries to break the reading process down along more phenomenological lines. A typical one of these comes from Emrys Evans (1992). He comes from a school of thinkers found in educational circles who have used the 'reader-response' school of criticism in order to establish a more democratic approach to literature in classrooms. Others from this field are Corcoran (1978) and Benton et al (1988) Hayhoe and Parker (1990) Sarland (1991) and Many and Cox (1992). These writers have essentially adapted the work of, say, J.N. Britton (1970) *Language and Learning*, Jonathan Culler's ideas of 'literary competence' *Structuralist Poetics* (1975), Louise Rosenblatt (1978,1985), Wolfgang Iser (1978) in *The Act of Reading: A Theory of Aesthetic Response* and Stanley Fish (1980) with *Is There a Text in This Class?* in order to free young, inexperienced and non-academic readers from the burdens of textual exegesis, historical commentaries, and a general critical apparatus. In this context, *and only in this context*, I have found the phenomenological approach highly sympathetic, and indeed influential on how in classrooms I have approached young readers of my own work or of other people's work.

Here, for example is Evans' schema.

There are different kinds of 'satisfaction' in reading he suggests:

'1. Unreflective interest in action
2. Empathising
3. Analogising
4. Reflecting on the significance of events (theme) and behaviour (distanced evaluation of characters)
5. Reviewing the whole work as the author's creation
6. Consciously considered relationship with the author; recognition of textual ideology, and understanding of self (identity theme) and of one's own reading processes.' (Evans 1992: 32)

The hierarchy here is probably quite difficult to sustain and may simply be self-serving as a way of defining Evans himself as a 'stage 6' reader. However, it alerts us to certain possibilities of some of the reading processes, without probing too deeply into where these processes come from – or why. Other reading processes such phenomenological critics have tried to identify include: testing for plausibility, suspension of disbelief, engagement, recreating, identification, negation (the upsetting of expected outcomes and patterns), anticipation, prediction, retrospecting or 'harvesting' (my own term), selecting or 'dropping' (my own term), resisting, accepting and so on (Corcoran and Evans 1978). One theory posed by Britton is that reading involves 'spectating' and 'participating' as different kinds of reading.

The problem Evans et al have to face is *why* it is that one person's reading can differ from another. Rosenblatt offers an answer when she suggests we need to see the act of reading

' . . . as an event involving a particular individual and a particular text, happening at a particular time, under particular circumstances, in a particular social and cultural setting, and as part of the ongoing life of the individual and the group.' (Rosenblatt 1985: 100)

This places the reader firmly in time, place and social context but raises the question of what exactly is this 'ongoing life of the individual'? Is it an individualistic 'self' and does each self 'do its own thing' when faced with a text? This was the challenge that Fish tried to take up when he noted that interpretation cannot be 'random' (Fish 1980: 172). He says, 'ways of interpreting' are learned and change with time and different contexts. These different ways of interpreting seem in Fish's eye to cluster into 'interpretive communities' (Fish 1980:171), that is to say those who 'share interpretive strategies' (Fish 1980: 171). This sounds perfectly plausible but lacks teeth. 'Interpretive communities' is perhaps a weak way in which to describe the social formations and class identities expressed by people who happen to read. Fish himself seems to recognize this when he writes:

' . . . no one's interpretive acts are exclusively his own but fall to him
by virtue of his position in some socially organised environment and
are therefore always shared and public.' (Fish 1980: 335)

For a moment it appears that Fish has moved towards an idea that we read with a sensibility born of a position within society, or even within some social group or class, (as Johnson, Hill and Bennett show, see above). But then a moment later Fish moves away from talking about a reader sharing interpretive acts by virtue of his or her position in a socially organised environment (i.e. a materialist model) and moves towards a more post-structuralist idealist stance when he writes that we have to see the self

' . . . not as an independent entity but as a social construct.' (Fish 1980: 335)

All one can say here is that if our essence, our being is that we are 'social constructs' we would not be able to sustain ourselves to write the books that are then read and interpreted.

Perhaps some synthesis of the two statements by Fish would give us a more coherent picture in which we accept that readers occupy 'positions' in society, and that these positions are one way in which to describe how readers live their lives in order to survive and indeed explain the shape of our 'interpretive acts', but that within that dynamic, we describe (socially construct ?) others and ourselves in ways that challenge, accept or alter the prevailing ideas of our day. In turn these prevailing ideas are not abstract but live and change in the context of the material possibilities and conflicts of the day. When we read, we cannot escape the fact that we are situated in a specific time and place in history.

Some of this territory has been explored by Jauss and others as cited in Holub (1984).

It is usual to identify a major challenge to reader-response theory as coming from any theorists who want to consider how texts summon readers, ask readers questions, or 'position' readers (Meek 1988, Stephens 1992). The school of rhetoric that considers the effects that texts have on readers might be included here (see Eagleton 1983: 205-207 for summary) as well as the notions of 'implied reader' and 'implied author' (see Iser 1974). It seems to me that these various approaches around texts are not as contradictory as first appears. Thus it is surely uncontroversial and undeniable to state that a text is:

firstly, an inanimate material object and, strictly speaking, without the intervention of perception, consciousness and indeed the human labour of looking, eye-turning, thinking, page-turning and the like, cannot, of itself and by itself 'do' things to readers;
secondly, that it is only through a knowledge of culturally acquired sign systems that we can turn that material object (the text) into language with all its ability to convey emotions, ideas, feelings and so on;
thirdly, once this has been done, or rather, *in the process* of turning the material squiggles into culturally accepted units of understandable language, we can talk loosely of texts 'doing' things.

In fact, though it might be accurate, it would be tedious to repeat each time that what happens is that the reader's social, material and intertextual experiences enable him or her to unpack meanings from the squiggles and in the process, and because of these experiences, will follow, play with or resist some of the strategies that we recognise that the writer has put before us, or, by virtue of who we are, 'fall for'. It is often simpler (but wrong) either to say 'the text' does this or that, or more usually, the author does this or that.

Similarly, we can read a text looking for, or we can even unconsciously become, say, 'implied readers' but again, this can only be done because we are able, through complex material, cultural and intertextual processes, to search out for or recognize various conventions and textual structures. In other words, reader-response theory does not need to eliminate the writer, the act of writing or the construction of texts.

Just how free the reader is when faced with a text is what lies behind the debate between Eco, Rorty, Culler et al in (1992) *Interpretation and Overinterpretation*. Eco opens by saying:

'Someone could say that a text, once it is separated from its utterer (as well as from the utterer's intention) and from the concrete circumstances of its utterance (and by consequence from its intended referent) floats (so to speak) in the vacuum of a potentially infinite range of possible interpretations.' (Eco, Rorty, Culler 1992: 41)

In actual fact and in real situations, as opposed to the abstract 'situation', the range of interpretations cannot be literally 'infinite'. They are limited, made finite, by human experience in specific times and places (Eagleton 1983: 54-90). However, is one part of the limitation the text itself, i.e. what is written?

In characteristically teasing style Eco postulates the nature of the coincidence between what is written and what is read:

'A text is a device conceived in order to produce its model reader. I repeat that this reader is not the one who makes the 'only right' conjecture. A text can foresee a model reader entitled to try infinite conjectures. The empirical reader is only an actor who makes conjectures about the kind of model reader postulated by the text. Since the intention of the text is basically to produce a model reader able to make conjectures about it, the initiative of the model reader consists in figuring out a model author that is not the empirical one and that, in the end, coincides with the intention of the text.' (Eco, Rorty, Culler 1992: 64)

So Eco suggests that the coincidence between interpretation and author-intention revolves around empirical readers trying to guess the author's model reader. The problem here is that it leads us back to the possibility that the empirical reader could, in theory guess anything. Do readers have a carte blanche to do what they want with a text – e.g. say that *Hamlet* is really about the Olympic Games?

I would prefer to break this problem not with Eco's philosophical juggling but as follows: no social act gives us a 'free rein'. It is an idealist concept to imagine that we enter the world unattached to our social and material formation, the formation that delineates our possibilities in life. Similarly, within each interaction, there are possibilities but these are within certain constraints. Thus it is not usually possible to go into a fish and chip shop to get your car filled up with petrol.

When we read it is not that we have a 'free rein' but that we are

1) constrained by our own material, cultural, personal and intertextual experiences and

2) in the process of unpacking the signs in the writing, we recognise, play with and challenge the writing's conventions, symbols, patterns, strategies and the like, which were in their time and place constructed out of the material, social and intertextual circumstances of the writer(s).

It is at this point that we can say loosely that texts 'position' readers (Stephens 1992), or set up processes of e.g. distancing. In fact, and in longhand, it is the reader through the acts of animating, recreating, recognising, analogising and the like which enables him or her to be, say, positioned. Thus a text may say that e.g. 'letter bombs were sent to people who were married to blacks' implying (?), we might say, an audience of whites. But it is our work as socially, culturally, and materially specific readers that enables us to elucidate (perhaps) these explicit, implicit or hidden meanings in texts and writing. In any given time and place in history there will be agreed and/or contested meanings and to say that these persist across all time and all places is 'for all intents and purposes' impossible.

As Colin MacCabe suggests:

'In analysing literature one is engaged in a battle of readings, not chosen voluntaristically but determined institutionally. The validity of interpretation is determined in the present in the political struggle over literature.' (MacCabe 1978: 26)

I would express it by saying that meaning springs from the social negotiations with the material world or, in philosophical terms, reality precedes consciousness.

4) Some Ideological Considerations

I am aware that hovering over the previous three sections is the problem of ideology. I can ask of each of those sections, how or where does the concept of ideology fit in? So, in this section, I will try to locate some meanings of the term that will underlie the work of the next chapter when I situate myself historically and culturally, and of the chapter that follows when I try to show how a specific poem arises.

Looking back on the work of this chapter, I can say that whatever meaning

I take for ideology, it is clear that it bears some relation to what I have called material reality. Then again, in the field of intertextuality, there are some who would incorporate all ideological activity into a notion of a text, an 'already', available for a writer. And in respect of literary response, as we have seen from Bennett there are some who would see the process of reading as in part a matter involving negotiations and conversations with 'ideology'.

> ' . . . the literary effect is not just produced by a determinate process, but actively inserts itself within the reproduction of other ideological effects: it is not only itself the effect of material causes, but is also an effect on socially determined individuals, constraining them materially to treat literary texts in a certain way. So, ideologically, the literary effect is not just in the domain of 'feeling', 'taste', judgement', and hence of aesthetic and literary ideas; it sets up a process itself: the rituals of literary consumption and 'cultural' practice.' (Balibar and Macherey 1992: 50)

or as Eagleton puts it:

> '[a text] generates a field of possible readings which, within the conjuncture of the reader's ideological matrix and its own is necessarily finite.' (Eagleton 1976b: 167)

But what is ideology? It is a word that poses a good few problems in its casual use because it can be found to be doing quite different tasks. Eagleton has identified sixteen different meanings:

> 'a) the process of production of meanings, signs and values in social life;
> b) a body of ideas characteristic of a particular social group or class;
> c) ideas which help to legitimate a dominant political power,
> d) false ideas which help to legitimate a dominant political power;
> e) systematically distorted communication;
> f) that which offers a position for a subject;
> g) forms of thought motivated by social interests;
> h) identity thinking;
> i) socially necessary illusion;
> j) the conjuncture of discourse and power;

k) the medium in which conscious social actors make sense of their world;
l) action-oriented sets of beliefs;
m) the confusion of linguistic and phenomenal reality;
n) semiotic closure;
o) the indispensable medium in which individuals live out their relations to a social structure;
p) the process whereby social life is converted to a natural reality.'
(Eagleton 1991: 1-2)

This is a bold attempt to gather up and summarise current usage, and Eagleton may well be right that these ways of using the word are currently in circulation. However, I would like to suggest a different, more portable, way of looking at the word, painted with larger brush strokes: most of the time, the words 'ideology' and 'ideological' are used to signify not much more than 'a body of ideas'. Sometimes the words are used like this as a way of distinguishing between

1) an outlook or a pattern of behaviour that seems to be random, intuitive or pragmatic and
2) an outlook or a pattern of behaviour that seems to come from a body of ideas, some kind of shared set of beliefs, an 'ideology'.

This way of using Ideology is essentially a 'neutral' usage as any group of language users can use the terms in this way to refer to *any* body of ideas. So it is that it has become acceptable even to Conservative politicians to refer to parts of their party as 'ideological' without necessarily meaning it in any derogatory way. 'We've got to get our ideology right,' as some Tories have said following the election defeat of 1997. For convenience sake, this neutral sense of the word I will refer to with a lower case I', as in 'ideology'.

The second area of usage concerns Eagleton's c,d,e,f,g,i,j,m,o,p. I find it quite acceptable that Eagleton has teased out the various usages of the term as it has been used and contested by e.g., Marx, Althusser, Foucault and others. However, the broad sweep of the concept here, and it is one that I will be adopting, is that there is a body of ideas at work in society which in complex ways (much disputed between Marxists, post-Marxists, post-structuralists and others) is linked to

i) power in society and
ii) the maintenance of that power.

This usage of the word is technical, confined to critiques of capitalism and totalitarianism and is frequently inflected with a sense that this kind of ideology is hidden and therefore needs to be exposed, made visible, confronted or opposed.

This ideology, it is said, helps maintain the status quo through such textual processes as 'naturalising', 'mystifying', 'universalising' (Eagleton 1991). Or, it can be looked at societally as Althusser (1965) did (albeit in a deterministic sort of way) and be seen operating through the dominant practices within the 'Ideological State Apparatuses' of e.g., education, law, family, religion. Bennett described this kind of ideology (derived from Althusser) as 'interpellating' the subject, placing a person in a position in society. For convenience sake, I can call this *area* of usage, 'Ideology', Ie with an upper case 'I'. (By the way, Bennett here is being too idealist for my liking, leaving out, as he does, the inexorable ways in which *material* need Interpellates' the individual, say, to go out and get a job, and in that way leaves the individual being 'positioned' in society, and *thereafter* taking up various ideologies, or being subjected to Ideology.)

However, it is not my intention here to engage in a debate with the contested meanings and usages of Ideology. If 'Ideology' were to be used to explain in toto the genesis of my work, I would be left with another form of idealism, but quasi-Marxist in kind. It seems to me this is partly why Eagleton in *Criticism and Ideology* (1976b) tied himself in several knots in trying to create what was a kind of ideology-Ideology map within which writers write. However, I will make the following observations:

1) My parents and I are in possession of a fairly coherent set of beliefs that could be described as 'left-wing' or Marxist ideology. The historical and cultural origin of these ideas in my life is teased out in the following two chapters.
2) My writing and the ways in which I insert that writing into society and education (as I describe later) is informed by this ideology.
3) My body of writing cannot be reduced to 'ideology'. The scenes, images, phantasies, dialogues, monologues and the like that are the poems are not simply expressions of left-wing ideology. However, it is undeniable that in many and diverse ways, these scenes, images etc. are *related* to this ideology. When I say 'related to', that is they variously 'encode aspects of', 'connote',

'are inscribed with', are 'congenial to', 'sympathetic with', 'confluent with', 'compatible with', 'of the same milieu and ethos as' this ideology.

4) My body of writing and my social practices in and around it e.g., performances, stand in a particular relation to Ideology, that is in relation to some of society's dominant practices in e.g., (at the level of the sign) formal poetry, use of standard English; as well as in the social practices of parenting, upbringing of children, education, literary criticism, the National Curriculum and so on. This relation could be (and has been) described generally as non-dominant, mildly subversive or heterodox and will be explored in the next two chapters.

5) It would be wrong to expect there to be an absolute consistency about this. One individual poem may subvert dominant ideas more or less than another. Indeed one individual poem may confirm dominant ideas more than another. Or again, between poems and within poems there will be contradictions, which will be manifestations of e.g. a contradiction between my collectivist ideology and my class-siting in society as a well-off artisan-artist in non-collective work; a contradiction between being a parent but writing about being parented. There will also be contradictions between my intentions and my actual practice, between my ideology and the ideological effect. Much of this is difficult (or some would say, e.g. Macherey 1978, unavoidably impossible) for me to detect as I am inescapably inscribed with Ideology. Thus it could be argued that at the very moment when it might seem that I am celebrating children's autonomy and 'free' spirit, I am, in a one-hour monologued performance in a school, policed as it might well be by teachers parading up and down weeding out 'trouble-makers', *dominating and dictating*. (!)

6) Neither ideology nor Ideology is a thing. Neither has an absolute autonomy enabling ideas to float free of:

i) the social and economic situations in which they are articulated;

ii) their class, race, gender and national provenance

iii) the historical time and place in which they surface;

iv) the mode of production in the society in which they are expressed;

v) the level of power maintained by the dominant economic class;

vi) the level of power maintained by the state;

vii) the level of activity of those opposed to the dominant economic class and/or state.

The precise ways in which I pick my way through some of these thorny questions will become clearer in the next two chapters.

5) Some Thoughts on the Writing Self

At the end of the day, the writing we are talking about in this thesis has been done by one person, one biological entity. I have offered some ways of seeing how this writing is related to

1) material existence
2) other texts
3) the processes of reading and understanding and 4) ideological contexts and effects.

I would now like to turn my attention to the question of how should I understand the writing 'self'? As I dwell on actions and thoughts of an 'I' in the next two chapters, what model of personality should I work with? At various times in the previous sections of this chapter either I or cited authors have opened up the field of how it is the individual writer or the self functions. Thus, Balibar and Macherey were quoted saying:

> ' . . . the writer . . . is a material agent, an intermediary inserted in a particular place, in conditions he has not created, in submission to the contradictions which by definition he cannot control, through a particular social division of labour, characteristic of the ideological superstructure of bourgeois society, which individuates him.' (Balibar and Macherey 1992: 49)

Here Balibar and Macherey are trying to juggle with several ways of looking at the writing self all at the same time:

1) he or she is an 'agent', meaning, one can assume, a kind of representative of a certain layer in society;
2) an 'intermediary', meaning, one can assume, a kind of go-between or messenger bringing news of society to its members;
3) someone caught up in the 'contradictions' of society, which one can assume might include such ideas as contradictions between, say the desires unleashed by a consumer society and the lack of possibility of satisfying them if one is not incredibly rich;
4) someone locked into a certain site in the mechanisms with which society is organised to produce, service and distribute things;

5) someone made individual by the institutions of, say, family, school, law and religion.

It is a difficult juggling act to perform, as evidenced by Balibar and Macherey's odd syntax.

I cited Roy Bhaskar tackling the matter like this:

'On the relational view a person's individuality is primarily constituted by his or her social particularity. In other words, what they are is mainly a product of what they have done or what has been done to them in the particular social relations into which they were born and in which they have lived. What they do or have done to them must be understood in terms of their historically and socially conditioned capacities, powers, liabilities and tendencies.' (Bhaskar 1989: 7)

Once again, this fixes the idea of the self as created within social activity which is limited and constrained by what is possible in the given historical place and time. Bhaskar is at pains here to show that the individual is neither wholly a determined product, nor wholly an omnipotent actor. He says instead: 'a product of what they have done or what has been done to them . . .' Ie 'actor' and 'acted-upon' simultaneously and dialectically. This struggle to counter simultaneously common sense individualism and crude determinism began, perhaps, with Wilhelm Reich (whose ideas later in life have tended to leave him stranded in disregard). What is unique about Reich's approach in the 1930s was that he was anxious to incorporate into materialist understandings of capitalist society, ideas surrounding desire, repression and sexual energy i.e. some of our most powerful emotions. It is in Reich that one finds someone attempting a synthesis of materialism, Ideology, the self and its history.

' . . . every social organization produces those character structures which it needs to exist. In class society, the existing ruling class secures its position, with the help of education and the institution of the family, by making its ideologies the ruling ideologies of all members of the society. However, it is not solely a matter of implanting the ideologies in all members of the society. It is not a matter of indoctrinating attitudes and opinions but of a far-reaching process in every new generation of a given society, the purpose of which is to effect a change in and mold psychic structures (and this is in all layers of the population) in conformity with the social order. Hence, natural scientific psychology and characterology have a clearly defined task: they have to put their finger on the ways and mechanisms by means of which man's social entity is transformed into psychic structure and, thereby, into ideology.' (Reich 1972: xxii-xxiii)

So Reich is trying here to avoid crude notions of indoctrination in order to explain ways in which society's norms are inculcated into each new generation. He wants to say there are 'psychic structures' which are 'molded' – a term that surely does not totally free him from a simplistic view of the matter as indoctrination. However, later in the same passage he tries to get closer:

'Ever since the beginning of the private ownership of the means of production, the first and most important organ for the reproduction of the social order has been the patriarchal family, which lays in its children the character groundwork for the later influencing by the authoritarian order. While, on the one hand, the family represents the primary reproduction organ of character structures, the insight into the role of sexual education in the educational system as a whole teaches us that, first and foremost, they are libidinal interests and energies which are employed in the anchoring of the authoritarian social order . . .

It is in this anchoring of the social order in the character structure that we find the explanation of the toleration on the part of the suppressed layers of the population toward the rulership of an upper social class that has the means of power at its disposal, a toleration that sometimes goes as far as to affirm authoritarian suppression at the expense of its own interests. This is far more obvious in the sphere of sexual suppression than it is in the sphere of the material and cultural gratification of needs.' (Reich 1972: xxiv)

So here is a model of the self in Reich's society (1930s) tied into and collaborating with the authority structure by means of repression of infant sexuality. However, Reich did not want to leave the self helplessly trapped with no way out:

'And yet, precisely in the formation of the libidinal structure, it can be demonstrated that, coeval with the anchoring of a social order, which completely or partially obstructs the gratification of one's needs, the psychic preconditions begin to develop which undermine this anchoring in the character structure. As time goes on, an ever widening divergency springs up between forced renunciation and the increased strain on one's needs.' (Reich 1972: xxiv)

Very few writers have tried, like Reich, to conceive of

1) class society,
2) the individual,
3) Ideology and
4) desire (and its repression)

all in the same breath. When I look at my work as a whole I can see ways in which I, like many children's writers, play with libidinous feelings, particularly in the permissible area of food. (On one occasion I made the libidinous feelings more explicit as with 'Who Likes Cuddles?' (Rosen 1985).) Again, like many writers for children I play with the minutiae of rule-governed behaviour that dominates children or which children subvert. So it is that the Reichian processes of suppression and subversion that were so powerful in our childhood development, reappear in various (dis)guises in the poems and stories we write. It could be said here perhaps that the very fact that I am a children's writer has some strong relation to how these matters were dealt with in my own childhood. Or even more convolutedly, it could be said that the kinds of gratifications I derive from writing and performing are related to permitted and forbidden childhood desires. Why am I seeking gratification through this channel? Who precisely am I trying to please? Children or the child in me? Teachers? Or the teachers who were my parents? And with my 'naughty' poems or poems that explore parenting, am I also trying to offend? If so who? Teachers? Or, again, the teachers who were my parents? However, this thesis, like Reich, would want strenuously to avoid splitting these considerations off from the particular social formations that precede, constrain and induce the contradictory feelings of repression and desire; the same social formations that are themselves affected by how the mass of individuals handle repression and desire.

How the self is found within social formations was explored nearly thirty years ago by Lucien Seve (translated in 1975, 1978). For Seve, a human being is firstly part of the 'productive forces'; secondly a human being is situated in the 'relations of production'; and thirdly a human being is conscious within the available ideologies of the time. (Seve 1975: 31-32). This is directly derived from Marx writing in Capital and *The German Ideology*. To relate this schema to my own situation would leave me defining as:

1) part of the productive forces of the communication industries, and part of the productive forces of the state apparatus i.e. education;
2) defined within those industries variously as client, artisan, jobbing worker and mercenary;
3) my consciousness developed within the dominant Ideologies of e.g.,
i) late British capitalism, monetarism, social democracy,
ii) the resisting ideologies of municipal and state socialism, and the politics of my dissident parents,
iii)various dominant Ideologies surrounding e.g., education, parenting, childhood, 'high' art etc.

It is not hard to detect here that Seve has chosen to overlook the defining characteristic of 'self' that dominates psychoanalytic and psychotherapeutic discourse: namely the relation between the individual and his or her family groupings, first as a child and then, if relevant, as lover and parent. A massive body of literature written from a whole variety of perspectives (and what is now a shared understanding all over the Western world) shows the emotional life of the individual developing from within these triads and dyads. Where Seve chooses to ignore this literature, Reich, in just a few sentences, poses a fundamental challenge to it: namely that the nature of our desires and gratifications (or lack of them) are not simply a consequence of relationships within a family, but rather, they are a consequence of the *kind of job Ideology wants the family to do*, in order to assist in the survival of class society. He breaks open the way in which our personal and social development has been rendered domestic and then reduced to it.

If we try to make some synthesis between Reich and Seve we see individuals in terms of

1) how they find the means to feed, clothe and shelter themselves;
2) the position(s) in society (as available in the mode of production of the day) in which they find themselves to do this;
3) accepting or resisting (or in usual contradiction, accepting and resisting) the dominant Ideological forces of the day;

4) occupying position(s) within the systems of upbringing and co-habiting (that have developed within class society in order to help maintain the status quo) positions that control and shape our desires.

In a sense this is no revelation. People describe themselves and each other all the time in terms of:

1) the job they do (and how much money they get);
2) how they see themselves in relation to people 'above' or 'below' them in society;
3) whether they 'go along' with this or that idea or 'can't stand' another idea and
4) whether they can get what they want as mothers, fathers, children and so on.

The problem, and it is the one that I am tackling in this thesis, lies in making the difficult jump to being able to make a model in one's head of *how all these elements are connected, all the time.*

A 'passive father' may, let us say, be described as 'having once been a dominated child' (i.e., according to narrow psychologistic, domestic explanations, his personality is located as developing *within* the family) But what is being said in this thesis is that there will always be all-important extra-familial forces at work, working their way into the family and to the individual. So it is that the boy who became the 'passive father' may have experienced his own father as:

1) having been desperately anxious about climbing the social ladder,
2) having forcefully expressed ideas around respecting your 'betters' and
3) having restrained all signs of self-gratification in his children as they were signs of waste and dangerous excess.
4) Crucially, the 'passive father' will also have been both actor and acted-upon within the institutions and work-places of his life: employment, school, hospital, shopping-structures, leisure-structures, health/disease institutions, legal structures, religious structures and so on.

As will become clear in the following chapters, I will try to avoid seeing my family (and, importantly, the feelings that were *seemingly* generated within it) as a self-enclosed unit – or to put it another way: I will not take the dynamics of my family as being the 'sufficient condition' for explaining the genesis of my poetry.

(For lengthy and sophisticated analyses along these lines see in particular Peter Leonard (1984); for a critique of psychology from a materialist standpoint see John Robinson (1993). For a Marxist view of 'human nature' see also W. Peter Archibald (1989) and an attempt at a humanist Marxist approach to the 'self' is made in Seidler (1994)).

This brief final section should point the way to my showing in the next two chapters how there is a constant interplay between the differing elements of existence – an interplay that does not simply produce the individual 'me', but also constitutes me as active agent (writer, performer, critic, father) in the world.

Conclusion

In this chapter I have tried to provide:

1) a rationale based on a Marxist form of materialism that underpins:
2) a specific and limited form of intertextuality,
3) a model of reading and what I have called reading-writing,
4) a view on ideology/Ideology
5) a view of the writing self. This is the theoretical basis for Chapter 3, in which I will try to locate historically myself and my writing self and Chapter 4, the analysis of the poems.

Chapter 3

IN THIS CHAPTER I WOULD LIKE to situate myself historically within

1) the socioeconomic fields of
i) my childhood,
ii) my writing life
2) the specific 'fields of cultural production' in which I have found myself working, which include:
i) the cultural institution of poetry as a whole,
ii) the cultural institution of poetry written specifically with children in mind.

In order to avoid repetition later in the following chapter (when I analyse the material, textual, ideological and cultural origins of specific poems), sections 1 i) and 1 ii) of this chapter are intended to be no more than broad pictures, in summary.

1) The Socioeconomic Background of

i) my childhood

> In acquiring one's conception of the world one always belongs to a particular grouping which is that of all the social elements which share the same mode of thinking and acting . . . The starting-point of critical elaboration is the consciousness of what one really is, and is 'knowing thyself as a product of the historical process to date which has deposited in you an infinity of traces, without leaving an inventory.' (Gramsci 1971: 423)

This passage takes us to the core of what I am trying to explore here: to describe and delineate the 'historical process' and those 'social elements' into which I was born. I cannot escape being part of a 'social grouping' or being a 'product' of certain historical processes. However, this is not the whole picture: as human agents in historical processes, we interact with historical processes and in small ways (as single individuals) we make some impact on those processes. It is sometimes convenient to dub this interaction an 'intervention' and as Alan Sinfield points out,

> ' . . . the kind of intervention intended by the writer is not usefully considered as merely personal inspiration; it occurs within a framework of socially constructed possibilities . . . ' (Sinfield 1989: 36)

The first question I have to ask myself, is what were those 'socially constructed possibilities' as I grew up, in the period 1946-60? My mother and father were teachers and we lived in a London suburb, socioeconomic facts that fit precisely the kinds of changes going on in society at this time.

Firstly, my parents, upwardly socially mobile from working-class Jewish backgrounds, were part of a change going on in society as a whole at that time. A layer of ex-working-class young people moved into new employment. Civil Service, managerial and professional jobs increased by 50 per cent between 1938 and 1951 (Sinfield 1989: 53). Lowe notes that in 'the period after the Second World War' there was

> 'a marked shift towards the tertiary sector of the economy, as service industries, distributive trades and administrative occupations assumed a growing importance.' (Lowe 1988: from Introduction)

There was what he calls a 'reinforcement of the professions' (Lowe 1988: 10). Secondly, my mother, being part of this 'reinforcement', was part of what was another kind of societal change: the proportion of married women in paid work rose from 10 per cent in 1931 to 21 per cent in 1951, 32 per cent in 1961 and 47 per cent in 1972. (Sinfield 1989: 206).

Thirdly, the fact that we lived in a London suburb also placed us at yet another point of change: there was what Lowe calls a 'drift to the South' and it was there that the 'professions became more dominant' (Lowe 1988: 10). As part of this, there was a 'rise of suburban commuting on a scale which was quite unprecedented' (Lowe 1988: Introduction).

We lived right in the heart of 'commuter-land' on the Metropolitan Line into London so my living environment, Pinner, Middlesex, was shaped by the fact that during the day it was depopulated by a great proportion of the men, and many of the women, travelling into London and back again in the evening. For much of my childhood, my parents too had to travel on this line, even if it was sometimes in the opposite direction, and I spent many hours on Pinner station collecting train numbers or waiting for my mother to come back from work (and wrote a poem about it (!) 'Platform' – (Rosen 1983: 80-82)).

The high expectations of the commuter-culture of Pinner of a certain standard of life in housing, education, parkland, shops and restaurants was central to my upbringing, and framed our way of life. It was the culture of school-friends, the neighbourhood: the large disposable incomes available to sustain the shopping centres and provide huge Conservative majorities and solid Conservative councils in the area. It sustained the selective education system that dominated and structured so much of my childhood. As we shall see when I come to look at the poems in Chapter 4, my parents and their friends whether as Jews and/or as left-wing dissidents were, in one sense, stranded in this environment I should point out here that Jewishness in my parents' lives was not expressed through Judaism. The complicated matter of exactly how my and my parents' class, ideological outlooks and Jewishness interacted, is taken up in Chapter 4 in relation to some specific poems. Suffice it to say at this juncture that the view expressed in this thesis is that class is not abstract but is expressed in everyday existence. In the case of my parents, this was manifested in the objects and social interchanges of a particular, class-specific layer of British, Ashkenazim Jewry.

However, no matter how particular their cultural and ideological origins, objectively and economically my parents were playing a part in some of the important social changes of that time. They had joined a social grouping, that has become the dominant social unit in post-war Britain, courted by the media and politicians for over fifty years. It would be a mistake to see the grouping as unified by attitude and so I will place my parents, and ultimately myself, within this grouping in two ways:

1) in the specific profession: education and
2) as 'left intellectuals'.

Education dominated my childhood in both the usual way, by my going to school, but also in that my parents were active, committed teachers who brought their work home whilst engaging in left-wing campaigns within education at that time. The situation for schools in our area was itself fairly privileged:

The new suburbs usually have good school buildings (with the additional advantages of good houses, books in the home and social family contacts).' (Central Advisory Council for Education, 1947: 12)

But as was noted at the time, the system was divided:

Public schools, secondary schools, technical schools, modern schools – here we have a regular graded hierarchy.' (Giles, 1946: 70)

And even within official publications there was some anxiety about this:

'Until good secondary schools are available for all, we cannot escape from the harmful competitive system whereby certain pupils are admitted to well-staffed, well-equipped schools, and the remainder treated as unsuccessful and sent to schools which have merely changed their name.' (Central Advisory Council for Education, 1947: 16)

But in Pinner and inside the Conservative governments between 1951 and 1964 the system and its grammar schools was defended along these lines . . .

The nation cannot do without them. It is their social function that is prized. These schools turn out an indispensable kind of citizen.' (*Times Educational Supplement* 5 Jan 1951 cited in Lowe 1988: 42)

. . . even though by 1949 . . .

' . . . it began to emerge that significant numbers of the pupils assigned to these schools by a selective examination were failing to stay the course' (Lowe 1988: 43)

and that that year nearly 25 per cent did not stay on at school till 16.

This kind of debate was a permanent fixture throughout my life from the time of my earliest memories right through to my leaving school. My mother having entered the profession as part of the wave of post-war 'emergency training' worked in primary schools that were geared up for the selection system. (Note: Lowe notes that emergency training ran during the period of 1946-1951. In one year, there were 34,000 entrants to the profession. By the summer of 1946, 44,000 men and 12,000 women had come forward and new applications were coming in at 1200 a week (Lowe 1988: 28).) My father entered the profession earlier and worked firstly with the beneficiaries of the selection system in the grammar school sector, then secondly, as part of a left-wing commitment, within the comprehensive secondary school sector, and thirdly within teacher training, where my mother too eventually finished up. I cannot escape from the observation that as I grew up I passed from the professional concerns of one parent towards the concerns of the other: primary school to grammar school. 'Growing up' – and all the feelings connected with that phrase – in my case reinforced a cultural trait of growing from the mother to the father in that it mirrored their professional concerns.

My parents' social and political engagement showed itself within education, my mother by taking up the 'progressive' cause within primary education and my father, by opposing selection and favouring progressive reforms of language and literature teaching, at the secondary level. My mother would identify strongly with reports like these:

> 'the most striking impression is that primary education is on the move . . . the emphasis is changing – away from a situation in which classes of children are being taught most of the day sitting at desks or standing rigidly in lines, towards one in which individual children are actively learning through experiences that appeal to their natural interest.' (LCC 1950: 3 cited Lowe 1988: 30)

Meanwhile, my father would be talking along these lines:

> 'Quite apart from the geographical disparities in 11+ pass rates, which tended to work in favour of the South-East, contrasts in buildings, equipment and staffing, to say nothing of the length of school life meant that the 30 per cent who attended grammar school received almost half of the expenditure allocated to the secondary sector. As Vaizey has shown: 'The award of a grammar school place at the age of eleven was equivalent to more than doubling the resources devoted to that child if it had gone to a modern school'.' (Vaizey 1958: 101-2 cited Lowe 1988: 52-3)

Or like this:

> 'The tests select for a predetermined number of places. The number
> of children capable of 'logical reasoning' . . . miraculously fits the
> number of grammar school places provided by LEAs A discipline which
> is capable of such manipulation is hardly likely to inspire confidence in
> its scientific objectivity.' (Max Morris, *Times Educational Supplement*,
> 24 November 1950 cited in Lowe 1988: 49)

Max Morris was a member of the Communist Party of Great Britain, as were
my parents, and as such they expressed their political commitments on a
wider stage, firstly as 'Party Members' until 1957 and thereafter as unattached
left-wingers. As a family, this put us in what was an identifiable grouping, as
Sinfield observes:

> This moment saw the formation and consolidation of a distinct class
> fraction: a younger-generation, left-liberal intelligentsia, with a quite
> specific subcultural formation. In his Declaration essay of 1957, Tynan
> discerned among some young people an 'instinctive Leftism' that
> needed only 'a rallying-point, social and political'. CND was to be one
> such; others were Royal Court drama, higher education, folk song
> and jazz.' (Sinfield 1989: 240)

Yes, as a family *we* went on CND marches, sat in the Royal Court (I even
wrote a play about my family that was put on there! *Backbone* (Rosen
1969)), we took part in higher education whether as students or lecturers,
sang folk-songs, went to folk clubs and collected jazz records. By the time
I reached university in 1964, I was in a sense ripe and prepared for the
student revolt of 1968.

Two passages from Lowe summarise with extraordinary precision the
period of my childhood both in an economic sense but also in relation to
education. I have annotated the passages within, showing the ways in which
we were part of societal wide shifts:

> (1)
> the years from 1951 to 1964 saw continuing uninterrupted full
> employment, with a 40 per cent increase in industrial output during
> the whole period. This newly achieved popular affluence was marked

by the acquisition of consumer durables. In real terms, wages rose by 20 per cent between 1951 and 1958, and by a further 30 per cent before the Conservatives left office in 1964. A few crude statistics can be used to demonstrate succinctly how this enabled what was nothing short of a social revolution. Between 1951 and 1964 the number of cars on the roads rose from 2 and half million to 6 million, as annual expenditure on cars and cycles soared from £90 million to £910 million.' [n.b. this coincided precisely with when we acquired our first car, i.e. 1956. MR] 'During the same period the percentage of households owning refrigerators rose from five to 37' [n.b. as with us and our first fridge, le 1960. MR] 'owning washing machines from 11 to 52' [n.b. as with us and our first washing machine, i.e. 1953 or 54. MR], 'and owning television sets from 9 to 85' [n.b. as with us and our first TV, i.e. 1956. MR]. 'This new middle class' [e.g. my parents. MR] 'aspired to mass schooling for its young people' [n.b. very much my parents' aspirations. MR] 'and could afford the necessary sacrifices. While there was a steady increase in the numbers of children in school in the 5-14 age range (from 6, 409, 000 to 7, 528, 000) the most striking advance was in the numbers staying on above the age of 15 (from 299,000 to 848,000)' [n.b. my brother and I were part of this. MR] 'and this was matched by a corresponding increase (from 85,000 to 126,000) in the number of university students' [n.b. my brother and I were part of this. MR]. 'This enhanced affluence enabled the beginnings of a revolution in schooling, through fuller participation in leisure pursuits and school visits than had been possible previously,' [n.b. both my brother and I were involved in a whole range of school outings and foreign exchanges, etc. MR] 'and it also meant that the secondary schools could extend existing elite practice by looking to their new clientele to provide such items as school uniform and ancillary sports equipment .' [n.b. as with us. MR] 'In these ways the nature of the educational expansion of the 1950s was largely determined by the economic upturn.' (Lowe 1988: 74)

(2)
' . . . the housing drive . . . was in reality aimed at those upwardly mobile elements of the lower-middle and working classes who could best afford homeownership . . . ' [n.b. we became home-owners for the first time in 1962. MR] 'It was a policy which heightened social

distance between the inner-ring suburbs and the new homogeneous overspill areas of the 1950s. Thus, housing policy predetermined the relative success of schools in these contrasting environments.' [n.b. we were part of this 'relative success' which was measured out and fought over in precise class terms in the locality in class attitudes between the old suburb of Harrow and the new upper working class suburb of Wealdstone. MR]

'A further consequence of this suburbanisation,' [n.b. of which we were a part. MR] 'which impinged directly upon family life and less directly on schooling was the rise of commuting . . . By the mid1950s the daytime population of Central London (one and a quarter million) was five times as great as the resident population. During these years this phenomenon was mirrored in all of the major conurbations. This meant that not only were unprecedented numbers of schoolchildren being drawn from homes where commuting was the norm for at least one parent (usually the male), but also that schoolteachers themselves became able to travel greater distances from home to work.' [n.b. as with us. MR] 'In the long term this trend came to influence the ways in which the teaching profession perceived its role, and it meant too that increasingly teachers in working-class schools chose to reside elsewhere in middle-class districts' [n.b. as was the case with my father when he began to teach in an inner-London comprehensive school. MR]. (Lowe 1988: 75-6)

In fact, the contrasts between old and new areas within Harrow was one of the key sites of class conflict in the locality. This was fought out in the crucible of education as was observed at the time:

' . . . so far from there being . . . 'parity of esteem' between different types of secondary school, there is a strongly established hierarchy, corresponding closely to the hierarchy of social classes. Despite the greater social mobility of post-war years, most professional and upper-business class parents . . . feel that they are losing face if they cannot afford to send their sons to Headmasters' Conference Schools. The rest of the upper middle-class families similarly prefer one of the direct grant or older grammar schools to the state grammar schools. To them and to the lower middle classes the failure of their children to achieve a place in any grammar school tends to be regarded as a social disgrace.' (Vernon 1957: 20-21 cited in Lowe 1988: 108)

On a more personal level, the whole of my childhood was marked with a contradiction: as a child of school-teachers I was objectively cast into a middle-class role, but the combination of their working-class background and membership of the Communist Party placed me in a not-easily described and ambiguous relationship with working-class children, especially as it involved activities such as collecting for a local bus strike, election leafletting, or even arguments about the Soviet Union's foreign policy with the local butcher's son, who, as it happens, went to my primary school but thereafter, the local secondary modern school. I have a distinct sensation of having lived a life in my childhood which was in problematic ways in opposition to the lives and backgrounds of most of my middle-class friends, (unless they were part of our 'dissident class fraction') and yet, it is inescapable from the socioeconomic phenomena I have described, that we were part of what was in effect an onward and upward and *optimistic* march of a growing and privileged sector of the middle class in a London suburb.

This contradictory position made itself manifest most clearly at the grammar school where I came into huge conflict with a society-wide phenomena of the time: the grammar school ethos. This was reflected in what were called 'behaviour problems' and outright revolt, as over the question of refusing to accept 'prefectship', i.e. the right to rule over younger pupils. Nearly always, this brought me into finding myself involved with 'the new clientele': those pupils of working-class background who found the grammar school ethos fairly unbearable.

> The grammar schools, particularly, saw themselves as suddenly acquiring a new clientele, and their response was to emphasise their traditional function and their long-term contribution to national life.' (Lowe 1988: 106-7)

Frances Stevens, an educationalist, wrote in a letter to the *Times Educational Supplement* January 4 1952

> 'the staff of a grammar school can no longer count on the strong ... desire of both parents and children for something which their school had to give: perhaps it was partly a regard for scholarship, partly, a

concern for the establishment of certain patterns of behaviour and ethical standards, and partly, let us admit, a sense of middle-class superiority . . . In the old ethos of the grammar school [there] was something worth preserving . . . with patience and skill a way can be found of transmitting it to these new 'first generation' pupils.' (cited in Lowe 1988: 107)

Or not!

Lowe (1988: 110) cites Gross, who by coincidence describes one of my two grammar schools, Watford Boys Grammar School:

'The actual content of the basic curriculum in the school has probably altered little in the last forty years . . . The situation is dominated by the ever-present external examination system, wherein teachers are examined as well as pupils, and this limits flexibility and experiment to a certain extent.' (Gross 1965: 274)

In many ways, I was chafing at the day-to-day details of how in Britain, the social hierarchy was being produced – or more particularly how my particular section of that hierarchy was being produced. Lowe cites one Toby Weaver, from the Ministry of Education, who was in no doubt what was going on and what it was all for:

The world of work may be crudely analysed, for the purposes of this discussion, into jobs at three levels, which are reflected in secondary school courses and organisation:

(i) Major professional and administrative jobs, for which a university degree or its equivalent is the normal qualification, which require in turn advanced courses up to the age of 18 at secondary school: I shall use the term 'fliers' to denote boys and girls who show at 11+ or subsequently that they are likely to achieve this level of educational and employment career;

(ii) Minor professional and executive jobs (e.g. physiotherapists, production manager) for which a group of GCE passes at matriculation level or equivalent is the normal qualification, and which require in turn '0' level courses up to the age of 16 + at secondary school: I shall call these people 'hurdlers', i.e. children who show at 11+ or subsequently that they can take a basic 5 year course in their stride;

(iii) Clerical, craft, semi-skilled and unskilled jobs which require no prior paper qualification before entry into employment. These children will receive a four year course and the majority will leave school at 15 – though many children will obtain some qualification by part-time study. I shall call these people 'pedestrians'? (Weaver 1954: 160 cited in Lowe 1988: 114115)

I was, then, a 'flier' but twisting and turning and kicking in the cockpit all the while.

1) (continued) The Socioeconomic Background of

ii) my writing life

In the previous section I have considered my *formation* within a particular class and particular class-fraction. The period of my adult writing life is perhaps less powerful as an influence, in that I arrive in adulthood already situated, and in my case remained in the same class and fraction, albeit with certain minor shifts. Thus, I went to university (1964-1969), took up a traineeship in the BBC (1969-1972), and after a short period of unemployment and then further study (1972-1976), became a freelance writer, performer and broadcaster (1976-?).

Virtually the whole period of the time when books of mine have been published has been marked by two important features: Conservative governments (1979-1997) and a downturn in the economy. (GDP slid into negative growth in 1973 and bumped along with small growth rates or negative growth rates (1990-1992) until the upturn of 1993 (Johnson 1994: 343).) Without going into great detail here, suffice it to say, this has meant that the whole time that I have been visiting schools, attending teachers' conferences, lecturing and the like, I have been placed at the heart of raging debates about

1) ideology, initiated in the last days of the Labour Government of James Callaghan (October 18 1976, Ruskin College) and carried on through all the Conservative Governments with their initiatives of the National Curriculum and Education Acts and
2) a mix of cuts, stagnation and failure to expand education spending

(Government expenditure on education expressed as a percentage of GDP declines as follows: 1975-76: 6.3%, 1980-91: 5.4%, 1983-84: 5.2%, 1989-90: 4.6% (Cook and Stevenson 1995: 113)). This, if you like, has been my working environment.

As a freelance writer, and more particularly a freelance writer for children, one is confronted with a set of stark choices:

- should I keep going with waged work and/or membership of a trade union or take up the role in society of the artist-artisan who is detached from wage-labour?
- should I maintain links with those people who are in waged work with children i.e., teachers, librarians, care workers, play workers etc., or stand to one side of them?
- should I distinguish between the kinds of institutions to work in e.g., primary or prep schools, state schools or public schools or should I take an undifferentiated view?
- should I participate in ideological debates concerning language, literacy, bilingualism, racism, sexism and overall class issues in education, or stand aside?
- should I take part in struggles over the equality of provision of education and equality of opportunity or regard these as irrelevant?

On each of these questions I took up the former of the two alternatives posed.

As it happens, one never makes these choices in isolation and throughout this period it was possible, given my formation, to find people interested in both identifying these as real and important choices and making them the same way as I did – to name a very few, authors such as Bernard Ashley, Robert Leeson, Beverly Naidoo, Grace Hallworth, John Agard, Chris Powling and Ziggy Alexander (from Brent libraries), editors such as Rosemary Stones, critics like Bob Dixon, and educationalists in the literary field such as Michael Simons (of the English and Media Centre), Myra Barrs (of the Centre for Language in Primary Education). Various journals such as the *Children's Rights Bulletin*, *Dragon's Teeth*, *The English Magazine* (from the English and Media Centre), *Language Matters* (from the Centre for Language in Primary Education) and *Books for Keeps* have all helped create a home or 'locus' for what is in effect, a committed, dissident view of literature-in-education that could be described as humanistic, alert to the questions of class, race, gender and disability.

So, the period of my writing life has been one of making those choices. Between 1976 and 1993 I took up various residences and salaried work within comprehensive and primary schools in inner London and Brent involving schools such as Vauxhall Manor (girls' comprehensive) (1976-1978), Holloway School (boys' Comprehensive) (1979-1982), Highbury Quadrant Primary School, (1980-1982), Gainsborough Primary School (1982-84), Brondesbury (mixed comprehensive) and a network of feeder primary schools in the London Borough of Brent (1983-84), John Scurr Primary School (1984-1989), and Linden Lodge School for the partially sighted and wholly unsighted in Wandsworth (1993). These long-term attachments to schools affected my work in many ways, but primarily it can be put simply by saying that I was brought into close daily contact with children and students who came from backgrounds far removed from my own: new arrivants from the Caribbean, the Indian sub-continent, Turkey and West Africa; white working-class children who were either migrants within the British Isles — or their parents were; white working-class children who came from long-established and relatively stable homogeneous communities, blind children, girls, and so on. This has been my experience of 'audience'. When I come to look at individual poems in Chapter 4, I hope to show how this audience made its presence felt. While I found myself in these kinds of schools, I also made the move in my living environment, taking up home in the inner London Borough of Hackney which, it is said, has one of the largest proportions of migrants and their offspring in Britain, one of the highest concentrations of unemployment and the usual markers of urban deprivation. (Three out of four residents live in council or rented homes; two thirds of households survive on less than £10,000 a year (Why Hackney is so full of Optimism' Edward Welsh: *Evening Standard* Nov 11, 1996); unemployment in 1997 still stood at 20% ("Hit Squad" goes in to rescue failing schools' Liz Lightfoot: *Daily Telegraph* June 13, 1997); two out of three secondary pupils take free meals; ('That'll Teach you a lesson' Dave Wooding: *The Sun* Sept 19, 1997).)

All this has brought me into contact with the immediate concerns and tensions of teachers put into the situation of delivering government policies whilst fighting for better conditions (smaller class sizes, better resources, better pay, better buildings), demanding job control in their daily work to suit their actual conditions of work (teacher-led assessment), and seeking professional development to improve their intellectual commitment to their work.

Though this has not been the only milieu I have worked in during this time, having also spent a good deal of time in particular in BBC Radio studios and on occasion working in television, the core of my activity for most of this period has been within education. Another aspect of this link with education has been in a less 'attached' way, as a visiting writer. In this time, I must have visited something like a thousand schools in the British Isles.

In other words, in the present situation, and whilst producing the creative work for this thesis, I have occupied a core socioeconomic sphere within education as a writer but also within broadcasting as a presenter of programmes either aimed directly at children such as *Everybody Here* Channel 4 (1982-1984), *Black and White and Read All Over* Channel 4 (1984), *Talk Write and Read* ITV (Central) (1986, 1989, 1991), *Readabout* ITV (Central) 1989-1991, *Eureka* Channel 4 Schools (1996), or indirectly as with BBC Radio 4's *Treasure Islands* (1989-97), which dealt with children's books for parents. Feeding into these activities from a purely literary angle has been my work for radio programmes for adult audiences on books and poetry such as *Meridian Books* BBC World Service (1990-1995), *Poems by Post* BBC World Service (1987-?) and *Best Words* BBC Radio 3 (1995?).

My economic activity then is diverse, deriving income from school residencies and visits, lectures at education and children's literature centres and conferences, school visits, broadcasting, advances and royalties on books. It is subject to changes and pressures within all these fields: education cutbacks, reorganisation within the BBC and mergers within publishing – all three phenomena being a direct consequence of monetarist 'solutions' to what was the downturn in world capitalism between 1976 and the present time. So it is I find that in each of these sites where I intersect with the economic system, I meet, say,

1) an increase in class sizes, a withdrawal of grants to sustain writers in residence and cutback on school book budgets;
2) a downsizing of a BBC Arts department and a cutback on a programme I might be involved with;
3) the removal of backlist titles of mine in an attempt to 'rationalise' the distribution of children's books according to the length of time a given title remains on the warehouse shelf.

Apart from teaching me the subtle ways in which the world economic system touches that seemingly most uneconomic activity of writing children's books, it also teaches me, as I hop about from sector to sector, a necessary cunning in order to maintain my family's well-being with a certain flexibility and agility.

The creative work under review here, is then, in part, a reflection of, or a product of that agility.

2) The specific 'fields of cultural production' (Bourdieu 1993) which I have found myself to work in, which include:

i) the cultural institution of poetry as a whole,
ii) the cultural institution of poetry written specifically with children in mind.

The question here is not a matter of giving a critical outline of these fields, but rather to explore the process of my formation as a member of a particular part of the middle-class intelligentsia.

i) The cultural institution of poetry (as I found it to be)

I was brought up in a home where poetry seemed to have some kind of sacred quality attached to it. My mother seemed to have an emotional reverence for poets, individual poems and at times the whole presence of poetry in our cultural life. She would give the name of W.B. Yeats, a special inflection that placed him and his poems into some undefined zone of yearning, gratitude and nostalgia (Yeats 1933). She gave off a feeling that Yeats had affected her in ways that were beyond explaining to a child, or perhaps to anyone; that Yeats had said things to her that meant more to her than things that were said in everyday conversation, or indeed that anyone in the world had said to her. The mystery and the inaccessibility of this cloud of feeling was replenished by her unwillingness or inability to recite the poems that had touched her. It was her private world and yet she, perhaps unknowingly, had passed on to me a sense that poetry had the potential to reach people in extraordinary, mysterious and exceedingly powerful ways.

Alongside this sense there was a more practical process at hand. My mother taught poetry and by the time I was at secondary school, was involved in poetry programmes for BBC Schools Radio. The way this affected me directly was that I became aware that my mother was always hunting for poems. I would often find her exploring the book shelves at home, or combing through collections, some intended for schools, to find the poem she needed. There was here a sense that poems could fit the bill, could be starting points for something else, could, in her hands, act as some kind of catalyst. Poems could be a point of influence. I would see her slot in markers and slips into books, put the books in her bag and take them off to school with her. And later, she would be doing the same thing as she wrote her scripts for the radio. I remember her saying things like, 'I need a poem that looks closely at an object.'

From this, I think I took several notions:

1) that poetry lived in books;
2) that it was terribly important (even if I was not sure why);
3) that individual poems could be embedded in processes other than pieces of writing that one could simply sit about and read, and
4) that these processes, in my experience, were almost always situated within the field of *education*.

Meanwhile, my father provided a complementary but different approach. I think I felt, perhaps wrongly, that the books in our house were mostly his. There were several shelves of poetry books in the house which, as a child, seemed to me to be one of the least interesting parts of the overall book collection. They were a mixture of the musty and the obscure. The musty element was, I think now, made up of pre-Second World War books, some from my father's university education – a mixture of classics and moderns. So here was his school prize, a copy of Keats' *Collected Works* in a soft blue leather binding, with an inscription inside. The edges of the pages were marbled and the lettering on the cover was in gold leaf. Though I never read the book, I can remember playing with it, flicking the India paper pages and turning it over and over. There was an academic edition of *Beowulf*, fascinating for its complete incomprehensibility and its strange letters, but even more so for the line-by-line notes, scribbles and translations that my father had written on the text some twenty years earlier during that mysterious and exciting time called 'The War'. In this 'musty' section there were, I remember, collections by Browning, Burns and Thomas Hood none of which I ever opened but felt I knew. They were, I now see, part of the furniture of the house and part of what made the place my home.

Where my mother had expressed a sense of poetry having an out-of-reach, deep, emotional quality, the presence of these books in my life gave poetry a historical, ancient, monumental quality. And it could be *studied*. It could, so it seemed, in my father's hands, be pored over, written about, annotated and stored on shelves. And certain volumes could themselves have a special aura around them, either because of their weight, their appearance or the honourable Latinate inscriptions inside.

Simultaneously, my father brought new poetry books into the house. I have a sense of Ted Hughes's early collections being bought the moment they came out and conversations taking place between my parents that this was something special. As I was fairly unquestioning about what my parents thought was special or important, this set up a problem for me. On the odd occasion that I opened one of these new books, they seemed to me to be utterly dull, dry and mostly incomprehensible. Titles and phrases seemed to make sense but the moment the eye began to follow a line, it all became instantly confusing and strange. The pages would strike me as odd, lonely places full of words that did not amuse or thrill. And yet, these parents of mine, whose views I thought were right, important (and of whom I had some impression early on that they seemed to matter to many people beyond the confines of our home), thought that this bizarre poetry stuff was important. I could not make the bridge and from early on there was a sense of inadequacy here. So, from my father I learnt :

1) that poetry had a long history;
2) that it could have an elevated status (school prize-worthy);
3) that it could be studied;
4) that it could, and perhaps should, be difficult and obscure and
5) that it probably wasn't for me.

There was one further resource that my parents seemed to have available in this area: in their pre-war, exciting, loving, politically active youth, poetry had aroused them together. They had shared something here. They would recount their excitement at seeing Auden and Isherwood read and the slightly mournful figure of Margot Heinemann was pointed out to me at social events as the woman who lost her lover, the poet John Cornford (1915-1936), in that most sacred of events in our household, the Spanish Civil War.

It never seemed to me odd that my parents did not write poetry. I know now that in fact on occasions they did, but I did not know this at the time. So the institution of poetry could in their hands be something that you possessed without making any of it yourself. That seemed normal and appropriate. In one sense, I developed an impression from both of them in their different ways, that poetry was so special and that it was so hard to write great poems in great books in the way that Keats and Ted Hughes could, that there was not much point in either of them trying to reach for that. So, even my important and clever parents who knew the difference between good and bad poetry could not do the business of writing it.

To my knowledge my parents did not go to poetry readings when I was a child, (theatre was of much more interest to them) but I did develop a slight sense that poetry was attached to poets through the media of radio, records and later, reel-to-reel tape. I can remember the voice on disc of Dylan Thomas (and Richard Burton reading Thomas) filling our front room: 'And death shall have no dominion . . . ' (Thomas 1995: 51).

What was this peculiar noise? It sounded like prayers in school assembly and yet my parents were atheists . . . Surely they wouldn't fill the house with prayers. Why did Burton's and Thomas's voices so shake with emotion and yet I couldn't figure out what the emotion was about? On the audio tapes, there was Robert Graves with his crusty upper class voice seeming to having jokes without explaining the jokes. My parents were laughing, my older brother was imitating Graves' voice and I was standing there trying to figure out what it was all about: there were individual phrases that made sense but I couldn't grasp the connections: 'And down we went with nothing in our pockets . . . ' 'Not you, not old Eagle' 'I started as a lift boy . . . ' (from 'Song : Lift Boy '(Graves 1975: 54)).

Meanwhile, on the radio, on that most unfriendly of stations, 'The Third Programme', people with clothes pegs over their noses introduced 'rare recordings' of 'poets reading their own poems'. They had to apologise for the 'rather poor quality of the recording as it was recorded on wax cylinders.' Or again they would explain that we should listen out for the 'rather extraordinary incantatory style of delivery of the poet William Butler Yeats, now reading his poem 'The Lake Isle of Innisfree' (Yeats 1933: 44). And again a weird prayer-like voice surrounded by recording hiss chanted about a strange place and a strange time. My parents would nod and sigh.

Now this powerful cluster of feelings and ideas formed my habitus, the institutional apparatus that ensured formation into a particular fraction of the middle class: Grammar school and university (see Bourdieu 1993: 162 and Giroux 1983: 84). I will look at my experience of poetry in primary school in the next section on *children's* poetry. At secondary school, it feels to me now that poetry came in four separate waves:

1) an almost vain effort by teachers in the first three years to find one or two classic poems that might interest us,
2) my 'O' level English course which, rather oddly, I followed at home with

my father,
3) my 'A' level course, and
4) university.

In that first wave, there is one moment that to this day still affects me. One teacher, a young, incredibly shy woman who wore the kind of clothes, make-up and jewellery that none of us had ever seen before decided to teach a unit on the dramatic monologue. We read Browning's 'My Last Duchess' (Browning 1908: 30-31) and spent hours discussing whether the Duke had killed the woman in the painting, and if he did, how did we as readers know he did? She then set us the job of writing our own monologues. Homework was 'Write a Dramatic Monologue'. I wrote a long monologue in rhyming couplets. The persona was a man killing someone on a beach for reasons of an unstated betrayal and the poem ended with the persona's suicide. This was 1959, me aged 13. It was printed in the school magazine and Mrs Liebenthal, (German Jewish refugee and school secretary at my primary school, whose son Robert was in the year above me), rang me up to tell me that she thought that my poem was marvellous and 'quite extraordinary for my age'. Somehow or another I had at that moment crossed the line. It was now (absurdly) me and Browning. I had gone through a door into this poetry place.

The next wave came with my father teaching me 'O' level English Literature at home. Here for the first time in my life was an anthology that had to be studied: it was *A Pageant of Modern Verse* selected by E.W. Parker (1949). Here, amongst 41 poets I met Thomas Hardy, Robert Bridges, A.E. Housman, Gerard Manley Hopkins, W.B. Yeats, Siegfried Sassoon, Rupert Brooke, Wilfred Owen, T.S. Eliot C.Day Lewis, W.H. Auden, Louis MacNeice and Stephen Spender.

This was a key book and a key period in the process of my initiation into poetry. I became aware of a whole new range of ideas most of which I accepted at face value:

1) that poetry came in historical periods,
2) that though you could talk about the separate elements of a poem – its techniques, its tone, its theme, a poem's meaning had to be seen as one, it was some kind of blended unity.

The key text here was my father's copy of *Understanding Poetry, An Anthology for College Students* Cleanth Brooks and Robert Penn Warren (1938). The book was stamped on end papers with 'Library Section American University of Berlin', 'HQ. 94th ENGR. REGT. (GS)', '1151st Engineer Combat Group OFFICIAL' and it had my father's signature on it.

I know now that this and the authors' other books are among the most influential texts in the twentieth century's perception of what poetry has been, what it might be and how we should talk about it, as they were the progenitors of 'New Criticism', as it is known. The book is constructed as a kind of narrative, in which we are introduced at the outset to what poetry is and then by means of a combination of

1) 'explication de texte',
2) a kind of interrogation of the reader and
3) exercises,

the authors take the student up a developmental ladder: from 'Narrative Poems' 'Implied Narrative', 'Objective Description', 'Tone and Attitude', 'Imagery', to 'Theme'. There are 240 poems in the collection ranging from anonymous ballads and Shakespeare sonnets right through English and American poetry of the twentieth century. With the commentaries and explanations, the book comes out at 680 pages. I studied *The Pageant* and *Understanding Poetry* for two years and I will try to reconstruct the kinds of notions that I added on to the base that I had already constructed around my parents' ways of using poetry.

The massive and overwhelming apparatus of criticism implied to me that the job of the poet was in some way to impress the critic. In my deferential way, I felt that these books, with the backing of my father, possessed the final judgement on what is a good poem. Brooks and Warren spend some time dealing with bad poems. The shame of it! To appear in a book like that only to be exposed as bad! But more than that: some of their commentaries said that poems could be flawed, not quite as good as they first appear. There were specific crimes that a poet could commit of which 'sentimentality' seemed to be the worst. There were individual poets whose works could be dismissed, even if you thought they were at first attractive. With an American audience in mind, Edgar Allan Poe came in for a pasting (Brooks, Warren 1938: 358-362).

There was then an invisible league table of poems and poets vying with each other for greatness. Perhaps I felt at this time, it was more important to be able to construct a league table that coincided with other critics' league tables than, say, to enjoy a poem, or of, course, to write one. In this period, though I was massively excited by the poems, and the discussions about them, it was here that I was drawn into a discourse that bestows upon itself the right to deliver final judgments on poets. What is deeply mysterious about these judgments is that they make no reference back to the outlook, minds, backgrounds or experience of the person delivering them. They pose as objective. A poem might be described as 'monotonous' and the critical apparatus that Brooks and Warren have constructed 'proves' that it is. Complementing this approach is that the criticism itself, with its eschewing of what came to be known as the 'intentional fallacy', deliberately sought to leave out the outlook, minds, backgrounds and experience of the poet too. It is this supposed objectivity and delivering of final judgments that made poetry so suited for examinations within the stratified education system I have described earlier (Mulhern 1979: 318). It was my being successful at this process that enabled me to continue to the next stage in the process.

At the time I do not think I was baffled or troubled by this approach, nor was supposed to be. It was simply another aspect of the discourse that I wanted (and, as part of my formation within a particular layer in society, was supposed to want) to acquire. Less consciously it was an aspect of the discourse that would affect the way I (and thousands of others) would write. That is to say, Brooks and Warren laid down the yardsticks that we would have to perform against and in so doing we would find ourselves performing against each other.

One other important way in which I was taken into a completely different aspect of the world of poetry at this time was through theatre. As a member of a theatre group, we entered poetry performance competitions (see later). I became aware, albeit in a rather hazy way, that there was a place somewhere where poetry could be public and social. It meshed with my awareness that there was a poetry connected in the public political space because I had seen Adrian Mitchell performing on the plinth at Trafalgar Square at the end of CND marches ('Tell me lies about Vietnam . . . ' from 'To Whom it May Concern', (Mitchell 1968: no page no.)). And yet this public poetry seemed to have very little to do with private or school study of poetry.

In the sixth form (1962-64) I was taken through the poetry of Keats, Milton, Gerard Manley Hopkins and Matthew Arnold, alongside Chaucer's *The Knight's Tale* (Chaucer 1957: 25-47) whilst taking poetic approaches to *Antony and Cleopatra*. In my spare time I read D.H. Lawrence's poetry (Lawrence 1977) and began to try and read the first publications in the Penguin Modern Poets series. For the first time, in particular with Hopkins, I began to sense that poetry could be connected to a poet and a poet to his or her time. Using the Penguin edition (Hopkins 1953) which included Hopkins' letters I grappled with his ideas of 'Inscape' and his technical ideas of 'sprung rhythm'. It all seemed wonderfully complicated and, again, mysterious. Hopkins was a fascinating mixture of narcissism, masochism and single-mindedness and, (thrillingly), suffered neglect and early death. It did not matter at all that he wrote about the glory of God being in all things while elsewhere in my life I was speaking out in debating clubs for atheism. What mattered was that he was an ecstatic; that he had grabbed hold of language and treated it as if it were a material, twisting it and squeezing it beyond the customary limits of syntax. In my day-to-day life and politics I was keen on expressing unorthodox and subversive views; in the field of poetry I was attracted to someone whose poetry was in its time unorthodox and subversive at the level of the signifier alone. However, I remember being delighted that Hopkins on one occasion in a letter described himself as some sort of 'communist'. It was at this time that I began to write poetry fairly regularly and wrote obsessively with a Hopkins-esque style.

At this time, I rarely saw poets in performance, and to my everlasting shame, turned down the opportunity of going to see Allen Ginsberg et al at The Albert Hall in the first of many of the great poetry happenings of that time. If I was going to see performances I was interested in the poetry expressed through folk music, blues and rhythm and blues (R 'n' B). My poetic input in the public space came through the words of 'anon' in traditional ballads and folk songs, Ewan MacColl, Peggy Seeger, Pete Seeger, Bob Dylan, Sonny Terry and Brownie McGhee, Leadbelly, Elmore James, Big Bill Broonzy and The Rolling Stones. I turned myself into a minor expert on the history of these kinds of music and studied quite independently of any course, folk lyrics, the theories of ballad composition and the passing on of folk music. This seemed at the time to encompass a heady mix of political, cultural and poetic issues. Poetry per se in my mind's eye was either private or academic.

The next phase in my formation – now within an even smaller elite – was at university where this schism continued. Academically I was inducted into the Oxford system of literature (1966-69). This in essence was what I might dub the 'baton-passing' theory. Whether it was stated explicitly or whether it happened simply by dint of the sequence in which we studied literature, the Oxford system was based on notions of chronology and tradition. That is to say, the overwhelming impression one learnt was that literature proceeded by dint of authors handing over their works to the next generation down through the centuries. In poetry, poets existed as receptors of 'influences' from previous poets or handers-on of influences to others. The task before us was often a question of trying to divine what a poet had done with the poetry that came before 'him'. In the three years study I have very little sense that it was of any importance, for example, that Wordsworth lived through and was excited by the French Revolution. I have no sense that I questioned who the 'Metaphysical Poets' thought they were writing for or publishing for or why they were engaged in such minute theological disquisitions on material objects around them. With the Oxford course, at that time cutting off at 1900, poetry ignored the seismic tremors of the First World War and the nuclear age and, with its strict adherence to British literature, ignored worldwide movements of modernism, surrealism, 'engagement', and the like. It also determined a peculiar notion of insularity, firstly in that Irish, Scots and Welsh poets were dubbed 'English' literature and secondly that the internationalism of poetry (e.g., Shakespeare and the Italian influence, Swinburne and French poetry) was sidelined or obscured altogether.

Meanwhile, the immediate matter in hand was that I had to negotiate a metrical analysis of *Beowulf,* and under the tutorships of Ian Donaldson (now professor in Cambridge) and the critics Wallace Robson and F.W. Bateson was brought face to face with continued close textual looks at poets from John Skelton through to, again, Hopkins. I imported my interest in the oral tradition into the course as a way of wrestling with my unease with all this purely literary and, as I saw it then, 'upper class' poetry (English course at university 1966-69).

From 1966 onwards I started to explore in my writing what was to grow later into 'children's poetry'. Poetry seemed to offer at this point a means by which I could reflect on and celebrate my childhood. The sixties was a time in which it was 'OK' to say 'kids are great' and with flower power, the Arts Lab, and the magazines Oz and the *International Times*, the milieu I lived in expressed a general rejection of 'adult' bourgeois values to do with mortgages, marriage, patriotism and war. In fact the 'kids are great' thesis was given a theoretical backing by figures such as Richard Neville in *Playpower* (1970). This meshed neatly with several social (or are they psychological?) influences of mine: my parents' lifetime involvement in education and celebration of children's language and creativity. I had an arrogant and futile sense at the time that while people around me were 'discovering' childhood and 'play' I had done that already – hadn't my parents already 'discovered' it?

So I began to write what I thought were fragments of an autobiography, written somewhat like E.E. Cummings (Cummings 1991) or the early pages of Joyce's *Portrait of the Artist as a Young Man*. (Joyce 1914-15, 1916). At the time I thought these were contributions to that world of adult poetry about which I was writing essays. I could quite consciously place them, as I have done here, in different traditions of poetry – whether it was Lawrence, Cummings, Joyce or others. I'm not sure I had any idea then *why* I was writing them. I just had a sense I needed to enjoy on the page such things as sharing my bedroom with my brother from ten or fifteen years earlier or the oral traditions of our household.

When a body of poetry had been written I made various desultory efforts to get it published, whilst having no notion that these poems could be given a live public airing to adults or children. However, I had had one important experience of reception. My mother's producer at the BBC, Joan Griffiths, had seen some of the poems and they had been broadcast. Moreover, she followed this up by asking me if I would both read some myself and then, later, construct some poetry programmes for the radio myself (1970). These too celebrated the oral tradition by mixing my poems, with folk songs, riddles, proverbs and folk rhymes. At this stage in my writing I wanted to believe that there was a continuity between what I was writing and this other, wider, social and, for me 'political', sphere. I wanted to act as some kind of bridge between private writing about personal and family experiences and verbal traditions that were possessed in common, i.e. the oral and folk traditions. I have a sense that I dragged my poetry away from the obscure syntactical violence of Hopkins and towards the oral styles of Lawrence, American poets to be found in Untermeyer (1942). This volume was on our shelves at home, and some of the poets in Untermeyer's selection could be found in our house in editions on their own Cummings (1991), Marquis (1951), and Carl Sandburg (1950).

Quite soon, I found both through my work with Joan Griffiths and as a result of negotiating with publishers that these poems had a public and commercial home in that thing called 'children's literature'. Where one publisher was disconcerted that they wrote about the experience of being a child from a child's point of view, another, Pam Royds at Andre Deutsch, in consultation with Margaret Spencer found the first collection a home on her list (Rosen 1974). I was a children's poet. However, that placed me inside a different kind of institution, with a long tradition of its own. In my head there was an awareness of what this institution was all about and I shall look at this in the next section.

ii) The cultural institution of poetry written specifically with children in mind

Historically, it is quite clear that the idea that a form of poetry can be written by adults with a child's audience in mind (hereafter called 'children's poetry') has been in evidence right from the beginnings of children's literature as a whole. The Puritans of the seventeenth century wrote verses specifically for children, most memorably John Bunyan (1686). Similarly, it is often overlooked that 'the first children's book', John Newbery's A Little Pretty Pocket Book (1744) is in fact a sequence of verses and, more importantly in the history of children's poetry, the publisher Mary Cooper's Tommy Thumb's Song Book and Tommy Thumb's Pretty Song Book Voll. [sic] II (i.e. 2), both of 1744, were both books of poetry, or what we usually call 'nursery rhymes'.

Since these times, various traditions have run through children's poetry which I will describe like this:

1) an oral tradition of rhyme and song that encompasses lullabies, obscene verses, fragments of ballads, parodies, sports rhymes, nonsense poems, riddles, chants, counting out rhymes or 'dips', and much else. It is this oral tradition that produced
2) the nursery rhymes, first put down in print in 1744 (Cooper 1744a) but which drew on the oral tradition. However, since 1744 there has grown up a written canon that has mostly frozen some two hundred or so of these rhymes and these have been constantly produced and reproduced in illustrated texts that are sold to parents and read to children.
3) A popular ephemeral verse, often with no author credited that can be found in chap books, annuals, comics, magazines, tracts, joke books, miscellanies from the seventeenth century to the present day;
4) poetry once written for an adult audience but which through the processes of anthologising and education has come to be accepted as 'for' children, or 'suitable' for children, or 'adopted' by children, and
5) poetry written specifically with a children's audience in mind, and which aims to be beyond the ephemeral by appearing in whole books of poetry as written by one identified author.

When I was a child in the 1940s and 50s I came across all five traditions.

1) The oral tradition of playground rhyme and song seems to have been particularly strong where and when I was a child. I have a clear memory of

girls' skipping rhymes, obscene rhymes, dipping rhymes, parodies of hymns and carols, boy scout chants, football songs and fragments of army songs and chants e.g.,

'Oh The Yellow Rose of Texas and the Man from Laramie
Invited Davy Crockett to have a cup of tea.
The tea was so delicious they had another cup.
And left poor Davy Crockett to do the washing up.'

(to the tune of 'The Yellow Rose of Texas')
(circulating orally, Pinner, Middlesex c. 1955, as remembered by MR 1997)

and

'There is a winding passage that leads up to my heart
and what comes down this passage is commonly called a fart.
The fart is very useful, it sets the mind at ease.
It warms the bed on wintry nights and disinfects the fleas.'

(circulating orally, Pinner, Middlesex c. 1955, as remembered by MR 1997)

I was never aware of anyone calling this 'poetry' until 1959 (when I was 13) when Peter and Iona Opie published *The Lore and Language of Schoolchildren*. This book became a family discussion point the moment it came out and though the authors treated their material with a slight disdain, it created in our house a mixture of comic amusement, a reverence for the 'genius of the people' and a sense that this was a kind of poetry too. It also acted as a trigger for me to hang on to my repertoire of oral rhymes which even at that time I was under the impression was larger than most of my companions'.

I should say here that there were some oral rhymes that I came across as a young child that seemed peculiar to our household: US army chants from my father's time in the American army e.g.,

'Shit, shine, shave and shower!'

(remembered from father c. 1955, noted here 1997, MR)

Yiddish and half-Yiddish rhymes that my parents knew from their childhood e.g.,

'Herschel shmerel went to the races
Lost his gatkes and his braces.'

shmerel = little fool
gatkes = trousers or pants
(remembered from father and mother c. 1953, noted here 1997, MR)

fragments of songs from the music hall e.g., 'If it wasn't for the houses in between'; 'My old man said, "Follow the van . . . " '; political parodies and left-wing songs from the 1930s: e.g., 'Just one more chance to save the Labour Party', 'There's a valley in Spain called Jarama', 'La Carmagnole'; French and German songs that my father sang e.g., 'Tout va bien, Madame La Marquise'; 'O wie wohl (?) ist mir am Abend'.

On reflection now, this total oral repertoire, whether it came from my child companions or from the home, strikes me as being an extraordinarily wide-ranging and profuse body of verse and rhyme. Even now I carry a large amount of it in my head.

2) The canon of nursery rhymes was brought to me by my mother, nursery school and infant school. Both my parents knew plenty of them off by heart; there were books of nursery rhymes at home and nursery rhymes and songs were part of the educational principles in post-war nurseries and infant schools. In this, I was not much different from any other middle-class educated child in a British family of this time.

3) The ephemeral verse could be found at this time in the comics and annuals that came into our house. Sometimes these were the verses that tell the story of Rupert Bear (Tourtel 1920, Bestall 1935), or the rhymes and riddles that were in annuals and 'Bumper Fun' books. None of these seem to have been particularly memorable for me, and if anything, I can remember being irritated by the rhyming couplets that accompanied one or two of the stories in The Beano or The Dandy and Rupert Bear. I have no sense even to this day of anyone regarding this material as 'poetry' even though it conforms to two traditional requirements: rhyme and regular rhythm.

4) The poetry once written for an adult audience but which through the processes of anthologising and education has come to be accepted as 'for' children, or 'suitable' for children, or 'adopted' by children was also available to me. At home, we had a copy of de la Mare's (1923, 1928) *Come Hither, A Collection of Rhymes and Poems for the Young of all Ages*. I was aware that my mother used this as a source book for her teaching and have memories of looking through it and stopping to read things, especially the Shakespeare songs from the plays: 'Hark, hark the lark' (de la Mare 1928: 6), 'Come unto these yellow sands' (de la Mare 1928: 119), 'Where the bee sucks' (de la Mare 1928: 121) and so on. But there are also poems here by Blake, Bridges, Chaucer, Clare, Coleridge, Crabbe, Donne, Flecker, Robert Frost, Goldsmith, Herbert, Herrick, Keats, Marvell, Milton, Owen, Pope, Sassoon, Shelley, Sidney, Southey, Spenser, Swinburne, Tennyson, Vaughan, Wordsworth and Yeats – in fact almost a taster for a course in English Literature at Oxford University! What is being proclaimed here (and was reinforced at school at the same time) was a message along the lines that said 'there are 'great' poets whom adults know of and like and bits and pieces of their work are suitable for you smaller people'. This was done with the very best of intentions and I do not intend by describing the message in this way to disparage the effort. It is, however, clear that this is very much part of the process described elsewhere in this thesis, of creating a 'habitus' (Bourdieu 1993: 162 and Giroux above). It was an initiation into a sphere of taste and appropriateness. The fact that this book (and books like it) were available at home, alongside the 'adult' poetry books on my parents' shelves, was absolutely crucial to my cultural and class formation – and, as I have found later in life, to the cultural and class formation of a very particular layer within the English cultural elite.

Symbiotically, school and home fed into each other: Miss Howlett, at Pinner Wood County Primary School, 1952 had our 'first year junior' class reciting 'When icicles hang by the wall' (Act 5 Scene 2 *Love's Labour's Lost* Shakespeare 1988: 307) and the phrases 'Dick the shepherd blows his nail', 'Marion's nose looks red and raw' and 'greasy Joan doth keel the pot' were discussed, laughed over and remain with me now as portable oral citations. Marion in particular had a resonance at the time, because there was a Marion in our class who had to suffer some finger-pointing and giggling here.

Similarly, Mrs MacNab at West Lodge County Primary School, 1956 had a choral speaking group which was entered for inter-school poetry competitions. Our entry was Edward Thomas's: 'Adelstrop' (Thomas E. 1964: 48). The poem opens with the words,

'Yes, I remember Adelstrop . . . '

At the time, this seemed like an extraordinary departure from what I had understood to be poetry. This was a metrical and rhymed poem but the lines were broken up in what seemed an odd chatty way, with an informal modern tone. My feelings at the time appear to me now as being caught in a strange duality, a lack and a presence: on the one hand the poem seemed to lack so much – strong pulsing rhythm, literary fame, clear obvious point, whilst at the same time the poem conveyed a sense of rural nostalgia that chimed with our rural summer holidays camping on farms. Indeed, not long after reciting the poem, I was taken, en famille, on a car ride through Adelstrop. By being part of this choral speaking group, poetry was taken off the page and put into a public space, albeit formal, and very controlled, right down to the school uniforms and the pressed down, combed hair that was essential for a good showing in the competition.

A very short while after this, as a member of a youth theatre group, I was again standing on a stage reciting adult poetry deemed suitable for young people. This time it was Louis MacNeice and 'I am not yet born . . . ' (from 'Prayer Before Birth' (MacNeice 1988: 93)). On a tatty stage in a converted chapel in Ealing, the 'Young Questors' of the Questors Theatre were cajoled and conducted through this poem, with solo parts, duets and choruses. Without referring back to the poem at this moment, I have a sense that at the time this was a poem that was both profound and oppositional. It protested and warned. The older girls in the group seemed excited and moved by it, perhaps more than I, and they were much more passionate than I was in performing their lines. But here was another space for poetry: a back street theatre, where another kind of 'intellectual' seemed to dwell: the group of people who were so passionate about theatre and poetry that they gave up all their spare time to create what was to become one of the best equipped amateur theatres in the country. There was commitment in their work, and the person who ran our group, unpaid, was described as 'a teacher' and our attendance, as 'training'. Regular, punctual attendance was insisted upon and preparation had to be thorough. I think I learnt here something along the lines: 'this arty poetry stuff isn't just simply about hanging about and scribbling the odd thing there's some hard work involved too . . . '

So, finally, I can consider

5), the poetry written specifically with a children's audience in mind, and which aims to be beyond the ephemeral by appearing in whole books of poetry as written by one identified author. This is the kind of work I have been engaged in since 1966. In fact it began when the kind of writing about my childhood I was doing was identified as 'suitable for children' in the early 1970s which, in turn, led to the publication of my first book of poems, *Mind Your Own Business* (1974).

A line of classically middle-class initiation is clearly discernible here. The first author I can remember as being part of this project is that disaffected member of the Scots Protestant Ascendancy, Robert Louis Stevenson. He was a figure of some fascination for me in childhood, in that I read *Treasure Island* (1883), *Black Arrow* (1888) and *Kidnapped* (1886) and owned copies of the three books that I kept on my shelves. In school, over several years, we read and learnt various poems from *A Child's Garden of Verses* (1885, 1912) including 'Autumn Fires' (Stevenson 1912: 49) and 'The Land of Nod' (Stevenson 1912: 12). I do not for one moment pretend that I unpacked that at the time of Stevenson's project, but he is an example of an adult writer writing about his childhood, in the persona of a child (or several children), an autobiographical verse, as if written at the time of his childhood. However, it cannot be purely a coincidence that ten or so years after reading these poems I began doing precisely the same thing. I should also say I did not know then that Stevenson is a fine example of the syndrome later known as the 'dropout'. In his case it seems that he used literature as a way of defecting from his particular class and cultural fraction.

The other poet who I read and who attempted in his work something similar to Stevenson was A.A. Milne. *When We Were Very Young* (1924, 1965a), *Now we are Six* (1927, 1965b,) and the 'hums' from *Winnie-the-Pooh* (1926) and *The House at Pooh Corner* (1928) were all present in my childhood. These seemed to have mostly arrived in my consciousness via the local library and a strong friendship with the boy who appears over and over again in my poems, Brian Harrison, or 'Harrybo'. At this time I know that together we read and talked about the Pooh 'hums' and such poems as 'Waiting at the Window' (Milne 1965b: 89), 'Rice Pudding' (Milne 1965a: 48) and 'The Good Little Girl' (Milne 1965b: 66). These seemed to match the tone of our own lives and speech very closely – an example of class identification on our parts. They were the subject of discussion between us and my mother, in an ironic, histrionic sort of a way, used sometimes to 'ask' me: 'Have you been a good girl?' from 'Rice Pudding' (Milne 1965a: 48).

Both poets succeeded with me in creating a view of childhood, sometimes contemplative, sometimes funny, oral, and always attentive to the incidental that I found attractive. Stevenson did not quite invent the genre, there had been poems before him that were written by adults in the voice of a child and intended for a child's audience. However, he was the first who created a sequence of poems that has this same addresser-addressee relation but was also clearly identifiable as autobiographical and, moreover, which provide a sequential, fragmentary view of a period in childhood (Rosen 1995a: 53-72). Around forty years later, Milne did something similar but not identical with his two volumes (1924, 1927). He seems to have been writing in part a kind of biography of his own son through the poetry, and of course, the Christopher Robin/Winnie-the-Pooh books (1926, 1928). Forty years after this, it is not totally fanciful to say that I was attempting to do what Robert Louis Stevenson had done, but using some of the oral techniques of A.A. Milne, particularly in the case of poems like 'The Good Little Girl' and 'Rice Pudding' which use the repetition of oral statements in a representation of how adults and children interact.

Parallel to this, but much less directly influential, I was inducted into the poetry of Walter de la Mare (1912, 1923, 1944, 1979). To return to the choral speaking, 'The Listeners' (de la Mare 1912, 1979: 84) was learnt and recited many times and, indeed, entered family folklore when my brother and I made pastiche audio tape renderings of it in what we imagined were Third Programme voices. De la Mare was very much the preferred fare of primary school teachers in the 1950s (at least, mine) and we read, or were read, many of his poems. For reasons I cannot wholly disentangle, I can sense in myself an attitude towards these at the time that was a mixture of irritation, boredom, distaste and a kind of fear. I think now that this is because they would have appeared to me then, and do still, as what I used to call 'lonely'. That is, his poems frequently establish an unconvivial mood: the moon sheds its light on a still world, ('Silver', (de la Mare 1944: 256)) cats sit quietly, one of whom has only one eye ('Five Eyes', (de la Mare 1944: 100)), and the traveller comes to the door, 'Tell them I came' he shouts, and no one answers . . . and, who, in heaven's name, are 'the listeners' (de la Mare 1979: 84)? I found all this uncomfortable and, if I was going for the sad or the nostalgic, much preferred Stevenson playing in bed while he was ill (Stevenson 1912: 11), or ending the summer holidays in Braemar (Stevenson 1912: 26). However, between them, these three poets helped create a generic intertext for me, which I have worked with since 1966. They also provided powerful affirmations of middle-class identity. The worlds they celebrate are places full of toys and leisure and highly verbal, educated chat. With the powerful backing of home and school, I turned this poetry into what I might call 'summonses', beckoning me towards membership of a highly particular fraction within the intelligentsia. One final touch needs to be added: the presence of first, James Britton and then Geoffrey Summerfield in my life.

Both were colleagues of my father's and friends of the family, and both created anthologies for schools. Britton's (1957) *The Oxford Books of Verse for Juniors* (4 vols) was for that most traditional of publishers, Oxford, and was, in its time, the major primary school anthology. Summerfield's *Voices* (1968) and *Junior Voices* (1970) was for the brash new revolutionaries, setting up Penguin Education. The men knew each other, and, in some ways, Summerfield's is a reply to Britton's. Both series of books had a strong presence in my household, in that I can remember discussions taking place between my parents and both Britton and Summerfield that were about choices of poems, choices of poets, reactions of children in my mother's classes to specific poems and the anthologies as a whole. Indeed, Summerfield came to our house and laid out on the front room floor his draft manuscript for *Voices* while his in-house editor, Martin Lightfoot, often visited and waxed enthusiastically about the kinds of revolutionary changes he was making both with the production of *Voices* and other books for Penguin Education. He brought samples of the amazing artwork and photos that made the *Voices* collections so stunning.

The impact of these two collections on my attitudes in the early 1960s, when I was thinking about writing poetry, can be put like this: Britton's series represented for me something very English, something slightly dated. It was analogous to *Come Hither* (de la Mare 1923, 1928) which was, I knew, something of the past. Summerfield was international, full of American poetry that excited me enormously, and with its design and artwork seemed to be of the moment, advanced, 'progressive' left-wing, 'groovy', dissenting, ahead of its time, and with a general buzz around its production. If I was going to get involved in this game, it was, I felt, going to be something to do with the Summerfield area, rather than the Britton. I knew both men and whereas I respected James Britton and quite liked him, particularly for the kindness he showed me in taking me and his daughters for swimming lessons for several years, Summerfield I admired and enjoyed. I loved his passionate enthusiasms and intense way of talking about an individual poem or story, in particular the work of Carl Sandburg. (The situation is delightfully complicated by the fact that at the time I was in a relationship with James Britton's daughter. Could one element in this whole matter have been an unconscious rejection and antagonism towards the father-in-law'? I'll leave that to a more Freudian perspective.)

As I have implied here, the preparation of *Voices* and its publication mark for me my discovery of Carl Sandburg. With the extracts from 'The People, Yes' (Sandburg: 1950: 439-617) that Summerfield used, I came across a new voice, Sandburg, and its publication in a book for children, legitimated for me a way of writing that I wanted to imitate. When he wrote,

> 'What's the matter up there?'
> 'Playing soldier.'
> 'But soldiers don't make that kind of noise.'
> 'We're playing the kind of soldier that makes that kind of noise.'

(Sandburg 1950: 529)

it opened up a whole new plane on which to write: in dialogue, episodic, fragmentary glimpses of the rough and tumble interchanges between adults and children. Or again:

> 'Why did the children
> put beans in their ears
> when the one thing we told the children
> they must not do
> was put beans in their ears?
>
> Why did the children pour molasses on the cat
> when the one thing we told the children
> they must not do
> was pour molasses on the cat?'

(Sandburg: 1950: 487-488)

I fastened on to the idea that there were moments of exasperation and incomprehensibility in the parent-child relationship whilst at the same time in the words actually spoken, there lie truths that need not be stated. Sandburg, in the second of these two passages does not answer the question and in so doing sets up a small but profound idea: that children engage with adults and test adults along the very fracture lines that adults try to steer the children away from.

So it was that as I wrote the poems (between 1966 and 1973) that were to become my first book, I worked within those aspects of the five traditions of children's poetry that I have sketched in here. It is clear to me now that not only was I initiated into a habitus, but, to use other terminologies, I learned a 'discourse' : I found out that poetry (as opposed to, say sculpture or bricklaying) was legitimated and valorised, and within that field, certain *voices* in poetry were legitimated, prioritised and valorised. In brief, I yearned to be part of a very specific socio-cultural activity. Or to be more precise, I *learned how* to yearn to be part of a very specific socio-cultural activity. Summerfield and Penguin Education helped create an audience of teachers and children. I made myself confluent with it.

There is not the space here to paint the full picture of how I see the nature of my intervention into what I have described earlier as the fifth of these traditions. Twenty two years span the dates of publication of *Mind Your Own Business* (1974) and the publication of those parts of 'the work' under consideration here that has become *You Wait Till I'm Older Than You* (1996). In this time I have become aware that I am liable to cause two very distinct, very different reactions: enormous enthusiasm and great distaste.

When *Mind Your Own Business* (1974) first appeared the critics John Rowe Townsend and Brian Alderson both welcomed it. Townsend (1974) put it in this context:

'A strange stony little field is that of modern children's verse: overshadowed by the well-known names of the past and strewn with the bones of recent failure.' (Townsend 1974 in *Guardian* 3.4.74)

He praised de la Mare, James Reeves and Charles Causley and finished the paragraph with the observation:

There is a wide vacancy for verse that can catch the feeling of everyday life as experienced by children of today.' (Townsend 1974: *Guardian* 3. 4.74)

Alderson, ('Leading young readers from mere verse to great poetry', *The Times*, 10.4.74) also tried to look at the broad context:

'Between the playground of children's verse and the landscape of poetry there lies a profound chasm.' (Alderson 1974: *Times* 10.4.74)

He praised Summerfield's *Voices* for trying to bridge that chasm, alongside Charles Causley and Ian Serraillier.

The critics' comments overlap. For them I was 'cheerful, casual-sounding' (Townsend) 'approachable' and showing 'cheerful informality' (Alderson). Both critics drew up what have turned out later to be battle-lines. Townsend describes me in opposition to what he calls 'solemn realism' and to the fact that

'Several good modern poets have failed totally to find the right eye-level or tone of voice.' (Townsend 1974)

Alderson writes:

' . . . his uninhibited enjoyment of the whole operation standing in sharp contrast to the well-meaning but rather stiff-jointed attempts of more famous poets to write 'with young people in mind' . . . ' (Alderson 1974)

I should say here that this was never an opposition I intended or created and yet over twenty years later an anonymous writer in the *Independent on Sunday* could write in 'Poetry in need: Please send money'.

' . . . generations of teachers – hardly know where to begin if they do want to teach literature, especially poetry. It's all mysterious, ivory-tower stuff, too difficult . And if teachers are at a loss, they will fall back on whatever is safe and easy, and children will learn to consider the works of Michael Rosen as the highest point of poetic achievement.' (*Independent* 26.11.95)

When I read a passage like that, I become more aware than usual that battles over literature do not always occur at the level of an argument over text. Quite often they are waged between those who would champion an author and those who, for whatever reasons, want to argue with these supporters as much as with the author's work. So it was that Maura Dooley wrote in 'Poetry Books for Children' *British Book News* (Autumn 1983 pp. 7-9)

'Michael Rosen has long been a favourite amongst many teachers and children. I have yet to understand why.' (Dooley 1983: 9)

The poems

' . . . shed no light, they offer no insight and in no way work the imagination.' (Dooley 1983: 9)

The criticism is interesting in that it engages as much with the 'problem' of the poetry's supposed or actual popularity as it does with the poetry's failure to do what poetry should do. It was from this time that I have been aware that there is a school of thought that believes I frequently produce work that children should be taught to avoid, or worse, that I have been partly or wholly responsible for launching a new school of children's poetry. The writer on poetry for children, Sandy Brownjohn, once announced to her parent governor (I was told c. 1988) that she banned Michael Rosen's work from the primary school she worked in. Morag Styles in a kind frame of mind put it this way:

'In the early 1970s a new type of poetry hit the market in the rumbustious form of Michael Rosen.' (Styles 1996: 202)

I do not think it is appropriate for me to engage with these arguments here, if only because the hostile criticism I receive is not frequent, not usually in writing and often hearsay. What is more important is that I acknowledge the fact that I am working within a dialectic of defenders and detractors. As Morag Styles points out, it is not always clear what the argument is really about:

' . . . his work caused a stir with many critics. Is it really poetry ? He employs a form of free verse close to the rhythms of speech. Is it subversive? Could it be regarded as quality literature for the young?' (Styles 1996: 202)

She goes on:

' . . . it centres on the everyday experiences of children, sometimes exaggerated, written in ordinary language, peppered with jokes, insults and slang. It is cheeky, sometimes rude, often poking its tongue out at adult proprieties.' (Styles 1996: 202)

The problems posed like that begin to look *ideological*. There is then a sense that I have engaged with two issues at the same time: the nature of poetry and the nature of the child-adult relationship. To be specific, that I have both challenged the accepted forms of poetry for children and at the same time created poems and scenes that challenge adult authority. I have to say that I find this description of my work ironic, in that all I ever *thought* I was doing prosodically was imitating past poets. My problem is that I chose *American* poets like Sandburg, Marquis and E.E. Cummings as models who, in British eyes, even after over 80 years of publication in Sandburg's case, are seen as odd and experimental. Then again, on the matter of subversion of adults, all I *thought* I was doing was representing something of the banter and argument that actually took place in my own home. Where adult authority was challenged there in real life, it was often, but not always, seen as some kind of joke. The line: 'Shuttup stinks. You can't rule my life' from *You Can't Catch Me* (Rosen 1981) was something I said to my parents when I was quite young, and then was repeated many times by them back at me as a kind of family jokey punch-line.

I can now see that these poems entered contexts in which such lines, when matched with readers' lifestyles conducted in what are perhaps more conventional, less bantering households than ours, could appear as ruder and more subversive than I ever intended. Perhaps this lack of awareness was and still is naive on my part. However, at the end of the day this is the classic problem of literature: writers do not control reception. I am now aware that many of my poems have intervened in the process by which adults and children in home and school relate to each other but this was never the original intention even if now, and with 'the work' connected to this thesis, it is much clearer to me.

I think then that the nature of my intervention is not so much at the level of exposing or subverting 'adult proprieties' as Styles puts it, though this kind of approach is in evidence. Rather, I appear to myself to be doing, in broad terms two things:

1) exploring the ironies and contradictions of adult fallibility whilst at the same time
2) giving credence and worth to children's (from either my own childhood or my children's childhoods) experiences.

If this is 'subversive' that is because in our culture these two views, especially if held up to the light instantaneously, are unorthodox. They run counter to the prevailing ideology (see Leonard (1984) and James and Prout (1990) for descriptions of societal constructions of childhood).

I have mentioned here that writers do not control the reception of their work and yet, as an inseparable part of both the cultural and material part of my work, I am constantly entering into face-to-face relationships with audiences through school visits, teachers' workshops and conferences. I have no doubt in my mind that since the publication of *Mind Your Own Business* in 1974 these face-to-face encounters are what has sustained my interest and, as no coincidence, my financial wellbeing.

To put it another way, on the publication of that book, I found that I could make some connections that up until then I had never been able to make: connections between

1) a huge enjoyment of, and participation in live performance, usually through theatre;
2) an ideological belief in 'popular' art and entertainment, in particular of the face-to-face kind as represented by folk-singing and the like;
3) my great enjoyment of sitting on my own and writing;
4) an antagonism towards the obscure and abstruse in literature.

In other words, I found through oral performances of my work that I was able to create a kind of mini popular theatre, a one-man show that was available and accessible to almost any kind of audience, something I had failed in doing firstly with a play I had written that was performed at The Royal Court in 1969 (*Backbone*, Rosen 1969), secondly with a huge amount of comedy sketch writing and performing at university and thirdly, with my association with Ewan MacColl and The Critics Group 1970-1972.

What happened at that moment was a kind of conjuncture of interests and activities. However, what must be stated here is that this oral theatre was not simply something dreamed up by me. Its economic life was only made possible by institutions already in place. I discovered immediately following the publication of that first book that there was a network of people who managed writers for children. Some, like the National Association for the Teaching of English (NATE) were professional teaching organisations. Even more professional were the various forms of local authority financed teachers' development institutions which at that time were called 'Teachers Centres'. Others were parent-led as with the

Federation of Children's Book Groups. Yet others were run by librarians either locally or nationally through the Youth Librarians Group and the like. Moreover, individual schools who 'discovered' an author could, through the publishers, or through personal contact, find an author and book her or him for a school visit whether as part of a 'Book Week' or as a one-off. Prior to being published, I had no idea that such a flourishing and enthusiastic network existed involving thousands of human hours of unpaid labour, a labour that supported the children's book publishing world to a degree that can never be calculated.

This was a time of enormous teacher-optimism. Several local authorities, in particular the Inner London Education Authority, where I worked as a writer-in-residence, saw themselves as pioneers, in particular in relation to ideological attitudes to class, race, and gender. I suddenly found myself plunged into the middle of cultural, educational and ideological debates, whether literally at the very point where I was working with a group of children or teachers, or at one remove, in the way that my poetry was used by teachers without my being there.

If a writer can be described as occupying a site, a position in which he or she works, then this was from that time to now, my site. I acknowledge that some or even many of my books sell through bookshops and reach into families that way, but I have come to realise that for the most part, my work swims in the sea created by those teachers and teacher-advisers and trainers who are enthusiastic about children's literature. As the debate around education polarised as a consequence of the Conservative government's initiatives from the mid 1980s onwards, so I found myself drawn into those debates taking up what might be described as the 'progressive', anti-selection, anti-cuts, anti-national curriculum, anti-SATs, anti-Ofsted stance. In effect, this meant a fusion of two approaches:

1) an experimental, libertarian, subversive tone and content in the poetry I was writing for children and
2) the ideological interventions through talks, demonstrations and newspaper articles.

This reached something of a climax in 1994 when I helped organise a boycott of the nationally prescribed list of approved children's authors, one of whom happened to be me. So it is that at the very moment at which I might be standing in front of a group of children in a school-hall or a group of teachers on an INSET course, I might find myself over and over again engaged in a politico-cultural exchange produced by the very specific economic demands made on education in the post-boom era:

Am I in an all-white school in a leafy suburb? Is the gesture I make in a mime, an inner-urban one, one derived from 'commedia del arte', an imitation of a public performer like Billy Connolly? When I do imitations of my old school teachers and my parents, does this provide a platform for others to do the same or is it some kind of release for the people watching, in that I am playing the role of the outrageous one, given permission to do and say the unsayable? (See Freud's observation that the pleasure derived from reading might be

'... due to the writer's enabling us thenceforward to enjoy our own daydreams without self-reproach or shame.' (Freud 1985: 141))

- Does what I am performing marginalise or affirm the people watching, many of whom have parents who come from countries once dominated by British imperialism?
- In the cross-currents of power and control going on in this school, can I detect racism? sexism? anti-working class prejudice? plain old-style authoritarianism? How should I react to the ambience of the National Curriculum, testing and Ofsted inspections that I can see and palpably feel is going on around me at the very moment of my reciting a poem or telling a joke?
- Why is this school falling apart physically?
- Why are the class sizes bigger here than in the school down the road?
- Why is it that on the rare occasions I have been inside schools in the private sector everything is so different: the facilities, the relationship between staff and pupils, the relationships between the children?
- Why are some children being banned from seeing my performance?

And so on and so on. There is scarcely a moment when I have walked into a school that these ideological thoughts are not all swirling around in my mind.

In conclusion, I can see that out of the crucible of my childhood with its various economic, cultural, political and psychological elements, I found myself producing a particular kind of poetry. The moment that became an economic fact, I found myself shifted into a slightly different milieu, with its own economic, and above all ideological considerations. Being who I was,

136

coming from where I was coming, I then actively and intentionally intervened at various levels simultaneously. 'The work' under consideration here comes at a point in time after some twenty or so years of this intervention

Chapter 4

IN THIS CHAPTER I WILL BE exploring 12 poems, one by one, selected for the following reasons:

1) each poem comes from each of the main categories in the work.
2) the ways in which the poems differ enable me to write about them selecting different critical approaches with the emphases varying between, say, largely materialist, largely intertextual and so on.

I will be selecting one or more elements from the following scheme in order to apply the theoretical approaches worked out in Chapter 2, and using the class and cultural positioning worked out in Chapter 3.

Here is the scheme:

1) Roots in material reality
i)in my childhood and
ii) at the time of writing
2) Roots in intertextuality discourse and ideology
3) How I have been affected by reception
i) my own responses and reactions and
ii) others' responses and reactions.

'The Work'

This is a collection of poems written between December 1994 and February 1995 and which was submitted as below with the provisional title *Wait Till I'm Older Than You* to Puffin Books, and, as part of the supervision of this thesis, to Dr. Jean Webb and Professor Ruth Merttens.

The poems can be found in the Appendix and they are (in alphabetical order):

Adverbs
Aldermaston March
Australia
Berwick-on-Tweed
Butcher
Butter or margarine
Calculator
Conversation with a six year old
Don't tell your mother
Eddie and the car
Eddie and the Supermarket
Essex
Found Poem: a reading wall-chart for children in about 1840
Found Poem: Safety Instructions on United Airlines 1994
For Naomi
Great Day
Gypsy
Harrybo
Hospital
Invisible Ink
Leosia
Miss Stafford
Moishe
Motto
Mr Baggs
Mr Vassar the newsagent
Mum's School
Muss i' den
My Books (forty years ago)

My children's rules
My friend Roger
Never-ending poem (for Sam Hurd)
Never Have
Northumberland
On the Question of whether it is possible to sleep on a train
Pneumonia
Proverbs
Raw Food
Robin Hood's Bay
Running
Sam
Sandwich
Shirt
Stealing
Stobs
Sultanas
Sweetshop
Talking-tubes
Teachers' helper for end-of-assemblies
Ted
The cupboard
The Deal
The Langham Cinema
The Line
The Nest
The Shop Downstairs
The Torch
The Wedding
Three year old boy says:
Top Board
Trousers Down
Trying to find out what my kid's homework is
Useful instructions
What politicians mean when they say they are against other countries having
    nuclear weapons.
Who started it?
(65 poems)

Some observations on the collection as it stood completed in April 15 1995

This is a non-thematic, unplanned collection. It is brought together and classified here only as part of this thesis and not as part of the writing process:

1) poems about my childhood
i) some written as if I am still a child,
(poems underlined are the ones analysed in this chapter)

Butcher
Great Day
Hospital
Pneumonia
Proverbs
Stealing
Talking-tubes
The cupboard

ii) others written as a reminiscence,

Aldermaston March
Don't tell your mother
Gypsy
Harrybo
Miss Stafford
Moishe
Mr Baggs
Mr Vassar the newsagent
Mum's School
Muss i' den
My friend Roger
Never Have
Northumberland
Raw Food
Robin Hood's Bay
Sam
Shirt

Stobs
The Deal
The Langham Cinema
The Line
The Nest
The Shop Downstairs
The Torch
The Wedding
Top Board
Trousers Down
Who started it?

2) poems written as a parent

Australia
Conversation with a six year old
Eddie and the car
Eddie and the Supermarket
For Naomi
Invisible Ink
My children's rules
Sandwich
Sultanas
Three year old boy says:
Trying to find out what my kid's homework is

3) poems from an adult perspective but not directly involving parenthood as a theme

Adverbs
Essex
Leosia
My Books (forty years ago)
Ted
What politicians mean when they say they are against other countries having nuclear weapons.

4) various word-playing poems

Butter or margarine
Calculator
Motto
Never-ending poem (for Sam Hurd)
On the question of whether it is possible to sleep on a train
Useful instructions

5) various 'found' poems with or without a comment from me

Berwick-on-Tweed
Found Poem: a reading wall-chart for children in about 1840
Found Poem: Safety Instructions on United Airlines 1994
Running

6) poem written as if it were a child's voice (not mine)

Sweetshop

7) poem written as if in a teacher's voice

Teachers' helper for end-of-assemblies

Further notes

1) Some of the poems were written in draft form or a different version as long as ten years ago.
2) The 'work' in this form was not going to be put in the public domain as I knew that it would change in performance, be edited by an editor at Puffin Books, be amended, be selected down after discussion with people at Puffin.

Analysis of the Work Poem by Poem

What follows are analyses of 12 poems using slightly different approaches. With the first few I am attempting to explain the origins of the poem from a wide explicatory framework. In the later poems I am picking out specific aspects of the framework *without meaning to imply by that, that these later explanations are intended to be 'sufficient'. They are understood by me to be highly specific.*

The framework and its theoretical underpinning was established in Chapter 2, so part 1) 'Roots in material reality i) in my childhood and ii) at time of my writing' is derived from the passage above on materialism and the writing self. Part 2) *Roots in intertextuality, discourse and ideology* comes from the passages on intertextuality, and ideological considerations. Part 3) 'How I have been affected by reception' i) my own responses and reactions and ii) others' responses and reactions', derives from the passage on reading in general, but the particular theory that describes the feedback process comes from Voloshinov (1986: 95).

It should be said here that in one sense the scheme might appear to defeat the very purpose of this thesis. It has been my intention to show the links between the material and the textual, between reality, experience and representation, between the self and writing and yet in order to make analyses I am forced to break the process into component parts, and even (below) at times to select out one or two parts only. What I am requiring of the reader then is to consider the twelve separate analyses of the twelve poems below as parts of a whole.

The cupboard

At the top of the stairs
there's a landing
that's where the bedrooms are
our bedroom
and mum and dad's bedroom

At the top of the stairs
there's a landing
that's where the bedrooms are
our bedroom
and mum and dad's bedroom
and the cupboard.

The walk-in cupboard
with no floor at the back
where the walls slope down
with the roof of the house

down to narrow grey corners.

The walk-in cupboard
with no light
where the old brown metal trunk
and the old grey metal trunk
stand on end
tall and empty
like caves
that would welcome you in
and shut tight behind you.

The walk-in cupboard
 where two gas-masks
lie between the timbers
like crazy skulls
and dad's army jacket talks of tanks
and dead heads.

The walk-in cupboard
where my brother showed me
behind the trunks
was a little low door
leading into a lightless nothing
where
with a wriggle
he said you could get through
– go on
and I did
and once in,
there was nothing
and nothing
and nothing
until
my head hit a box.

A slit of light leaked through a slipped slate
in the roof.

I opened the box
it was stacked to the top
with sheets of paper
written on
letters to mum from dad
when he was away
as the war was ending
when my brother was small
and he was coming home
and he was leaving home
and he was coming home
Just before I was born.

1) Roots in material reality

i) childhood

In the analysis that follows here, I intend to show how the very specific class and cultural positionings of my family unit provided a set of material contexts for the writing of this poem. The origins of our siting in the London suburbs in Pinner Middlesex, the exact physical nature of our living space, the origins of the objects in the poem, the cause of my fascination with these objects largely derive from these class and cultural positionings. Within the societal base-and-superstructure metaphor there is here a base-superstructure microcosm: the parental means of survival (i.e., their jobs, their migrations, and above all my father's positioning in response to that most base-determined activity, war) provides the base for the superstructural musings of the poem.

We lived in a flat over an estate agents that was arranged on three floors, a room on the shop level, on the first floor – the living area of kitchen, bathroom, a spare bedroom and a 'front room' overlooking the street and then on the third floor were two bedrooms . . . and 'The Cupboard'. The stairs and top landing always seemed to be dark. It was all yet more proof that there was something strange and different about the way we lived. Nearly all the people I knew lived in 1930s suburban semi-detached houses – Harrybo, Roger, Mart (all from this collection). A couple of friends lived in council flats and one old friend of the family lived in a Victorian terrace house ten miles away in Muswell Hill. I was always aware that there was something different about my family

– it was a cluster of feelings about being the only Jewish kid at my second primary school (8-11 years), having parents who were Communists, having a mother who worked, having a house full of books and paintings on the wall, going on camping holidays, having no car or television until I was 10, and – living in this strange flat. Now I can see that it was a question of my parents being in a way *displaced*. If we had lived in Hampstead, Highgate, Crouch End, Muswell Hill then it would all have seemed quite normal. It was the seemingly strange fact that we were living in an area of London where there were no other like people. Part of the origins of this poem (and others) rests in this sense of otherness. Other kids did not seem to have cupboards on third floor landings, and if there were nooks and cubby holes in their houses then they were full of seemingly less weird objects. Their attics and sheds had old wireless sets and leather suitcases. Where there was old army gear it was *British* army gear. The other strange and not quite explicable fact about my father was that his army gear was American. He spoke with an English voice but he had been in the American army. By about the age of 10 I had become aware that he was American because he had been born in America, he had come to England when he was about two years old (1921) but he had never naturalised because there was some problem (or feared problem) that Communists couldn't easily renounce their foreign citizenship and become British. They were, I gathered, likely to fall between two stools and become stateless. So whereas my friends had stories about their fathers fighting in the Eighth Army and the like, my father had lived through most of the war not being called up and then at the end of the war served in the Education Corps of the American Army, first in England, then in Frankfurt and then in Berlin. This was always of especial interest to me because this took place before and up to the moment I was born. There always seemed something strange and sad about my father being away from home in 1945 and 1946, thus the letters at the end of the poem. The metal trunks were also part of this cluster of foreignness and otherness. I gathered that they too were part of my father's and his mother's migrations. The black trunk had his mother's name written inside and because she was English, there was a cloud of meanings connected with her travelling to America with my father's father, returning several years later without him and my father never having seen him again. The grey trunk contained some of these memories, although these were overladen with memories of it being put to service on long camping holidays in Wales and France (1950-1962), carrying tents and being mislaid by British Road Services and S.N.C.F.

'The Cupboard' and its contents, then, is fixed in my mind as part of this Jewish, left-wing otherness with its roots in not-quite-understood migrations, family mysteries and enforced separation between my father and mother.

<u>ii) at the time of writing</u>

This is the moment of synthesis between reality and its representation and it is moreover, crucially the moment in which I wish to hold to the theoretical framework offered by Bhaskar and Ebert. In the analysis that follows I have taken as read:

1) my material situation as 'writer', 'writer for children', 'poet in schools' (as described in Chapter 3) which are the initial determinants in the writing process here;
2) my siting within a milieu and projected audience that is educated to receive the kinds of work I produce;
3) the socio-historical reasons for my embodying these ideas within the material reality of pen, paper, page, word-processor, print-ink;
4) my formation within a literary culture and a literary elite which gave me access to the pre-texts that fill my intertextual space – bearing in mind that that formation was enabled by my parents' material existence, their 'habitus', the socioeconomic milieu of my locality of origin, the expanding socioeconomic situation of the time.

In pre-writing reveries the image of 'The Cupboard' has often come to me. I have often seen it next to me as I view myself standing at the top of those stairs calling out to my mother who is in the bath downstairs, thinking: doesn't she realise I've got something stuck in my teeth? And again I am aware of the cupboard's presence when I remember how my brother's pet slow worm escaped out of its glass home and lay on the landing. The words, 'The Cupboard', have sat around in many of the notes to myself that I've made over the years intended to trigger me into writing.

Sometimes, quite independently of this memory I've thought about 'the box' of the last section of the poem. It was a box that my father made when he went to carpentry classes. It too was and is part of a past that belongs just before and after I was born. I have only ever looked in it once, when I was in my twenties and it was stored in a cupboard next to my bedroom in another house. It was brim to the top with the letters mentioned and I began to read one of them. In it, my father talked to my mother about my brother. He was offering some advice to her about what Brian would be saying and how he would be behaving and what she should do about it I suddenly did not want to know anymore. It seemed like an unwanted insight into the worries and fears that they must have had following the death of a boy younger than my brother but older than me, Alan, never mentioned by my mother, only a handful of times by my father. It seemed like an unwanted insight into the lifelong monitoring and overseeing that my brother had lived with. It seemed like an unwanted insight into my parents' intimacies. If I read further wouldn't I find things that they would want to keep private?

My father kept the box of letters after my mother died in 1976 when I was 30 but I do not know whether he has kept them after his second marriage or after he moved house. The box remains something of a mystery and yet represents my parents' literacy and intimacy and my father's determination to be skilled with his hands even as he was striving for intellectual attributes.

What happened in the writing of this poem was that I brought together the two mysteries, the cupboard and the box. And as I wrote I found that as I went deeper and deeper into the cupboard, a 'true' description of actual trips there, I found myself getting to the box. But I am fixed in a post-Freudian world and the sense of the secrets of parents, the secrets of the parental bed, the secrets of their intimacy that can never be reached by the child came to me too. The 'coming' and the 'leaving' came to me first as an unthought-through image and then made it on to the page when I accepted that it had come to me in reverie; recognized it as a partly repressed image coming to light and put it in the poem as a conscious effort to write an image of sexual activity displaced onto the toing and froing of travel. Clearly this way of writing comes about in part as a result of education and reading around Freudian ideas. This too, is of course a function of a university education which in turn is in part the consequence of that educated bookish background.

Having seen the conscious effort to represent the repressed, then I can look back at the poem and see unconscious representations of Oedipal longings too.

2) Roots in literary texts

In this section I am drawing on a classically literary intertextuality in which I want to show how I negotiate with some obvious pre-texts. Once again, I have taken certain matters as read, e.g. the specific class and cultural origins of, and reasons for my original encounters with these texts which, as I have, described, were part of my induction into a habitus (Bourdieu 1993: 162 and Giroux 1983: 84).

I can hear in the poem any or all of the following: the poems by Robert Louis Stevenson and A.A. Milne that are written in the present tense about the emotional life of a boy. These sit in my mind from two phases in my life – from when I was between 7 and 11 years of age and again, reading them as an adult in the last ten years. The poems in particular that sit near the front of my consciousness would be Stevenson's 'Block City' (Stevenson 1912: 35), 'The Land of Counterpane' (Stevenson 1912: 11), 'The Land of Story-books', with its lines:

'Now, with my little gun, I crawl
All in the dark along the wall,
And follow round the forest track
Away behind the sofa back.'

(Stevenson 1912: 36)

'North-West Passage 1. Goodnight', with its lines:

'Must we to bed, indeed? Well, then,
Let us arise and go like men,
And face with an undaunted tread
the long, black passage up to bed.'

(Stevenson 1912: 27)

'Waiting at the Window' (watching the drips on the window pane) by Milne (1965b: 89), 'Lines and Squares' (lines on the pavement in London) (Milne 1965a: 12), 'Halfway Down' with:

'Halfway down the stairs
Is a stair
Where I sit.'

(Milne 1965a: 81)

and 'Disobedience' with the disappearing Mother from *When We Were Very Young* (Milne 1965a: 30).

I can also hear the sound of James Joyce's opening pages of *Portrait of the Artist as a Young Man* (Joyce 191415, 1916) which I first read when I was 16 and have not looked at since. Yet this was the book that first excited me to the idea of exploring my own childhood with the voice of a child. In a sense much of the writing consists of layers and layers of trying to do what I thought Joyce was doing there. Of course this means that I have departed from the original effect that book had on me because I now feed off the intertextuality offered me by my own poems. Some of the rhythms and repetitions of this poem I have experimented with before, for instance in the poem 'Nightmare' from *Don't Put Mustard in the Custard*, (Rosen 1985), which is a rhythmic, stream-of-consciousness type of poem about a recurring nightmare I used to have of falling between the lines in the London Underground at Baker Street Station.

Finally I can hear just a few faint echoes of D.H. Lawrence's free verse narrative poems that also sit in my mind as examples of the way in which a writer can narrate, interrupt a narration with and take detours as he does with 'Snake' and 'Bat' (Lawrence 1977: 340, 349).

Unconsciously, I might guess that *Alice's Adventures in Wonderland* (Carroll 1865) has been at work here too with my trying to get through a 'little low door' and the idea of disappearing into a dark space.

2) Reception

i) mine

In this section I want to exemplify the reading-writing process I have tried to describe earlier. I have already mentioned the poem 'Nightmare' which I have read out loud on several occasions both to adults and children. What people have said to me in response to my writing, enters my writing head as a kind of catalyst or as a nudge of encouragement. This then reappears at the moment of writing. It is one of the many ways in which I internalise an audience: the stated feelings of past readers. One teacher in Canada (Montreal 1993) asked in relation to the poem 'Nightmare' did I realise that postwar Jews are forever writing about trains? At the time I thought that this was a slightly fanciful, possible sentimentalised view of Jews as forever haunted by the Auschwitz transports but it stuck in my mind as an example of the way in which a stream-of-consciousness poem, in which a writer can give relatively free rein to semi-conscious and previously unconscious thoughts, can release other texts that are behind the surface text. I knew that I wanted to try and do that again and was, in a way, waiting for a time when that might happen again. When I read 'The Cupboard' I feel that I have done that, and it is in part as a result of what that person said. I would like to think – and I do hope – that the poem leaves enough 'gaps' for readers, child or adult, to fill in feelings of their own about secret places and spaces in their family lives, and just as the writing of this poem brought to the surface feelings about my parents of which I was hardly aware, so readers of the poem might find something similar happen to them.

In the act of writing, and reading what I was writing, I wanted the repetition of the opening few stanzas to give the sense of closing in on something important derived in part from the folk rhyme 'In a dark, dark wood' and Alan Brownjohn's poem 'In this city . . . ' (Brownjohn 1963: 12 in Hollo 1963) which ends up with someone sitting on their own in a room, crying. I think the momentum of writing like this propelled me on to the final phase of discovery of the inner secret, the letters about and of the toing and froing before I was born. As I read this now, I can see that this is all a highly structured construct of a cluster of feelings and events. The poem reads to me like a double act of discovery – the surface discovery of the letters but a second deeper discovery of my own curiosity about my parents mysterious pre-me intimate lives (see above my observation on Marx's comment that in changing nature we change ourselves).

ii) by others

At the time of writing this passage, the only other people I knew to have read this poem were the editors Liz Attenborough, Rosemary Stones and Emma Matthewson of Puffin Books, none of whom passed comment other than for Emma Matthewson to have included it in the section marked 'Probable Definites' (!) for the then intended book, now retitled as *You Wait Till I'm Older Than You* (1996). Unlike some of the other poems, she made no recommendations about changes. However, I then discussed with Rosemary Stones on one occasion and Emma Matthewson on another. The idea that it would be good to re-cast the poems that are reminiscences into the present tense, i.e. along the lines of 'The Cupboard.' In her letter of June 2 1995 Emma Matthewson says, 'You were thinking of looking through [the collection] and adapting some of the poems to be less obviously retrospective.'

These conversations and this note turned me round in the way I came to look at this collection of poems. As a result of many public performances I had become used to telling stories and poems about myself with locutions like 'When I was a boy . . . ' As I've got older it seemed less and less appropriate to say things like: 'I share my bedroom with my brother . . . ' But writing a poem like 'The Cupboard' reawoke a feeling I had when I first started writing about my childhood in 1966, namely that I wanted it to be immediate and 'as if I am there, now.' I can see the danger of this being a bogus authenticity, a backdoor attempt to win the child over on to the implied author's side. It is a sensation that I have had myself on reading certain kinds of coy and simpering present-tense poems about 'likkle me' that were very much the vogue in humorous magazines in the first part of the century (see Ginnett 1916?: 4,5,7). I tell myself that by attempting tougher and more heartfelt moments and feelings that I will avoid this sentimentality. This is a way in which writing is in part a kind of response to other writing, it is not only what it is, but also what it is not. By internalising my and others' responses to other poems, in a similar field or with a similar style, I try to avoid making what I think are the same mistakes. I can see ways in which 'The Cupboard' carries signs of (in negative response to, or in reaction to) this kind of reception to some of these sentimental first person poems of the past.

Butcher

In the butchers
there are
rows and rows
of bits of animals
bits of leg
bits of belly
bits of neck.
The butcher goes
chop
chop
chop
and the bits get smaller.

When he opens his mouth
I see all his teeth

and his tongue is as red
as a bit of animal's leg.

1) Roots in material reality

i) childhood

Once again in this section I want to cite the specific material situation that
offers the context to the objects and feelings in the poem. Butchers and
butchering are not abstract concepts nor are they, I am asserting here, simply
signifiers manifesting difference, divergences or variants of e.g., 'botcher', 'I
betch ya', or whatever. I want to show here that 'butcher' is incontestably
linked with various material acts of butchering that I have encountered as part
of my socioeconomic existence.

As I have said, our material situation, derived from my parents' migrations
and socioeconomic existence, was that we lived in a flat over a shop (1948-
1962). This meant that our front door was really a back door, which opened
on to an open alley shared by the delivery vans and services to approximately
twelve shops. Six of these were on my own road and the other six were on
a road running at right angles to it, making two sides of a kind of courtyard,
the other two being made up of a builder's yard and a Catholic Church. One
of these shops was a butcher's, managed by the father of a friend of mine, Mr
Townsend. I spent a great deal of time in and around the Townsends – they
were one of the first houses around to have a television, they had a wonderful
Golden Retriever to play with and there was something odd and intriguing
about playing around at the back of a shop, watching the deliveries of the
carcasses, talking to the butcher's assistants, looking at their bloody overalls,
watching Mr Townsend making sausages, boiling bones, making lard in sizzling
pots and at Christmas, seeing the hundreds of chickens, turkeys, geese, ducks
and pheasants coming in, being plucked and hung up in the shop. This piece of
social interchange can be seen in the wider material context of the locality's
increasing disposable income as described in Chapter 3.

He was also the butcher my mother shopped from and he was seen by my
mother and her friends as someone rather special. She and they had nothing
but a good word for him. According to them, his steaks, mince and poultry
were the best you could buy and there was some slightly mocking story in
the family lore about how even Lily Kriss who would, one might expect, buy

from nothing less than a top-notch kosher butcher, would come across from North Harrow some three miles away to shop at Mr. Townsends – all on the evidence of roasts that my mother had dished up in the past.

So meat, hanging up in great quantities, being manhandled off the back of lorries and being broken down into joints and cuts was something with which I was especially familiar. One extra touch to the picture was Tony. He was Mr. Townsend's top butcher. He was the one called on to do the cutting and sawing. It is his arms and hands that I can picture most clearly slicing through liver, hacking through bone, flinging end-pieces into buckets. I can see his veined forearms and his big hands round the chopper. He was a jokey warm sort of a man who knew me from the time I was born until we moved away from the area when I was seventeen. But that said, I can sense a certain unease about my memory of being at eye level to the wooden counter, watching his sharp knife going through the liver, and the big metal chopper hacking away at the massive joints. I liked it when he sharpened the knives, I liked the noise and the rhythm. It was the cutting and hacking that bothered me. I can see his fingers, so near to the blades, and I can hear myself wondering if Tony might or could slice or sever a finger.

In class terms all this was an encounter between the literate, educated middle class and the tradesman. It is always an uneasy relationship in the sense that economically it might be fairly equal but in all kinds of ways each offers a threat to the other – the tradesman frequently feeling uneducated and despised by the intellectual who, in turn, can often feel threatened by the skills, strength and practical indispensability of the the tradesman. Perhaps my hostility and wariness in the poem derives from some of this class unease.

ii) at the time of writing

In this section, it becomes clearer that my siting as 'writer in schools', in direct contact with an inner-city children's audience is crucial.

I wrote the first draft of the poem at John Scurr Primary School, London. I was working with a group of Year 4 children. We were writing what I had called 'Seeing Poems', poems where the entire piece was made up of what you could see at a given moment in a given place We would not say what we thought, or what we could hear, or what people were saying. It would be just like a photo or a little silent video, pictures in words

In this sense, the poem comes out of a pedagogic experiment, one designed in a particular phase of late twentieth century education in inner city, London schools. The literary origins of the experiment lie in Imagism and its cultural predecessor, Ancient Chinese poetry. The writing of the poem, then, is a conjunction of my intellectual formation (which included finding Imagism etc.,) and my role as writer-in-residence in an inner city school (a project dreamed up by progressive English teachers and arts administrators in the late sixties and early seventies).

2) Roots in other texts

In this section I diverge from the literary sense of intertextuality. The predominant texts here are non-literary:

1. Francis Bacon's paintings. In my mind's eye they merge and blur into bloody faces, bodies, carcasses, limbs – all mysteriously suspended, motionless in empty dark spaces. They are uncannily visceral and seem almost to express what is on our insides by putting them on our outsides.
2. The dissection rooms and anatomy labs of my short medical training at the Middlesex Hospital Medical School (1964-1965) and Oxford University (1965-1966). My access to these particular texts is another aspect of my very specific class formation. I enjoyed dissecting rabbits and rats and became quite good at it. When I moved up to dissecting the human body, it all seemed to become too complicated and the inside of the body became unknowable again. From this time, I have possession of the texts of anatomy and physiology, the diagrams, photos, and dissection procedures of pre-med courses (Grant 1958; Aitken, Causey, Joseph, Young 1964; Le Gros Clark 1965; Keele, Neil, Jepson 1965). The human body exists in my mind not only structured by sensation and physical experience but also by this abstract detailed and highly material pattern of thought The body in anatomy labs is an object structured according to logic and routine. The cranial nerves have to be learnt off with a mnemonic. In the lab itself, we would treat the bodies as if they were parodies of bodies and would hold bits of them up in bizarre positions, present bits of genitals to each other as gifts or even fling bits of them at each other. In this situation, the body is at the furthest possible point from its sensuous, dynamic, responsive nature and much more akin to a comic shop rubber mask, or a gingerbread man. Part of the poem's viewpoint is informed by this treatment of the body through the discourse of medicine – or, I should say, medicine as re-interpreted by

students in anatomy labs, behind tutors' backs, and compensating for their own inhibitions and self-consciousness.

3) Reception

i) mine

In this section I want to show more of a sense in which I am a literary reader-writer involving myself in literary judgments culled from my formation.

I read the poem to myself, not as a performance piece but as a kind of film montage akin to an Eisenstein sequence (see *The Battleship Potemkin* Eisenstein 1925). Very few people in the English-speaking world who choose to write poems about dead animals can escape from the presence of Ted Hughes but when I read this, I find myself relieved that I have not explained the interconnectedness of the bodies dead and alive; I have not inferred spirits, myths or any spectral meaning to what is going on. I can sense in myself a semi-conscious reaction against a New Age and Hughesian investment in the animal and the inanimate. I kid myself that I have reduced powerful bloody processes to factual hard reality. Of course I have not. In fact, it feels to me that by pretending to reduce it in this way, I have made it all the more macabre and bizarre. What strange ritual seems to be going on here and why is the butcher like the very thing that he destroys? Are we all linked through our blood, bones and exoskeletons? The poet does not tell us but it seems as if he thinks so. Why else would he have juxtaposed the meat with the butcher's mouth?

ii) by others

Once again, the material situation as a writer in residence in a school is of prime importance.

Writing and sharing writing with children is a quietly emotional thing. Children become quite willing to treat you as a co-worker, someone trying to get on with the job, facing similar difficulties and like them possibly not succeeding. I remember the day I wrote this, two girls I was working with seemed to think that what I had written was a trivial matter. It did not catch their attention, they were too busy doing their writing. I do not suppose they remember my poem, but then I do not remember theirs. This does not, however, render the whole episode meaningless. The process of writing together has lasted in my mind at the very least. But it has also reminded me that some of what I write, does not take place in the rowdy, public arena. Some of it does not involve laughter and immediate pleasure. I have a body of material that hangs about more quietly than that, makes small elliptical comments, is possibly ignored by most of my readers – but not all of them.

Rendering the familiar unfamiliar has been the task of much English and American poetry (particularly since Gerard Manley Hopkins and Emily Dickinson were 'discovered') whether this is effected by making language express true, unexpected essences of objects or whether it is motivated by the intention to break up the seamless normality of the visible surface. In my case, I think that working with children and watching how they read my work, has influenced how I take on the notion of rendering the familiar unfamiliar. On this occasion it was to show a surprising connectedness between things: a 'have you noticed how' way of bringing things together, but done without saying so, so as not to be obvious and heavy-handed. I can sense in my writing here a libertarian approach to readers, leaving them to make the same connections as I've made, as if I am saying: 'make the connections if you want to. If you don't, or make other connections, that's OK . . . ' I understand here, of course, that this libertarianism may be phony because I cannot escape from the authority that is invested in the notion of 'poem' in 'print' in a 'book' in a 'classroom' as written by an 'adult' for a 'child'. What I am referring to here is a semi-conscious libertarian attempt – not a possible or actual libertarian effect.

1.

Don't tell your mother

When my mum went to evening classes
my dad would say,
don't tell your mother – let's have *matzo bray* *
she always says I mustn't give you that greasy stuff.
she says it's bad for you.

So he broke up the matzos
soaked them in water
beat up an egg

159

dunked the matzos in the egg
and then fried them.

'They taste best fried in *hinner shmaltz* **
skimmed off chicken soup,' he says,
'but butter'll do.'

It tasted brilliant anyway
we loved it.
Then we washed everything up,
absolutely everything,
and we went to bed.

Next day,
mum says to us,
What did your father cook you last night?

Silence.
What did your father cook you last night?

Oh, you know . . . stuff . . .
. . . egg on toast, I think.

* *matzo bray* = the Yiddish name of a dish made of *matzos* and egg.
Matzos is the word for unleavened bread and tastes like water
biscuits.

** *hinner shmaltz* = the Yiddish word for chicken fat, which is
skimmed off the top of chicken soup.

2.

Don't tell your mother

When my mum went to evening classes
my dad would say,
'Don't tell your mother – let's have *matzo bray*.'

She always says:
"Don't give the boys that greasy stuff.
It's bad for them."
So don't tell her, alright?'

So he broke up the *matzos*
put them into water to soften them up.
Then he fried them
till they were glazed and crisp.

'It tastes best like this,
fried in *hinner shmaltz*,'
he says,
'but olive oil will do.'

Then he beat up three eggs
and poured it on over the frying matzos
till it was all cooked.

It tasted brilliant.
We loved it.
Then we washed everything up
absolutely everything
and we went to bed.

Next day,
Mum says to us,
'What did your father cook you last night?'

Silence.

'What did your father cook you last night?'

'Oh you know . . . stuff . . .
. . . egg on toast, I think.'

3.

Don't tell your mother

When my mum goes to evening classes
my dad says,
'Don't tell your mother – let's have *matzo bray.*
She always says:
"Don't give the boys that greasy stuff.
It's bad for them."
So don't tell her, alright?'

So he breaks up the *matzos*
puts them into water to soften them up.
Then he fries them
till they're glazed and crisp.

'It tastes best like this, fried in *hinner shmaltz,*
skimmed off the top of the chicken soup,'
he says,
'but olive oil will do.'

Then he beats up three eggs
and pours it on over the frying matzos
till it's all cooked.

It tastes brilliant.
We love it.
Then we wash everything up
absolutely everything
and we go to bed.

Next day,
Mum says to us,
'What did your father cook you last night?'

Silence.

'What did your father cook you last night?'

'Oh you know . . . stuff . . .

. . . egg on toast, I think.'

(Notes) (Sept 1995)

These three versions are presented here in chronological order. The first was written in 1993 and published in *You are, aren't you?* (Michael Rosen 1994b). The second version is the one originally sent in to Puffin Books for publication in the MS *Wait Till I'm Older Than You* and the third is how it has appeared in *You Wait Till I'm Older Than You* (Rosen 1996). For changes see 3) Reception (below).

1) Roots in material reality

i) childhood

In this section, I want to explore another aspect of the material reality of my background: Jewishness. For some, to describe Jewishness as 'material' might seem odd if not plain downright wrong. However, what is being argued here is that individual Jews' different kinds of Jewishnesses, and their different ways of manifesting their Jewishness, have specific socioeconomic origins.

To be Jewish involves a complex web of conditions that are at one and the same time religious, secular and economic and some (most definitely not me) would argue genetic. The words 'Jew' and 'Jewish' obscure an enormous range of practices and perceptions depending on geographic situation, economic situation and sect allegiance. Historically, I belong to the group of Jews known as Ashkenazim (literally 'German') but refers to the Jews coming out of the 1500 years or so tradition of having lived in western and eastern Europe. The *lingua franca* of many of these Jews was and still is for a few, Yiddish – a language resembling medieval German with elements of Hebrew and Slav (Geipel 1982).

The actual and finite reasons for my being Jewish and living in Britain owe their origins to the pogroms against the Jews that took place in Greater Russia in the latter part of the nineteenth century. Along with hundreds of thousands of other Jews my forbears on all sides of my parents' families moved westwards. My parents' families fetched up finally in the East End of London, occupying a position in society that could be described as a mix between working class and impoverished petit bourgeois. Thus my father's mother was unable to work because of polio and lived with her parents. Her father worked for a tailor. My mother's father worked in a cap factory but my mother's mother tried at various times and unsuccessfully to run a shop, in one case a small corner dairy. In both homes Yiddish was spoken, more so in my mother's than my father's.

My parents represent the professionalisation of this section of Jewry, both of them winning scholarships to local grammar schools and then, again following a pattern of this generation of Jews, moving north-westwards out of the East End – in our case to Pinner, Middlesex. This poem represents in my mind a fragment of this experience. If I were to answer the questions, why matzos? why *matzo bray*? why hinner shmaltz? The answers all lie in this background. The political and religious origin of matzos lies in the story of Moses and the Jewish slaves fleeing Egypt:

> 'The dough they had brought from Egypt they baked into unleavened cakes, because there was no leaven; for they had been driven out of Egypt and allowed no time even to get food ready for themselves.' (The New English Bible, Exodus 12, 39; 1970: 53)

Like most Jews that I knew, we ate matzos all the year round, and not only (or in our case not at all) at *pesach* (Passover). We ate them just as non-Jews and we too for that matter (!) ate water biscuits and crackers with butter and spreads. However, eating *matzo bray* was something that I only knew from my father's cooking. Its origins lie clearly in the social conditions of Eastern European Jewry and so-called 'shtetl life'. Many poor Jews from this area in the nineteenth century lived in villages as tenant farmers, share-croppers and peasants – as shown in *The Fiddler on the Roof* (Norman Jewison 1971) and some of the stories by Isaac Bashevis Singer (see in particular *A Day of Pleasure. Stories of a Boy Growing up in Warsaw* (1980)). Every such community relies on staple crops and animals. For many Jews working on unfertile land (because of discrimination) these were rye and chickens. As can be seen from the recipe, this dish is a way of making one chicken go far. The chicken fat is skimmed off the soup, that was in turn made from the chicken skin and bones taken from the chicken eaten on the day after a feast day or a sabbath. The egg likewise comes from the chicken and the matzo, presumably stale, was a way of making the most of what was left over. So the dish survived urbanisation, (where Jews went on keeping chickens in back yards and even in tenements) and embourgeoisement. Though saying that, I repeat, I never came across my middle-class Jewish friends eating *matzo bray* – perhaps because it seemed too *haimishe* – a word meaning 'homelandy' i.e. too much like the poor Jewish peasants of Eastern Europe, and not modern and English and prosperous.

Perhaps my father, with his acute sense of class and solidarity, relished the haimishe quality of the dish and its humble origins. The poem records my mother's displeasure with the dish which she expresses through its supposed greasiness, but I know that tucked away in there is her ambivalence about certain aspects of her Jewish home-life that she felt glad to be rid of – the Yiddish cursing, compulsive card-playing and, as she saw it, the unhealthy food. Part of what she saw as her emancipation from a predetermined sex role as a Jewish housewife, and part of what she saw as her emancipation from the obscurantist aspects of Judaism was her eating of healthy, fresh, fat-free food.

The actual conditions of my father cooking for my brother and me, also relate to this emancipation. My mother always seemed to me to be someone who yearned for a better and fuller life for herself, the children she taught and – no matter how abstract this sounded – the 'international working class'. This entailed her reading an enormous amount, attending meetings and evening classes and always engaging in argument and debate with friends and colleagues. Of the evening classes that she attended, the one I remember most clearly was her Scottish Dancing Class. This may seem bizarre to others but to me now seems quite consistent. It was her way of keeping fit, learning a skill that she could share with the children she taught, and at the same time showed that she could be quite happily cross-cultural in her interests.

Meanwhile my father was thrown into role of cook. He operated with a narrow repertoire, born of the gender roles in Jewish families as much as non-Jewish ones but the fact that there was a repertoire at all represented the conscious ideological effort by both of my parents to break out of those gender roles and attempt some forms of equality of labour in the home. In actual fact, some of my father's cooking was a secret joke between my brother and me, particularly his dishing up of cold meat on Monday nights. In the privacy of our bedroom we would do imitations of my father cutting the cold meat from the roast the day before, smacking his lips and saying with relish – 'A nice bit of meat here, boys!' – while we found cold meat, with chunks of cold fat clinging to it, utterly ghastly. That said, we loved his *matzo bray*. It is fatty, but the egg makes it sweet and the matzo tends to burn slightly giving it a half crispy, half soft texture. It is a piece of childhood oral gratification, which incidentally, I had plenty of. I was not deprived of food – ever – and was by the age of ten something of a 'fatty'. My parents, my mother in particular, voiced a dread of poverty and hunger. They had seen starving families throughout their childhoods and had taken part in collections for the National Union of Unemployed Workers in the 1930s. I don't think either of them actually experienced starvation though my father's mother was reduced to asking for charity from the Jewish Board of Guardians to give my father a pair of shoes when he was a boy (Rosen H. 1993: 90-91).

There is also the tradition, (or is it the caricature?), of the Jewish mother (see below *Aldermaston March*) urging all the people around her to eat. The material origins of this are not hard to see: the pivotal role of mothers in most cultures but amongst Jews in particular, as cooks and carers; the situation of Jews in poverty and flight throughout the nineteenth century; the welcome relief they found in Britain and the USA; the anxiety that the relief would be temporary. Rather than follow a Protestant tradition of saving for a rainy day, (and moderation in all things), which perhaps reflects the stability and permanence of middle class settlement, Jews seemed to have developed an attitude of 'grab what you can while you're in this place because you might have to move on tomorrow'. I was always aware as a child that food, health and security were heavily involved with each other and any bad eating or under-eating was in some almost spiritual way, wrong. It was my duty to stay fit and alive even if it meant being a bit overweight in the process!

2) Roots in texts

i) (The 'text' of Yiddish and yiddishkeit' – a word referring to Jewish, not Judaic culture)

I want to use this poem as an opportunity to consider another aspect of intertextual contexts: a socio-linguistic consideration of dialect and idiolect.

Returning for a moment to the question of Yiddish, my parents spoke it in fragments, as ways of naming objects, as curses and exclamations, as ways of describing people and situations that English did not quite seem to manage to do. It was also a way of stating identity, but an ambivalent contradictory one. They were classic examples of what Isaac Deutscher referred to as 'non-Jewish Jews' (Deutscher 1968) or what Jonathan Miller described in *Beyond the Fringe* (1960) as not being 'a Jew – but Jew-ish'. My parents did not celebrate their Jewishness in any religious sense yet never expressed any shame, concealment or self-hate that religious Jews sometimes accuse secular Jews of. At the same time they clearly enjoyed the humorous, ironic quality of Jewish jokes, Jewish banter in the home and were deadly serious about opposing all signs of anti-semitism and racism. Yiddish phrases and expressions are part of my language profile and exist in my consciousness as quite legitimate and available ways of describing objects, moods, feelings and people. I have no other word for *matzo bray*, chicken fat is not the same as hinner shmaltz because 'chicken fat' I take to mean the fat under the skin on a roasted chicken, while hinner shmaltz is skimmed off the soup. These particular words then are fragments not just of Yiddish but of a whole social, economic and political history of which I am a partial inheritor.

ii) roots in textual and ideological argument at time of writing (taking part in the cultural discourse on 'Jewishness')

In this section I want to show how writing, (or more accurately, a writer choosing to write a certain piece) involves an intervention into a conversation that is already gong on. I do not mean to imply by that that this conversation or discourse is autonomous and sealed off from its socioeconomic base. The motives and the causes of the intervention originate in the class and cultural positionings that I have described elsewhere. Or to try and put it more subtly, the interventions inevitably bear the signs of the class and cultural positionings of the writer making the intervention.

In the last fifteen years or so, I have lived in an environment that has raised 'the cultural question'. By this I mean that the questions of feminism, 'black power', rights for the disabled and many other groups' rights for autonomy, self-organisation and equality, arrived eventually on the doorsteps of Jewry. For many Jews it was anathema and ran quite counter to the pattern of life that Jews had followed in Britain and America. This was to establish themselves as a totally distinct religious community, but totally assimilated socially. Thus, the picture of the queen appears in the foyers of many synagogues – and yet many religious Jews cannot eat with non-Jews – i.e. loyal but separate. My Uncle Ronnie cannot visit me and cannot allow me and my non-Jewish wife to visit him and thinks that my retellings of the late medieval Jewish 'Golem' stories (Rosen 1990b, 1997) might give non-Jews 'the wrong impression' of what we Jews are or should be – ordinary, respectable but separate.

Meanwhile, some Jews, both religious and not, took part in the discourse of cultural rights and claimed that Jews too are an 'ethnic minority'. Some went further and said that the experience of anti-semitism put Jews in a very particular situation vis a vis racism, expressed as it is today usually towards Africans, Arabs, Afro-Caribbeans, and Asians. Some said that Jewish ethnicity could be celebrated and mourned quite separately from the religion. One tendency amongst this grouped together round the publication *Jewish Socialist*. It was a tendency that tried to disengage itself from Zionism and in so doing put itself at odds with the vast majority of diaspora Jews. I found myself attracted by much of what the magazine has stood for, have contributed articles, attended meetings, helped with benefits and been affected by their political and cultural attitudes. One aspect of these is to deny the 'Jewish establishment' its claim to speak for all Jews. Quite the contrary, it has put forward the suggestion that the so-called 'Jewish community' is in fact extremely diverse and that the Chief Rabbi and others have no right to claim that secular Jews are not really Jews or that Jews ought to behave in this or that way.

This 'cultural turn' can be put in a harsh light by suggesting that it is a refuge from universality, from internationalism, from class politics. In the wake of the obvious failure of universal, socialistic internationalism (in the form of the Soviet Union), many people interested in these ideas have turned towards a 'cultural' way of expressing their politics, a kind of multiculturalism elevated to the level of organisation or coalition. My own position has evolved in this context, saying in effect that yes, indeed we are all cultural beings but that is not necessarily sufficiently strong or viable grounds for organisation or emancipation for all people. Or, put conversely, there are great dangers in simply and only organising culturally – namely that you start to express a kind of cultural nationalism, separatism and chauvinism. These arguments are all taking place in the context of unsatisfactory delivery of basic human rights to all people, and unsatisfactory political programmes and solutions. Put crudely, neither naked capitalism as expressed by Conservatives or Republicans nor diluted welfarism as expressed by the Labour Party or Democrats can provide jobs, houses and social care for everyone. In their wake flow discrimination, racism and violence and, within sections of the liberal intelligentsia and within some of the minority cultures, the cultural turn appears to offer solutions.

This poem is a very mild, very small and almost insignificant expression of cultural identity within this problematic. Because its eventual reception is likely to be in and around schools then I imagine its significance grows slightly. Multiculturalism in the present context of schools is under threat. Under the national curriculum, history was to be more English, literature was to be more 'heritage', bilingualism has been undermined and so-called anti-racist excesses were outlawed and ridiculed. A poem like this will enter this environment and may be, I imagine, slightly unmanageable. It's not R.E. and yet it is to do with Jews – or is it? Is it just about a boy and what his parents like to eat? Can it be made acceptable by being de-Jewified? In some contexts I imagine it will hit anti-semitism. It may even disappoint some people who quite like Michael Rosen's work but now find that this poem is too overtly Jewish. After all, it is always much easier to cope with cultural similarity than difference. But these may be defensive projections.

The poem then was written with an anticipation of this problematic. Meanwhile it was also written with a certain amount of enjoyment and relief that the cultural turn, whatever its political weakness, had liberated any self-consciousness, secretiveness, furtiveness I may have had about admitting that I was Jewish. Or, that intrinsic to the actual material way in which I have lived (here in the poem, *eaten*) is a form of Jewishness, which as a cultural structure also has material roots. In other words, the concerns of my mother and father expressed in the poem were expressed through and with Jewish ways of going on.

iii) roots in other texts

One ground text that is foregrounded here is of the bilingual parental idiolects. Part of the taste of the dish, its singularity, lies in its linguistic provenance in Yiddish. At the literary level, the scene is a kind of conspiracy, all boys together doing something disapproved of on the plane of matriarchal authority. In my memory this has chimes with several scenes in Great Expectations (Dickens 1860-61) where Pip and Joe take, or intend to take secret pleasures together, away from the tyrannical control of Pip's surrogate mother. The key phrase here is the exclamation my father used to say: 'What larks, Pip!' (Dickens 1996: 17, 45, 100, 217, 471). This resonates with me in several ways at the same time. My father read *Great Expectations* to the family one summer holiday. As a result, several of the phrases of the book passed into the family folklore, including 'What larks, Pip!'. (To be pedantic for a moment, in actual fact Dickens never uses the entire phrase, 'What larks, Pip!' but it is either simply 'What larks!' or the word 'larks' is in another phrase!) My father would call out 'What larks, Pip!' at times (I think) when he thought we were having a good time. In fact, thinking about this now, as I write, my father must have used a text like this to express (or is it mask?) his true emotions. He took great pleasure in having good times at home and on holiday. He loved home comforts and expeditions in particular. I guess he sometimes found it easier to express these pleasures through the medium of someone else's words. Or perhaps the words from literature lent a kind of aura or extra value to the episode taking place in reality. So in the background to this poem, I can hear 'What larks, Pip!' as taken from the two contexts – my father reading us *Great Expectations* and his frequent citation in the course of taking pleasure.

In a rather more dull way, the discourse of recipes is not far away, and in order to verify my first draft, I did in fact refer to Florence Greenberg's *Jewish Cookery* (1947, 1967: 412). I should say that this in itself was a kind of family joke. It was, for some mysterious reason always referred to as 'Fanny Greenberg' as in 'Look it up in Fanny Greenberg!' So for me to write the poem with 'Fanny Greenberg' at my side is a kind of private intertextual joke. The final irony here, though is that the recipe is not the one that my father cooked it by – see the later drafts. So the intertextual pathway goes like this:

1) my father's recipe
2) my memory of my father's recipe
3) my cross-checking with 'Fanny Greenberg'
4) my writing of the poem incorporating these texts – then
5) my father telling me that I had got the recipe wrong i.e. presenting me with a new text (!)
6) my producing an amended text based on this latter pre-text.

This intertextual pathway represents several movements – cultural transmission through food, parental authority and control, middle-class academic facticity with its reverence towards verity and empirical proof. Though this pathway is hidden in the final text (obscured? repressed?) this text I am writing here reveals it

3) Reception

i) mine

In this section I want to draw attention to my positioning not only as a writer but also as a performer in schools (already described in Chapter 3). Once again, it has to be stated that this positioning is not simply or purely literary but as I have shown, a consequence of some specific economic demands put upon the education system. Moreover, as a consequence of my own privileged position within the education system, I have the opportunity to take up a very specific site there.

The voice of the first draft is derived out of story-telling and anecdotalising with friends, family and in front of children in schools. As I wrote it, I checked it against this voice: did it conform to its constraints and requirements? Thus the 'So' and the 'Silence', the lack of conjunction between 'anyway' and 'we loved it', the repetition and emphasis of 'absolutely everything', all of which I hear and read back to myself as *oral devices*. The untagged dialogue – as in the last three lines, is born out of hearing myself tell and perform this episode. With no adverbial directives, no stage directions, it relies entirely on a reproduction of oral performance. The reader (either to oneself or to others) has to convey meaning through tone, gesture, amplitude, hesitation, pitch and intonation patterns. My reception of poems that I have written in the past, performances and conversations I have observed myself enacting, have contributed to this part of the writing.

As I read and re-read the poem, another theme emerges – lying to my mother. I am aware of a certain unease in myself here. Did we lie to her? Does it matter that I have put on public show a lie to my mother? She did not do anything to deserve that, I hear myself thinking. But it is also a question of split loyalties. It was after all 'What larks, Pip!', we had a good time, and surely we should not 'grass' on my Dad for doing that? I imagine in this reception space, that some teachers or parents might play with some of this. They might ask, why is it that Michael Rosen did not tell his Mum the truth? Should he have done? Would you? Do you always tell your Mum the truth? And so on. By saying this, I am stating that I am not unaware of the kinds of contexts this poem is likely to find itself in. In part, I wrote it with this in mind, and my satisfaction with it, lies, in part, in my knowledge that it feels to me like a poem that could easily find its place in this kind of environment. In other words the poem not only lives in the 'discourse of poetry', but it also lives in a pedagogical discourse – the contemporary one in which children read, discuss and write poetry in primary school classrooms. Or to be more specific – there are a number of teachers whose practice I am familiar with, who could (may? will?) insert it into their work, 'find it useful'. In the sense that we all write for an audience, I am aware here that this 'children's' poem is, in part, written for, or into, an institutional practice dominated by adults. However, because I am of the opinion that the institutional practice of reading, discussing and writing poetry on personal and social matters is itself emancipatory, then I am not too troubled by these considerations. In years to come, with some other means of children's access to literature, the present practices may appear ludicrously authoritarian, but I am writing in the historical present, and it is this context that impinges on my writing.

<u>ii) by others</u>

The key person here is my father. The first time he heard the poem was at a launch party for *You are, aren't you?* (Rosen 1994b) I could hear him muttering in the background immediately after, and when the reading was over he jocularly made the point that he would never cook *matzo bray* in the way that I had suggested he had. This was both funny and serious. It was funny that I had got it wrong just as I was trying to be culturally authentic and celebratory. It was funny that my father was, in a sense ticking me off, some forty years after the event. It was also serious, in that what is the point of writing a poem like this, unless you do get it right? Or, is what counts the memory, and there is no 'getting it right'? But then, as the poem is in a sense a celebration of my father's fatherliness, and may survive his passing, then surely isn't he entitled to know that other people, other Jews especially, will know that he cooked a damn good *matzo bray* and not some diluted, unpalatable hotch-potch that Michael said he cooked? In fact, I quite like it that the poem should celebrate and commemorate my father in this way, if only because in plenty of the other poems of mine he comes out looking irritable, authoritarian, or self-indulgent. At last, I say to myself, I have found a way of expressing a bit of my father's tenderness.

The transition in the drafts from past to present tense follows from the suggestion made by Rosemary Stones at Puffin Books that there was something inconsistent and perhaps hard for a child reader to follow – in mixing poems in one collection that referred to my childhood in both present and past tenses. I accepted this criticism, and liked the idea that I was returning to something I began thirty years ago, which was to try to write in the voice of the child I was, and so produce a text of poems that, like *A Child's Garden of Verses* (Stevenson 1885), gives a fragmentary sequence of images from a child's life.

Found Poem: Safety Instructions on United Airlines 1994

"If you are sitting in an exit row
and you cannot understand this card
or cannot see well enough

to follow these instructions
please tell a crew member."

I thought:
But If I can't understand the card
how can I understand it
to tell someone I can't understand it?

Note 1) The analysis that follows does not include a materialist explanation i.e. it is an analysis of some 'necessary conditions' but not 'sufficient conditions'. Beyond what I am about to say, I will not be examining in detail the obvious situation that the poem could not have happened without my being on board a plane to the States – a situation born of the material situations of my father's migrations and my position as a successful writer, invited to take part in conferences and school visits there.

Note 2) With the rest of the poems that follow I will be selecting only one or two elements from the scheme outlined at the beginning of this chapter. These have been selected as ways of exemplifying another aspect of the 'work's' contexts so far not fully explored. For clarity's sake, I repeat that all these twelve analyses should be seen as a whole, and no single poem's commentary be taken as exemplifying all the contextual parameters I am delineating in this thesis.

1) Roots in other texts (including educational discourse)

I first came across the concept of the 'found poem' in 1976 when the teacher anthologiser David Jackson was putting together the collection *Ways of Talking* (1978). In saying this, I would emphasise that merely because I 'came across' a concept does not explain any of the following – why I noticed it, why I enjoyed it, why I thought I would like to attempt to imitate it, why I chose the text that I did to follow the form. However, first I will examine the occurrence of the concept itself.

David Jackson was an inspirational force in English teaching in the 1970s and early 1980s (see in particular his *Continuity in English Teaching* (1983)). With *Ways of Talking* and the accompanying audio cassette he was moving towards a theory of texts, orality and children's writing to which I am greatly indebted. My understanding of this at the time was that the school students with whom he was working, were confronted by a massive quantity of heterogeneous texts, some written, some oral, some performed through the electronic media, some integrated with illustration (picture books and comics). Some of these were regulatory (rules, instructions), some were narrational (stories, anecdotes, lies, story-jokes), some were more purely expressive (song lyrics, poems). In addition there was a whole set of linguistic interactions (gossip, arguments, boastings) that had no literary status but seemed, on random observation, to be immensely important to these school students. What he identified in my work, he implied, was a willingness to engage with all these areas. I had not confined myself to the purely lyric, or the purely narrational and when I was working in that area, I seemed to be engaging with them in precisely these informal, non-literary ways. Because he had a commitment to students' own expressiveness, he made it clear to me that my poetry had helped him say to his students, 'Look what you can write – you can use the language that you hear and see around you.' The two aspects of my work in particular that he latched on to were the domestic arguments and the deconstructions of, say, news bulletins and the like ('Here is the News' from

Wouldn't You Like to Know? (Rosen 1977: 76-78)). As part of the conversations I had with Jackson, the visits I made to his school and the workshops I was involved in with his students, I found myself, in a sense, legitimated by some kind of theory. And it was a theory that seemed to work – the students wrote and what they wrote was interesting and enjoyable for all concerned. But also, and just as important to me, Jackson introduced me to writers and kinds of writing that I had not previously encountered. He did what a good teacher does – he showed me the possible: a writer such as Siv Widerberg (1973) who could catch a seemingly trivial moment in a child's life and in just three or four lines imply much, much more:

> 'I collected stamps.
> Papa gave me a whole bagful.
> I don't collect stamps anymore.'

(Widerberg 1973; Jackson 1978: 53)

And, of more direct relevance here, 'found poems' by Brian Jones (Jackson 1978: 39) and Ronald Gross (Jackson 1978: 36). Now there is no need for a long disquisition on the evolution of this form because what counts in this context is my encounter with it. Suffice it to say, that its origins are in Dada and

Surrealist art which 'found' objects, such as, famously, a urinal, and 'brought them in' to the hallowed space of the gallery and said, 'it's art'. In terms of my encounter with Brian Jones and Julius Lester's work (Lester 1971), care of David Jackson, the found poems connoted a great deal: the anti-orthodoxism of Dada, the uncommented-on comment that a found poem represents, the 'sideways' way of saying things, the photo-like freezing of a moment in the everyday, the reflection back on to, and implied questioning of the institution of 'Poetry'. Jackson introduced me to the work of Julius Lester in this area of 'found poems' (Lester 1971) and here, with his selection of dramatic items from newspapers, it seemed also to be a way of fracturing the normal, legitimated, dominant discourse. The method seemed to be that by pulling out and holding up for examination usual, quotidinial statements that in the normal run of life rush past as accepted views on how things are, the ideological intent or significance could be suddenly made bare. And you (the writer) didn't have to say what that significance was. The very act of excision and re-publication did the exposure. It was a way of writing without writing in two ways at the same time:

1) by not actually writing the words,
2) by not putting into words ideological intent or significance.

This seemed to me of great interest with regard to school students. Surely this was a way of being ironic, not-heavy-handed, about the world around you. Coming as I do from the perspective that sees that one of the functions and entitlements of going to school is that teachers can create situations which will enable students to see that ideas and texts are *constructed* and have ideological intents and significances that may not be immediately apparent, the 'found poem' seemed like a useful tool. But in case this seems like over-burdening this form, it is also a way of playing with the surface. In the school context, in which language can often appear to be 'given' and rule-bound (e.g., through text books, translation exercises, school rules, instructions, science experiments' formats for 'writing up' etc.) then here was a way of holding up for inspection some of the 'languagey' things about language, some of the lexty' things about texts – without making a big deal of it.

Parallel with David Jackson's alerting me to this phenomenon and my susceptibility to the concept, various other non-literary sources were playing with the same idea. *Private Eye* has had from the outset various spaces for readers to snip bits out of the endless stream of textual output – 'Pseuds'

Corner', 'luvvies', 'Colemanballs', 'Fancy That', 'True Stories'. *The New Statesman* has had 'This England' and writers such as Nigel Rees have produced a clutch of books such as *Eavesdroppings* (1981) and *Foot in Mouth* (1982) that are in effect woven-together fragments of daily speech and absurd signs. I have long enjoyed the mild antiauthoritarianism and anti-pomposity that a lot of this kind of work implies. Ironically, for such an obviously intertextual way of communicating, it is in its own way rather anti-postmodernist. Where the architect who 'quotes' various past styles in his building can be criticised for loading his or her construction with solemnity and reverence, this whole tradition of excision and republishing seems much more irreverent and ludic. Nor is it really akin to the postmodern TV ads that are often replete with allusion and play as these rework the pre-text and – more importantly have a determining intention and function to sell something that is imaged or textualised within its form. These found texts draw attention to themselves as themselves.

So in a way I have been educated into looking for 'found' texts! I have a friend who instead of saying 'one fell swoop' says 'one foul swipe'. He has no idea that this is 'wrong' and because he makes himself clear (both to himself and to his receivers) he is not 'wrong'. I cite this as an example of texts that I have conditioned myself into looking out for, disruptions to the surface, breaks in the smooth-running of representation.

There is one further autobiographical root to all this: my parents and my brother were great re-cite-ers. We had a tiled kitchen that they covered with felt-tip quotes from family, friends and general texts in the environment, selected for their significance, absurdity or wit. So here could be found my mother's comment: 'Ask your father what he's doing and tell him to stop it.' Or her dubbing the broken dishwasher a 'wishdasher' and my brother's comment on what he was doing with his Ph.D in Geology – 'I am pushing back the foreskin of knowledge'. This was only part of a more general playing with found texts that my home was full of spoonerisms, obscene alterations to book titles ('Nicholarse Nickleby'), deliberate misquotations from Shakespeare ('Hamlet, Hamlet I am thy father's gimlet' – an obscure family joke referring to the Russian film of *Hamlet* (1964) that pronounces the name 'Gamlet'), mispronunciations and games with French, German and Yiddish words, distortions of school prayers and hymns ('Our Father which art in heaven, Harold be thy name . . . ' – my father is called Harold), inversions of idioms and proverbs ('That's another gether altomatter'), mocking quotations from unlikely sources ('Here is Old Lob. Here is Mrs Cuddy. Run Rover run.' from the 'Beacon Readers' ([Various] 1922 but many editions thereafter). Looking back on all this, it seems now like a massive profusion of textual play. It drew attention in a relentless way to the sound of language and to its potential for fallibility. However, I do not take from that the Derridean conclusion that this is because language never finds its referent and works by referring to itself, its homonyms, near homonyms, echoes, contrasts, shadows and the like. I take almost the opposite position — that all this textual play directed me to the way in which we are all language-makers and that in face to face situations, in appropriate contexts, language-making and language-receiving produced marked and visible effects (laughter, thoughtfulness, excitement, and always further comment). This poem, then, comes out of these traditions. However, it can be quickly seen that I have broken one of the rules of 'found poems' – I have added a comment that 'explains' why) have excised it from its context and put it in this collection.

2) Reception by others

The addition to the found poem (i.e. the last three lines) is a direct consequence of the found poem's reception by children. After I had spotted it on the flight, I rushed into schools with it, thinking that children would be able to see immediately how absurd the literal meaning of these instructions are. They did not. I would say to them that I found this notice on a United Airlines flight I would read it. There would be no reaction. Then if I unpicked it, with almost the exact same words as I have appended, they would laugh, partly I think because of the absurd and difficult repetition of 'understand'. In a way I regret that I have done this, but I guess this is part of what I might dub my populism. I would rather find a way to make the point clear to most people than put something in a book that baffled or confused most people. By making a piece of patterned language myself (with the repetition of 'understand'), I think I have got around the problem in a playful kind of way. I should say here that in the editing process I have had to fight my corner on this one. My editor at Puffin books was rather keen for me to leave my added comment off. I insisted purely on the basis of my face-to-face encounters with live audiences.

Eddie and the car

The stupidest thing I have ever done
happened in France.

We were going to have a picnic,
so we were driving along the road
in our little yellow Renault 4.
Have you ever seen a Renault 4?
It's like a little square tin box.
If you lean on it
your hand goes straight through the side of the car.

We were off to have a picnic.
Have you noticed how long it takes
parents to make up their minds where to stop for a picnic?
It takes us longer to find where to have the picnic
than it takes to eat it.
We stop, we get out, we spread the sheet
we unload the boxes and bags and bottles
we sit down and it's
sniff
sniff
sniff
what's that?
what on earth could smell like that?
a dead dog?

OK
EVERYONE BACK IN THE CAR
Drive on.

We stop, we get out, we spread the sheet
we unload the boxes and bags and bottles
we sit down and it's
zzzzzzz
zzzzzzz
zzzzzzz
wasps.
Hundreds of them.
OK EVERYONE BACK IN THE CAR.
Drive on.

In the end we got to this perfect place.
Backed the car up a little slope
laid everything out on the ground
sat down.

'Eddie do you want some chicken?'
'Na.'
'Eddie do you want some crisps?'
'Na.'
'A drink?'
'Na.'
'Right, well, you toddle off
and leave us to eat in peace.'

So Eddie (who was three at the time)
walked off to the car
and he got into the back seat.
He looked out the window
and called out:
'Look at mee-eeeee.
I'm in the car.'
Joe, who was seven,
looks over and starts giggling back at Eddie.
'Look at Eddie, dad,' says Joe.
'Turn round, Joe. Don't take any notice of him.
It only encourages him.
Turn round.'

Then Eddie climbed into the front seat of the car.
He grabbed hold of the steering wheel
and shouted out at us:
'LOOK AT ME-EEEEEEE,
I'M DRI-VING.'
And Joe says,
'Look at Eddie, Dad
he's driving.'
I say,
'Turn round Joe,

don't take any notice of him.
It only encourages him.
Turn round.'
We went on eating.

Then Joe looked up and said,
'Dad.
The car's moving.'
I said, 'Don't be silly, Joe,'
and I turned round to look at the car.

He was right.
The car was moving slowly down the slope
towards the road
with Eddie at the wheel.
He is screaming:
'THE CAR'S MOVING. THE CAR'S MOVING.'

Now If you were a sensible, intelligent person
at this moment
you might perhaps go over to the car
open the door
get Eddie out
jump in
jam on the brakes
and stop the car.

That would be a sensible thing to do.

Slightly less sensible
but still quite sensible
would be to
go over to the car
open the door
get Eddie out
close the door
and wave goodbye to the car.

At least Eddie would be safe.

What I did was
try to stop the car.
I rushed over and grabbed hold of the pillar between the two doors
and tried to stop the car going down the slope.
Eddie was screaming out the window:
'THE CAR'S MOVING!'
And I'm grunting back at him,
'I know it's moving.'
All the time the car is moving down the slope
and I'm hanging on.

On the roof of the car is a tray of peaches
so Joe is calling out,
'Dad, look at the peaches.
the peaches are flying off the roof of the car.'
and I'm saying, 'Never mind the peaches,'
And Eddie is shouting,
'The car's moving.'
'I know it's moving.'

Now I know that what we've got coming up next
is the road.
So I think, it'll be flatter there.
The car will slow down.
I'll be able to stop the car.
We get to the road.
The car doesn't slow down.
I am not able to stop the car.
'Dad, look at the peaches.'
'Never mind the peaches.'
'The car's moving.'
'I know it's moving.'

We are now heading for a twelve foot ditch.

The car nosedives down the ditch

with me still hanging on.
it bounces once, twice on its nose
and lands up stuck head first in a hedge
with its wheels spinning in midair.

I opened the door, grabbed hold of Eddie
got him out
and he jumped into his mother's arms
and bit her.
He sunk his teeth right into her arm.
Joe is walking around saying,
'Look at the peaches
look at the peaches.'

Eddie is OK
now to get the car out of the hedge.
Get in
start up
into reverse
and
nothing.
The little yellow Renault 4 has front wheel drive.
The front wheels are turning over and over
in midair
and nothing else is moving.

What to do?

I got out the car and looked round
and there is no one anywhere.
We're in the middle of the French countryside.
We're stuck in a hedge
miles from home.

Then I looked again
up the road
and I could see in a field
someone's backside.

A man was bending down
digging potatoes.
So I ran up the road and spoke to him. 'Excusez-mol, monsieur,
je suis anglais et je suis stupide.'
(I'm English and I'm stupid)
and my little boy got on the front seat of the car
and the car went down the hill
and
BLUP
it's stuck.

The man stood up
and slowly wagged his finger at me.
'Jamais, jamais, jamais–'
(Never, never, never)
Never let a child on to the front seat of a car
they can easily–
'Yeah I know that now,' I said
but how do I get the car out?
He then raised both hands by his side and said,
'Bof!'
This is French for:
'I haven't got a clue
you're on your own, mate.'

Try it:
raise both arms
by your side
hands upwards
and as you say it
puff your cheeks out:
'Bof!'

So now what?

Far away in the distance
I see a man ploughing a field
so I started off running up the road

towards him.
As I am running along
I start to realise that I am only wearing my underpants.
When we had the picnic
I thought I would sunbathe.
So here I am running down the road
in my underpants.
No matter.
Must press on.

As I got nearer to the field
where the man was ploughing
I started thinking,
how *do* you get someone to stop ploughing a field?

So I climbed over the fence
and stood in front of the tractor
held up both my hands
and started waving.
I don't suppose the farmer
had ever seen a large hairy bloke
in his underpants
standing in front of his tractor waving his hands.
But he brought the tractor up to me and stopped it.
And he said, 'Ey bein?'
which is French for:
'Well? Have you got something to say or not?
Or are you completely stupid?'
As you say it you have to nod your head upwards
leaving your mouth open after you've said it.
The 'bein' bit sounds like 'bang' said through your nose.
Try it.

So I said,
'Excusez-mol, monsieur,
je suis anglais et je suis stupide.'
(I'm English and I'm stupid)
and my little boy got on the front seat of the car

and the car went down the hill
and
BLUP
it's stuck.
The man looked at me
and slowly wagged his finger at me and said
'Jamais, jamais, jamais'
(Never, never, never)
let a child get into the front seat of a car
because they can easily—
'Yeah, yeah, yeah, I know that *now*
but do you think you could help me?
I could pay you . . .
it would be very nice if . . . '

So three hours later
after he had lunch
he came along with his tractor
his wife
his dog
and a long chain.
They tied the chain round the back bumper of the car
and they pulled and they heaved
and they heaved and they pulled
(just like the story of The Enormous Turnip)
and they pulled and they heaved the bumper
right off the car.

Thanks.

Well, in the end
they got the little yellow Renault 4 out of the bush
and out of the ditch.
After we had kicked it a few times
it worked.
It was a bit difficult going round corners
but it worked.
We've got a photo of the

little yellow Renault 4
stuck in the ditch
in our photo album.
It's great.
It reminds me of
the stupidest thing I have ever done.

What follows is the fullest explication along materialist lines in this sequence
of analyses.

1) Roots in material reality

i) the event

This essence of this episode, the picnic, the event of Eddie my son climbing
into the car and letting off the brake, the ditch, the farmer and the eventual
outcome are all as I understood them to have happened. In 'realist' terms
(i.e. philosophically) I have of course mediated this event with language. I have
selected a tiny few of the multi-multi millions of atomic and molecular actions
and reactions of that day and patterned them and structured them in language
(using conventional and 'borrowed' articulations) in such a way as to have
made a text that is comprehensible to most users of English. These acts of
selecting and patterning (only possible through, and in language) were made in
a territory that was already made – or to be more precise in territories (plural)
already made. One territory was the economic and sociological structures and
processes in the activity of that day. The other was the linguistic and textual
resources at my disposal. However, these linguistic and textual availabilities
were also determined by my economic and sociological circumstances.

Let us take these in turn:

1) the economic and sociological structures and processes in activity that day'

What was in activity that day was part of the characteristic behaviour of
middle-class, white, British nuclear families on their summer vacation. Many
of them (us) go in a car to the south of France and *consume* aspects of France,
including its landscape. It is a behaviour that involves both a certain level of
material wealth (to pay for the trip), a certain kind of intellectual and social
formation (to think that France and the French countryside is desirable and

consumable), a certain kind of social formation to want to take on this activity in the social form of the family, and a certain kind of formation to be complicit with the dominant social unit of twentieth century capitalist society, viz., the nuclear family. The interaction of these material and ideological processes produces the material event of 'family-in-France-going-on-picnic'.

2) 'the linguistic and textual resources at my disposal, their availability being determined by my economic and sociological circumstances'

The linguistic and textual resources at my disposal (for it to have been possible both to have had the experience and to write about it) include the following: the ability to narrate events i.e. to create linked sequences that have intelligibility; the ability to narrate using such structures as dialogue, change of narrative perspective and modes of address; the ability to operate in two languages; the ability to use so-called narrative devices as

1) 'asides',
2) tonal processes such as irony,
3) structural patterning which when linked with meaning produces such features as tension, climax and anti-climax.
(I am sure this doesn't exhaust the resources here.)

The economic and sociological conditions that determined my access to these resources include:

1) my parents' disposability to education and learning (that created Bourdieu's 'habitus') which in turn helped me enmesh smoothly with the state's education on offer in the 1950s and 60s;
2) as a legacy from the past and the cultural and military bias of Britain towards France and away from Germany, France was the magnet site that was made most desirable in this period of the twentieth century.

But 'most desirable' for whom? It has to be said that the patterns of English holiday-making abroad in the second half of the twentieth century could be very crudely expressed as Spain and the Canaries – working class; France – middle class. It is out of the nexus of my 'habitus', my education in an English grammar school curriculum of the 1950s, and this economic and cultural structuring of holidays that enables me to operate in French in France.

The material roots of my ability to write in this particular way can be traced back to a combination of the following: the economic surplus of an advanced capitalist society that has the resources to pay for a privileged elite to spend time in the unproductive work of studying cultural artifacts (e.g., in my case, do A-levels and a degree in English Literature whilst receiving state and parental monies); the surplus which also plays a part in facilitating the specific institutional practices and ideologies of an English Literature course in the early 1960s, in England, in school in London and at university in Oxford; the economic situation of impoverished Ashkenazim Jewry migrating that was the condition within which individual Jews made use of the cultural practice of 'spieling', 'shmoozing', 'kibbitzing' all terms denoting anecdoting, gossiping, sharing familial and familiar stories.

2) Roots in textual activity

So the kinds of cultural practices and ideologies that come together in these circumstances are:

1. Pre-'Theory' literary criticism.
This was a process that was dominated, even as late as the mid-sixties, by a notion that literature was apart from and even superior to the economic and industrial conditions of life. There was a great deal of 'pure' textual activity, frequently on texts that were pastoral, pre-industrial or ones that inflected 'purely' personal desires, wishes and feelings. So there was a double act of turning one's back on the world outside both in the process of *how* one looked at texts and in the *choice* of texts that one was examining. It was very difficult at the time to see the irony that this turning of the back was in fact facilitated by the very industrial process we were ignoring, nor, more subtly, that it suited one section of the dominant culture (the conservative-traditionalist wing) that its critical and artistic cadres did not examine too closely what was going on in the contemporary outside world. Indeed, what we were taking part in was the creation of the category of the 'aesthetic', its separation (supposed) from the 'economic', and its restriction to matters concerning formal symmetries of e.g. rhyme and metre and to contemplation of past-oral pastoral times.

However, whatever its limitations, these practices are part of my literary formation. Indeed, the resolutely populist tone, the persistent use of the familial, the informal and the vulgar can be seen as a reaction against this formation. 'No, I will not conform to the norms of the academy. Yes

I will adopt the tones of those communicators and entertainers outside of literary discourse.' The poems are each in their own ways, different kinds of contestations with that literary discourse. I should say, however, I tend to 'normalise' what I am doing, as I am doing it, and am surprised if it causes offence, particularly to people claiming to represent 'literature' or an unseen academy, examples being criticism by the editors and critics Sandy Brownjohn and Anne Harvey as expressed at teachers' meetings, and as reported to me).

That said, some of the narrative and indeed prosodic characteristics of this piece derive from that very academy. It may seem a distant link but when Falstaff in *Henry IV pt. I* tells the story of how he fought off the ruffians, (Shakespeare 1988: 464-465) and again how he fought in the battle, he adopts a particular kind of bombastic, boastful tone. This was a moment that I treasured in my reading and theatre-going for many years.

There is a presence here I can detect of family readings of Dylan Thomas's autobiographical writings e.g. 'A Visit to Grandpa's' (Thomas 1966: 39-45). Again, though 'free verse' was excluded from my university degree, it was allowed at 'O' and 'A-level' and it was here that I discovered that this was a possible way of writing. Again, I don't find it impossible to hear behind this piece the voice of D.H. Lawrence recounting and commenting on his experiences with the snake and the bat (Lawrence 1977: 349, 340).

2. 'Spieling'

However, it can also be said that I have re-worked these ways of writing, using other traditions, influenced by other ideas. The 'spieling' I have referred to is part of what is known as the aggadic tradition in Jewish and Judaic culture, its complement being the halachic or legalistic tradition). So in the Bible one can see that the halachic is represented by, say, the Ten Commandments or Leviticus and the aggadic in the parables of Jesus, which various commentators have noted are characteristic 'exempla' tales of Jewish pharisaic culture (Maccoby 1986: 44). In short, you can explain what kind of behaviour is acceptable either by saying what the law is, or by telling a story (or both!). Both my parents were 'spielers' regaling friends and relations with family anecdotes, long embellished tales of what my mother thought of my father the first time she saw him, what the 'Top Sergeant' said to my father when he wouldn't bayonet the dummy, how the piano got stuck in the corridor, what the doctor said when he saw my brother's jaundiced face and so on.

In summary then, with this piece, we are looking at a Falstaffian-free-verse-spiel that contests the canonical and traditional discourse of 'Poetry'.

Its specifics can be traced to various material practices – some macro-economic (in providing surplus wealth for study and leisure), others micro-economic in terms of individual circumstances for the holiday, others socioeconomic in terms of 'family life'.

3) The relationship between the 'ideology of the poem' and material existence.

In this section I am departing from the scheme outlined at the beginning of this chapter in order to take up some of the questions around ideology raised in Chapter 2.

The practice I will adopt here is to describe what I consider are my ideological *intentions* whilst fully understanding that these might not be ideological *effects*. I am not even going to posit here an ideal reader who should 'get' these ideological effects. Nor will I read the ideology off the poem as if I were the ideal reader. Rather, what I will try to do is situate the moments and interactions of the poem in wider ideological activity. Then I will ask the second question of how this relates to material life.

For me the key moments and interactions of the poem are contiguous with, if not synonymous with, what I think happened that day. It is that kind of poem in which I have tried through writing to get at a kind of *essence* – for my own satisfaction before undue contemplation of an audience. These moments and interactions are:

1) the holiday-family-picnic-in-France institution;
2) the anarchy of very small children; the stupid behaviour of the family patriarch (me) in such circumstances;
3) the cultural clash of Brits and the French.

I think both in intention and in the process of discovery that happens in writing itself, I was working with the following ideas:

1) to undermine the idealised view of the perfect family plus beautiful car enjoying their ideal holiday-commodity. Everyone knows that holidays are not like this but we are presented with this notion as part of the way holidays are sold and as part of the way a certain view of family life is projected at us as ideal and proper.
2) to portray the way in which the micro-rules of family life are subverted by

someone who for whatever reasons does not obey them. I cannot escape from a sense that to describe these moments is also to celebrate them. There is here a libertarian, Reichian sense in which the uncontrolled libido of the very young child is something to be admired and perhaps envied.

3) to subvert the trope that the site and source of all familial and societal wisdom is the mature father. A peculiar fact has become clear to me through life: for practical reasons, and/or as a symptom of ideology, and/or as a consequence of my conditioning, my role as father is to dominate, to know best, to lead, and yet, in actual fact I am as incompetent, irrational, and as incapable as anyone – including the smallest person in the family unit.

4) to play with the mutual misunderstandings of two language groups as part of a way of showing that no one individual, no one group or one nation is the sole bearer of wisdom and truth. There is also a slight anti-Brit-abroad bias in order to subvert the dominant idea of Brit-civilised, foreigner-uncivilised that dominates many post-holiday conversations.

Here then are four subversions, which begs the question (also ideological) why should I be so interested in subversion? In brief, the function of literature that I have allotted myself (and this is not intended to exhaust all the possible functions of ail literature but merely to signpost one function that I intend) is to undo the seams that bind us into life and ideas or what Marx called the 'ruling ideas' (Marx 1965: 61) or has been dubbed since the 'prevailing ideology'. Part of our problems as a civilisation, in my view, is that our circumstances appear natural and unchangeable, even though many of the conditions in which we live are clearly unsatisfactory. Because I am interested in (nay, fervently hope for) a situation in which people will want to create conditions in which all human life and labour can be emancipated from poverty and drudgery, I have a notion that one tiny way of bringing about that change might be to produce texts that break up the seamless, the natural and the unchangeable. In this particular instance, that is by subverting various forms of the ideal that are paraded before us. I am under no illusions that this poem is either a very powerful example of subversion nor that even if it were, it would in any way be a sufficient or even a necessary condition for change. It is merely a fringe irritant in the functioning of Ideology.

This whole pattern of ideological intention on my part is linked to materiality (non-Foucauldian sense) through my societal, parental and self-positioning. As I have explained elsewhere, the material links with notions of universal emancipation derive in part from the circumstances of impoverished and oppressed Ashkenazim Jewry trying to find ways of emancipating themselves from their conditions. While some looked for *national solutions* − (the homeland), and some looked for assimilationist, bourgeoisifiying solutions, others looked for internationalist solutions through socialist and Marxist parties. I am, via my parents, an inheritor of this lattermost impulse, that survived a low-level bourgeoisification, a fair amount of assimilation but which was then given a powerful recharge by the events of the late sixties. It is then sustained by a variety of practices: observation of world, national and local events; a freedom from wage slavery; an interaction with movements for local and societal change; a sustained programme of reading and discussion only made possible by my position as a relatively high-earning, leisure-ful freelance writer − a position which in turn is only possible as a consequence of the high development of the productive forces of late capitalism.

4) Further observations on material roots, in relation to the poem's situation within the economic system

In this section I want to explore yet another way in which material existence impinges on creative work, namely how material reality, expressing itself through the market and money, manifests itself within texts.

There is one other way in which the poem links with material conditions. The poem is involved in commodity exchange. As part of our economic and cultural conditioning we come to see art-objects both as sites of enjoyment (use-value) and as objects to buy (exchange-value) (Marx 1954: 44-47). Or, to put an alternative, (which artists themselves become acutely aware of): though we come to see that some art-objects may be sites of *enjoyment*, we know that if they do not become objects to buy, no one outside of a few personal friends and acquaintances will be able to enjoy them. In effect this means that there is a subtle interplay between artist, art-producer-distributor and audience in which no one is singly responsible for what gets made, distributed and consumed. In my case this means that having tried some kinds of writing that neither art-producer-distributors (publishers) nor audience liked then I tended to stop producing them. Where both publishers and audience appeared to like what I had written then I was in the pleasant position of knowing that my art-object (poem) would be both useful and exchangeable. In some circumstances, I have known something of mine to be useful (i.e. an audience liked it) but for a variety of reasons the art-producer-distributor (publisher) did not and so that piece of work did not reach the audience, it was not exchanged.

The Eddie poems in *Quick Let's Get Out of Here* (Rosen 1983: 24-25, 28-32, 4245, 66-67, 76-79), first composed in 1982, began as use-value objects, performed spontaneously in response to children's questions, as part of trying to cope with sleepless nights and a restless, energetic two year old. I then transcribed my performances and ad-libs and these were accepted as commodities for the book. Since then I have had literally thousands of indications that children and adults enjoyed the five or so 'Eddie poems' in *Quick Let's Get Out of Here* (Rosen 1983). I have been performing this piece un-written for something like ten years – it has been shaped and re-shaped hundreds of times in performance (i.e. used) and is now for the first time being offered for exchange. I think I can say that very little shaping of it derives from its final destination as a commodity but much more as a consequence of the conventions of oral story-telling, stand-up comedy and the circumstances of school-based performances. Now these too are paid for and so the way commodity production has affected the poem is through these uses – and exchange-value circumstances not those of a book – though the decision to include the story-poem in this collection was affected by the success of the previous Eddie poems in book form as well as in performance.

5) A further material condition

There is one final way in which this piece is affected by a material circumstance.

Two or three days after Eddie was born he nearly died. He was in hospital with his mother and I had to return home at night. I spent one terrible and helpless night alone at home which seemed so terrible and empty that I could hardly bear to live through it. Then he recovered and I flipped over into a kind of absurd gratitude. For the first four years of his life, I looked after Eddie half of the time, and he came with me on school visits and the like. For years I never really thought about the episode in the hospital but one day I was thinking why is it that I think of Eddie as slightly different from my other children, why is it that I am over-indulgent? And it occurred to me that I am still grateful that he is alive. This episode with the car resonates with feelings about the previous near-miss. That previous near-miss is a kind of shadow or pre-echo of the car-in-the-ditch episode, which if psychologists are right, puts a kind of multiplier on the later of the two experiences.

It can of course be asked why all this should matter so much to me and I will avoid the 'naturalising' answer that 'it's only natural to think this way after you've nearly lost a child'. In a rather deterministic mode it might have resonances with the dead brother I never knew. More likely, it appears 'natural' only in so far as:

1) I am of a culture that treats its children as near-permanent fixtures in home life, because children die rarely;
2) that we treasure children as (perhaps mistakenly) aspects of ourselves;
3) that we project on to them all kinds of aspirations and compensations of our own lives and we try to make them turn out in certain ways often for purely conventional and socially acceptable reasons. These are the conditions of the late twentieth century bourgeois family. In these circumstances, my feelings are 'natural' but in other societies, in other times I might be much more philosophic, or indeed might have a religious schema with which to explain and dissipate what happened.

(Note: what follows are transcriptions of drafts so I have retained the original punctuation (or lack of it), the abbreviations and line spacing no matter how odd it might appear now.)

I.

Torch

My dad gave me a torch for my birthday,
it was covered in black rubber
my dad said it was waterproof
so that night I got into the bath with
it and went underwater exploring
deep sea diving.
Then it stopped working.

I went to my dad and said
The torch isn't working
He said what've you done to it?
Nothing.
You must've done something
No
You have, I can see you have
I was er

underwater exploring
in the bath.
The Fool. The
bloody fool. For
months he's
been
nagging
us
to get him one of these
torches – and then he
breaks it. What a waste
of money. Gor.
Following Sat. he says we're
going to take it back to the shop.
We go in
and he says I bought this torch last week
and it's just packed up. Won't work.
Scarcely been used.

The man in the shop opened up [sic]
and says:
And you haven't done anything to it
apart from switch it on and off.
That's right says my dad
And I go
Well actually I
And my dad stood on my foot and
I shuttup.
Then man went out the back for a bit.
Came back.
Well sir, I can't get it to work
I'll send it back.
and you can have a new one.

Outside my dad says.
What *is* the matter with you
o you want a new torch or not?
Here take it. And don't go in for one of yr

deep sea diving capers.

2.

Torch

[not redrafted from the previous text, but written in the knowledge that I had
put draft I somewhere but had now 'lost it'.]

I got a torch for my birthday
it was a waterproof one
covered in black rubber – /that night/
I took it into the bath
and went deep sea diving
for treasure.
After about 2 minutes
it stopped working.
 I took it to my dad
he said: just cos it says it's waterproof
doesn't mean you can take it underwater
 you fool,
Oh
it's ruined – now [? illegible] broken,
finished – cha-a-gh

Next day
he says
we're going to the shop to take it back
and Don't you say a word about
this business in the bath
we went in
and my dad said to the man,
'I bought this torch last week
got home
switched it on
didn't work.

The man picked it up
turned it over

Are you saying it never worked, sir
I said
well when I took it
underwa-
My dad stood on my foot
I stopped.
It never worked, is that right sir?
Yes, says my dad
well we'll take a look at it out the back
[illegible] if we can't get it to work
we'll get you a new one, sir
Thanks says my dad
and we walked out.

As soon as we were down the street
my dad says
What did I say to you?
Didn't I say – say nothing.
but you – you have to open your big mouth.

3.

The Torch
as in *Wait till I'm older than you*

I nagged my mum and dad for a torch.
'Oh go on. I'd love a torch.
One of those ones with black rubber round them.
Go on. Pleeeeeeese.'
It was no good. I wasn't getting anywhere.

Then came my birthday.
On the table was a big box
in the box

a torch.
My dad took it out the box
'You see that torch,' he says
'It's waterproof.
That is a waterproof torch.'

Waterproof. Wow!

So that night I got into the bath
and went underwater swimming with it.
Breathe in,
under the water,
switch on
search for shipwrecks
and treasure.
Up breathe
under again
exploring the ocean floor.

Then the torch went out.
I shook it and banged it but it wouldn't go.
I couldn't get it to go again.
My birthday torch.
So I got out, dried myself off
put on my pyjamas and went in to the kitchen.

'The – er – torch won't work. It's broken.'
And my Dad says,
'What do you mean, 'It's broken'?
It couldn't have just broken.
How did it break?'
'I dunno, it just went off.

'I don't believe it. You ask him a simple question
and you never get a simple answer.
You must have been
doing something with it.'
'No. It just went off.'

'Just try telling the truth, will you?
How
did
it
break?'
'I was underwater swimming with it.'

'Are you mad?
When I said the torch is waterproof
I meant it keeps the rain off.
I didn't mean you could go deep sea diving with it.
Ruined. Completely ruined.
For weeks and weeks he nags us stupid that he wants
one of these waterproof torches
and then first thing he does is wreck it.
How long did it last?
Two minutes? Three minutes?
These things cost money, you know.
Money.'

I felt so rotten.
My birthday torch.

At the weekend, he says,
We're going into Harrow to take the torch back.

We walk into the shop,
my dad goes up to the man at the counter
and says:
'You see this torch.
I bought it from you a couple of weeks ago
it's broken.
So the man picks it up.
'It couldn't have just broken,' says the man,
'how did it break?'
'I dunno' says my dad,
'it just went off.'
'Surely you must have been doing something

with it.'
No, no, no,' says my dad,
'it just went off.'
'Come on,' says the man, 'these torches don't just break down.'
So I said
'Well, actually, I was in the –'
and I got a hard kick on the ankle from my dad.
'I was in the, you know, er kitchen and it went off.'

So the man said that he would take it out the back
to show Len.
He came back a few minutes later and said that Len
couldn't get it to work either
so he would send it back to the makers. '
You'll have to have a new one,' he says.
'I should think so too,' says my Dad.
'Thank YOU.'

Outside the shop
my dad says to me,
'What's the matter with you?
Are you crazy?
You were going to tell him all about your underwater swimming,
weren't you?
Blabbermouth!'

4.

The Torch

I nagged my mum and dad for a torch.
'Oh go on. I'd love a torch.
One of those ones with black rubber round them.
Go on. Pleeeeeeese.'
It was no good. I wasn't getting anywhere.

Then came my birthday.
On the table was a big box

in the box a torch.
My dad took it out the box
'You see that torch,' he says
'It's waterproof.
That is a waterproof torch.'

Waterproof. Wow!

So that night I got into the bath
and went underwater swimming with it.
Breathe in,
under the water,
switch on
search for shipwrecks
and treasure.
Up breathe
under again
exploring the ocean floor.

Then the torch went out.

I shook it and banged it but it wouldn't go.
I couldn't get it to go again.
My birthday torch.
So I got out, dried myself off
put on my pyjamas and went in to the kitchen.

'The – er – torch won't work. It's broken.'
And my Dad says,
'What do you mean, 'it's broken'?
It couldn't have just broken.
How did it break?'
'I dunno, it just went off.

'I don't believe it. You ask him a simple question
and you never get a simple answer.
You must have been
doing something with it.'

'No. It Just went off.'
'Just try telling the truth, will you?
How
did
it
break?'
'I was underwater swimming with it.'

'Are you mad?
When I said the torch is waterproof
I meant it keeps the rain off.
I didn't mean you could go deep sea diving with it.
Ruined. Completely ruined.
For weeks and weeks he nags us stupid that he wants
one of these waterproof torches
and then first thing he does is wreck it.
How long did it last?
Two minutes? Three minutes?
These things cost money, you know.
Money.'

I felt so rotten.
My birthday torch.

At the weekend, he says,
We're going into Harrow to take the torch back.

We walk into the shop,
my dad goes up to the man at the counter and says:
'You see this torch.
I bought it from you a couple of weeks ago
it's broken.'
So the man picks it up.
'It couldn't have just broken,' says the man,
'how did it break?'
And my dad says, 'I dunno it just went off.'
'Surely you must have been doing something with it.'
No, no, no,' says my dad,

'it just went off.'
'Come on,' says the man,
'these torches don't just break down.'
So I said
'Well, actually, I was in the –'
and I got a hard kick on the ankle from my dad.
'I was in the, you know, er kitchen and it went off.'

So the man said that he would take it out the back
to show Len.
He came back a few minutes later and said that Len
couldn't get it to work either
so he would send it back to the makers.
'You'll have to have a new one,' he says.
'I should think so too,' says my Dad.
'Thank YOU.'

Outside the shop
my dad says to me,
'What's the matter with you?
Are you crazy?
You were going to tell him all about your underwater swimming,
weren't you?
Blabbermouth!'

1) Roots in its own textual changes

In this section I want to consider how writing a piece is layered within its own drafting process. To all the other contexts I have described all through this chapter, I am now adding an insight into a kind of self-regarding, self-referential intertextuality. It also reveals more clearly than I have been able to show up till now, the ways in which the writing process is inevitably a reading-writing process, or a reading-writing-reading process or a reading-writing-reading-writing-reading process and so on ad infinitum.

This is a poem that I have tried writing for about fifteen years. Its beginnings were in the memory of my family knowing me as the one who 'missed the point', or revealed things that should have been kept quiet. I had written a poem about revealing to our lodger that we laughed behind his back (in *Wouldn't You*

Like to Know (Rosen 1981b: 92-93)). I had not (!) written a poem about how just as my parents were trying to smuggle some over-the-allowance numbers of cigarettes through the customs, I was sitting in the back of the car saying, 'Don't forget the cigarettes!' And I remembered that I had done something similar with the torch that I had wrecked in the bath.

The first two drafts are attempts to get to grips with this aspect of the incident: me as the one who blabs. However, it can be seen from the third and fourth versions that the story has changed. It includes this aspect but more as a secondary motif. The prime motif is now the two parallel confrontations: one between me and my father over how the torch broke and the second between my father and the man in the shop. The question is how and why did this change come about?

1. Ideological.
I was affected in the time between writing the second and third drafts by the initiative made by the government over 'parents should teach their children the difference between right and wrong.' As is often the case with me, I played with the idea, trying to find ways to deconstruct it, both in conversations and in public talks or appearances on e.g. *Any Questions* on BBC Radio 4 (1994, 1995). I had not got much further than thinking about how one person's 'right' is another person's 'wrong' when I found myself thinking of whether my parents did or did not teach me the difference between right and wrong. Even to think about them in those terms seemed ironic, as my perception of them throughout my childhood was of people who critiqued the world. News programmes, teachers' comments, newspaper articles, my or my brother's random comments about the world, fairness, values etc. were all subjected to ideological examination and confrontation from an oppositional standpoint. In other words their 'right' was very different from the 'right' I received in the public arena. That said, I could not find or focus on a good, meaty, concrete example of one of these confrontations to write about until the torch episode, (already existing in two drafts), surfaced. What then happened was that 'draft 2' which I worked from, blended with what was to become 'draft 3'.

2 Rhetorical (i.e. concerned with 'speech-effects')
The key moment now became when the shopkeeper asks my father how the torch broke and, as I have it in the final draft, he produces exactly the same phrase as the one I had given my father when the torch originally broke:

'I dunno, it just went off.'

It will be seen that in draft 3 this reads:

' "I dunno," says my dad, "it just went off" '

whereas in draft 4 it reads:

'I dunno, it just went off.'

This is an example of how with my writing, the oral is structured into the writing so that it can reappear in performance as 'oral'. I will explain.

I have discovered through readings and performances that repetitions have a variety of powerful effects. Repetitions of a phrase can provide a rhythm which then sets up expectations. This enables the writer (me) to break that expectation to make a point as with 'See me in my trainers' in *Don't Put Mustard in the Custard* (Rosen 1985: no page number) where the exultant line 'See me in my trainers' is demolished when the trainers wear out and it becomes 'See my trainers.' Parallel to this playing with expectations, I have discovered through performance and reading how some of the episodes and anecdotes that I have written have (what audiences show through laughter) a 'crux line'. So in the poem in *You Tell Me* (McGough and Rosen 1979: 67-68) where I swallow the leg off my clock, it builds to the moment when I confront my dad with the problem and he says, 'You've ruined a perfectly good clock.' Before I performed that poem in public I had no idea that it would be one such 'crux line'. It was only in performance that I discovered audiences making it so.

In other words here are two rhetorical processes that I have in my repertoire that may or may not surface when I am writing: repetition and the crux line. What has happened in the drafting and re-drafting of 'The Torch' is that the two processes have come together: the repetition enables the crux line to happen. I have no memory of this being a very conscious moment: that I thought 'how about a bit of repetition here?' It seemed to have grown rather as one gropes for a familiar garment, or plonks oneself down in the familiar armchair rather than the unfamiliar one. In terms of causation then, it is hard to disentangle exactly what went on here, other than to adopt Iser's term 'repertoire' again (Iser 1974, 1978). However, because I performed the poem several times in draft 3 form, I discovered that the crux line worked better if I used the draft 4 form. 'Worked better' means here, brought about a bigger laugh, a bigger shout of recognition. To be more accurate: children produce more like a rapid intake of breath, a 'oh no, your dad lied too', whereas adults have tended, I guess, to be amused by the irony. So what happens is not simply that I make an act of selection from the repertoire of rhetorical devices and proceed to insert a perfect bit of rhetoric into place but that some kind of feedback process works on the repertoire, enriches it and helps it. This may take place in the actual act of writing – as in the producing of draft 3 – but it may also occur after writing one draft and so enables a redraft as for draft 4.

3. Performative
There are more performative aspects of the piece than are expressed by the notion of 'rhetoric'. Thus, though the crux line has been structured linguistically so as to enable a performance to work, the poem exists now as a kind of play-script for me (or anyone else) to work on in more physical and visceral ways. I play the poem out in roles,

1) me speaking,
2) me thinking,
3) the narration,
4) my dad,
5) the man in the shop.

These are the five perspectives of the poem and I differentiate them in performance. What this means is that every performance is slightly different, I insert extra phrases, I change the word order, I take out parts, I add in facial expressions, finger-jabbings, sad gestures of holding the torch out for examination, and so on. In other words, the poem, though it exists here on the page and eventually in a book as a static piece of print, does not operate like that for me as and when I deliver it to audiences in face to face situations.

This has repercussions on how I view what exactly it is that I write. To be more precise: when I look at something like 'The Torch' I see it as a kind of play-script, something that has to be worked on and worked up so that it can take on a full life when animated by performance. Writers talk about 'getting it right'. For me, this is what 'getting it right' means: getting it right for performance and in performance. As a follow-on from there, and in awareness of the kinds of situations that my poems find themselves in when I'm not there, I see the poems waiting to be performed by teachers, parents and children.

Now as Voloshinov, Bakhtin and others have pointed out, the social is embedded in every piece of language-use. What has happened here though, is that the part of the social which is face-to-face performance and reading is embedded in the writing too. Of course, there is a sense in which all language is performative, and some language (e.g. jokes) more so than others (e.g. tax forms) but I can see how as a result of establishing repertoires through performance, and as a result of exposing those repertoires to feedback, the performative aspect is even more pronounced (!) than usual.

In prosodic terms this is one of the ways in which this kind of writing is distinguishable from what is customarily known as prose. It is not that 'The Torch' is just a piece of prose chopped up into lines, nor is it just me simply telling the story on to the page (something that I often ask children to do, incidentally) but is fairly consciously shaped so that there is a kind of rhetorical orality about it, rather as an experienced speaker (vicar or politician) might structure a sermon or political speech.

4. Anti-moralistic

There is one other way in which the text is structured that seems to operate on me as a kind of constraint: that is of not wanting to explain significance. I find myself consciously avoiding commentating, explanatory and moralising voices, the kind that can be found in, say Enid Blyton:

> 'Here was Mrs Stick talking like that about old Spotty Face – and yet she had a little girl down in the dungeons – a child much younger than Edgar! What a beast she was.' (from *Five Run Away Together* cited in Fine 1997: 9-10)

It seems to me as I write, that situations like that in 'The Torch' are full of ambiguities and possibilities. When either the child, or my fairly naive narrative voice is the 'focalizer' (see Prince 1988: 31-32) then clever interpretation is inappropriate and too controlling an intervention. There is some way in which I want to keep the integrity and unity of the situation intact without breaking it with the intrusion of another voice that would explain the significance.

So, in this way, I internalise an active reader and/or an active audience of several readers who can rifle through the situations and phrases I have written about in order to speculate on such evaluative matters as 'who was in the right there?' or 'he shouldn't have done that!' and the like. By shifting the focalising to and fro between parent and child I hope that the reader has to shift too, and cannot rest too comfortably with one protagonist or one viewpoint only.

Then again, behind that wish to make reading as active as possible, is a hope (partly based on concrete experience in classrooms and from receiving letters from teachers) that active reading, is highly conducive to active talking which in turn, can ('can' but not necessarily 'will') be highly conducive to performing and writing.

This way, I see 'The Torch' coming at a certain point in a conversation. As a text it is in conversation with:

1) its intertextual forbears (e.g. confrontations between parents and children in William books (see Just William (Crompton 1922), *The Adventures of Tom Sawyer* (Twain' 1876), Dickens and many, many more);
2) the discourse around 'right and wrong' as mentioned earlier;
3) my own performance repertoires.

But it also begins conversations with children, teachers and parents (this is the usual constituency) who are busy thrashing out questions of what are 'right' ways to behave. This is of course a highly ideological matter and can be taken (I do) as being an ironic intervention into something that has been presented as neat, clear and fixed. There are, I insist (!) strong reasons, based originally in my materio-ideological origins and on-going life (covered elsewhere in this chapter) that create the possibility/likelihood that it is I who should be doing this.

Adverbs

Today we have adverbs.
As you can hear an 'adverb'
is something to do with a verb.
You remember the 'verb' from last week?
The adverb tell us how the word we call a 'verb'
does its business.
Except you remember the verb doesn't only 'do'
it also 'is' and 'feels'.
So the adverb tells the verb *how*.
But also remember a verb isn't strictly speaking
a word.
It can be two, three or even four words.

And also – strictly speaking –
we can't always be certain
which of these words the adverb is telling 'how' to.
OK?
Now the adverb is also a word
that describes adjectives.
You remember adjectives describe nouns.
So really these kind of adverbs should be called
ad-adjectives.
But they're not.
Sorry about that
but there's nothing I can do about that.
Same word – adverb –
doing its stuff to verbs
doing its stuff to adjectives.
But watch out here:
don't go calling any old word
hanging in there next to an adjective
an adverb.
It could be another adjective.
Watch out for that one.
Are you still with me?
Great,
because this gets even more interesting.
Sometimes there are words that
do things to adverbs.
You know what we call them?
Adverbs.
They could
it's true
be called ad-adverbs
 but they're not
my hands are tied.
And we might as well
do the job properly here:
there's even another kind of adverb
that is really all on its own but
 in a kind of way

does things to the whole of the rest of the sentence.
Don't ask me just for the moment to remind you
what a sentence is
but just remember there is this word
(not actually called an ad-sentence)
that is doing some business for the whole sentence.
And it's an adverb.

So there you are.
Get reading
and look out for adverbs
changing all sorts of things
all over the place.
It's a useful word isn't it?
Adverb.
Once you get the hang of them
they're good fun:

'Well, honestly,
they're really dead easy.'

well, adverb
honestly, adverb
really, adverb
dead, adverb

1) Roots in material and ideological circumstances at the time of writing

In this section I want to consider at greater length ways in which a poem operates at the level of ideology. However, ideology is not taken here as having its own autonomy but rather it is performing its role within the economic system.

The immediate circumstances of the poem was my reading one of the 'final' drafts of the National Curriculum (Schools Curriculum and Assessment Authority, May 1994: 1) which said that 'grammar' should be taught and that vafious specific terms such as 'adjectives', 'verbs', 'nouns' and 'adverbs' should be taught too. What was going on here? A section of the ruling class over a period of some ten years made it clear that it wanted to bring in much more defined curricula within state education and these curricula would be defined along certain lines that they favoured. This meant that at the highest levels of government, prime ministers and secretaries of state would frequently make pronouncements on what they thought would be desirable kinds of knowledge that all children should acquire, how they should acquire it, and how it should be assessed. This whole system of knowledge-acquisition would be put into place by fiat and statute. To put it crudely, if a government minister thought that it was desirable that all primary school children should read *Winnie-the-Pooh* then it emerged at one point in the history of the implementation of the National Curriculum that this might have become law; likewise 'adverbs'.

These are the ideological circumstances that teachers, parents, children and, on some occasions writers like myself, have lived through in the last ten years. For most of this time, there have been groups of people (NATE and the like) who have engaged in an educational argument over the content of the National Curriculum. They (and I) have tried to point out contradictions, inaccuracies, impossibilities – in other words we have been engaging with the ideas themselves as ideas and relating them to educational theories and practices. But ideas don't produce ideas, human beings in specific historical circumstances produce ideas. So what were the historical circumstances that produced the content and implementation of the National Curriculum? Whatever they were, this poem would share them.

From my visits to Australia, Canada and the USA (1987-1995) in this period, it became clear to me that this was not simply a British phenomenon. Politicians all over the English-speaking world were spending time in elections and in their respective parliaments at national and provincial level making very similar claims:

1. Educational standards had fallen.
2. Teachers weren't doing a good job.
3. It was time to return to a more virtuous, efficient and successful educational system of the past – located somewhere round the 1950s.
4. A key area for improvement was in the use of the English language.
5. What was needed here was a return to the methods of the past that correctly stressed accuracy and correctness i.e. conforming to the spoken and written forms of standard English.
6. The frequently stated reason for this programme in all the countries I observed was that it was necessary *because of the highly competitive world market*.

Here's an example taken from *The Evening Standard* 9.9.1992:

> ' . . . children are not being taught 'standard' English, grammar or literature under the present programme . . . '

> 'English is the most important of all the national curriculum subjects. The knowledge and skills are critical for success in the education system and in later life,' said Mr Pascal'. [chairman of the National Curriculum Council]

> . . . traditionalists have repeatedly called for a return to the old methods of drilling pupils in the rudiments of spelling, punctuation and grammar . . .

> Mr Patten [the Secretary of State for Education] said: 'English is at the heart of the National Curriculum. All other learning depends upon the mastery of the fundamental skills of language, which are vital not only for educational and cultural development but also for **our economic competitiveness**.' [my bold] (Nick Pryer 'Schools to Put English First, Patten orders big teaching shake-up' in *The Evening Standard* 9.9.1992:1-2)

It was stated in all countries that there was a great danger that 'we' would 'fall behind' or 'fall further behind' the 'others'.

Now it is a customary accusation to make of Marxists that they (we) 'reduce causation to the economic' but here, again and again, politicians (usually of the Right but not always) were doing precisely this, by saying that children should learn how to spell correctly because of the needs of international capitalism (the world market). The question that arises here, is what precise characteristics of world capitalism make the requirement to spell, so urgent? The politicians' argument seemed to equate items such as spelling and grammar with 'a skilled labour force' better able to compete with the other guy. This is where the Right appear to be indulging in 'vulgar Marxism' and I would want to draw out something more complex.

Can it be true that the politicians truly believed themselves that the teaching of spelling and grammar would/does produce a workforce better suited to capitalists' needs to compete in the world market? It seems unlikely. The only capitalists I have ever heard talking about what they wanted from employees said that they wanted workers to be 'flexible' i.e. to be prepared to be fired, re-train and change job or, to put a kinder light on it, to be prepared to do a variety of jobs in the same place of work as this was cheaper in that tough world out there. The invention of spell – and grammar-checks on computers was putting 'high standards' in this area quite low down on the agenda. Some capitalists I heard pleading in public for better training of scientists and engineers as this was, they said, the key area for generating wealth but I rarely, if ever, heard politicians saying that.

So it would appear from this line of argument that politicians have had their own agenda in this period that I might articulate as follows: the global market is tough for the English speaking world, the rate of profit for these countries is down, unemployment is up, social stability is under threat. One possible weapon in the competition might be (they do not actually know) to increase the educational level of the populace. However, this would cost an enormous amount of public money and this particular group of politicians have a monetarist ideology that believes the state should spend less money, not more. Therefore, rather than focus on the cutting edge of new technology as a way of 'raising standards' it is much easier to focus on those aspects of knowledge that cost the same or less. The most electorally suitable aspects of knowledge to focus on are those items and methods that are to do with surface order and child-control. These might (do?) have an ideological resonance amongst a population frantic with worry about disorder, crime and job insecurity, which, as it happens, are a consequence of the very economic order that is calling the shots here.

These are the material conditions of the National Curriculum's requirements on spelling, grammar and my poem. However, at first glance, the poem fails perhaps (or I appear unable) to address these wider material and ideological questions, its focus remaining firmly within the field of grammar terminology. Is it, like NATE, restricted to the field of arguing about what is the best thing to teach and what is the best way to teach it? Largely yes. However, poetry is a much more open-ended, 'sideways' kind of writing than straight polemic. The poem, is after all a dramatic monologue of sorts. This raises the question: who is speaking?

2) Roots in intertext

In this section I am considering more clearly than I have hitherto how a poem embodies a pre-existing form, or to put it another way, is at the formal level, in conversation with other pre-existing forms of the same or similar kind.

In the poem it is of course the teacher, someone who in this circumstance is 'teaching' a concept (i.e. 'adverb') and a name for that concept which quite clearly has no validity. The monologue is not genuinely 'realistic' because it would be self-evident to any teacher saying this that he/she was saying complete nonsense. So, though it is in one sense a polemic against old style grammar's terminology, by being dramatic it takes in the political situation of a teacher placed in the position of teaching this kind of grammar. Some already are. So though the poem does not raise any of the material arguments outlined above, it does engage with the political reality of teachers, in those conditions being forced to teach the unteachable, the absurd and the plain wrong.

A published or performed poem creates a space for itself. That is (more accurately), in the process of being read or heard and in the time and place that follows it, readers and listeners 'do things' with the poem. It is brought into conversations already going on, made to contribute something to them, alters, becomes involved in shifting those conversations. In the event of teachers or school students reading this poem then I would hope that it might raise specific questions about the failings of old style grammar. But because it is a dramatic monologue I would hope that it would also raise questions like: why are we doing this stuff? who told us we had to do it if it's no good anyway? The poem *answers* none of these questions – after all it does not even make suggestions of what other grammars might be more appropriate.

There are other ways in which the material is inflected in the poem e.g. why the dramatic monologue form has been used and why it is I who has written it. The second question I have dealt with elsewhere (i.e. my cultural inheritance and formation. The dramatic monologue question is an interesting historical question – historical both in the history of the dramatic monologue and my history of meeting it and choosing it as a way of writing.

The dramatic monologue is in essence a soliloquy, a lift from a Shakespearean mode of address. Such a form was only possible when the actual material behaviour of individuals had reached a point at which such a self-reflexive, self-perceiving, self-achieving notion could be given dramatic shape. Rather than being held within the constraints of feudal allegiances and religious positioning in the Christian cosmogeny, individuals were trading, buying and selling labour and seeking justifications for their activity in new religious forms, or in their own self-conceived motivations. After all Shakespeare's characters do not often hang about waiting for priests and divinities to guide their actions.

The transition of the dramatic monologue from drama to poetry had to wait until the nineteenth century with, most typically, Robert Browning who published his first dramatic monologues in 1842 (Drabble 1985: 291), but also the working-class poet Samuel Laycock (Harland 1882; Hollingworth 1977) and his cotton famine poems of the 1860s, poetry before then, as a largely non-popular form, was mostly written as a kind of private address and so

1) was dominated by the rules of the academy i.e. had in-built conservatism, and 2) could not include within its prosody a popular (vulgar?) oral form of address that pretends that neither the writer nor the reader was present i.e. the narrator is not the poet and the narratee is 'in the room' with the narrator (see Caudwell 1973: 92-93).

Once poetry was freed to incorporate it, (perhaps stimulated by the habit of slicing Shakespeare up into performable chunks and soliloquies done by star actors such as Kean and Garrick) the dramatic monologue took off both on the page and in the music hall and salon. Part of the complexity of a well-developed capitalist society is that it fragments life for individuals into hundreds and thousands of differing human encounters. Indeed, the higher up the social scale in the urban environment in particular, the more encounters there are: e.g., trade, servants, transport, vacations, entertainments and so on. The dramatic monologue of the nineteenth century onwards is a way of capturing one of these fragments and rendering it typical, archetypical, significant or symbolic. The aim of the writer or performer is often for it to resonate with the publicly recognisable. It found its most welcome home in the new entertainment halls of the industrial working-class – the music hall but the 'popular reciters', books of popular but more middle-class entertainment are crammed with them too (see e.g. Carpenter 1867; Morrison 1901; Anon 1904). These recitations (i.e. dramatic monologues) were then performed in the sitting rooms of the middle class, often as condescending, or plain racist accounts of the lower orders' habits and thoughts.

So this poem of mine inherits a popular as well as a literary form (thus there is no need for explanations and tagging to pinpoint that it 'is' a teacher talking, that it 'is' a class of children who are supposedly listening).

My own encounters with the form came through home (outings to Shakespeare), school (Browning's 'My Last Duchess' 1908: 30-31), politically motivated tracking-down of a working-class poet (Samuel Laycock) and a historically motivated tracking-down of the popular (the 'Popular Reciters').

Such a form then enters my reading-writing 'repertoire' (Iser 1974, 1978) available to me as a kind of langue' from which I make a 'parole' of the poem. I think I have already answered the question of why I choose this form to say what I want to say about adverbs by drawing attention to the way in which it politicises the criticism I am making of the inadequacies of old style grammar. However, I am frustrated that the form prevents me from politicizing the issue further i.e. prevents me from drawing attention to some of the underlying causes of the situation in the first place. It would be breaking the pseudo-realist rules of the teacher's speech. In this way, it can be seen that a form not only bears historical traces but also defines and confines a field of possible utterance.

On the question of whether it is possible to sleep on a train

Can I sleep on the train?
Can I sleep on the train?
Can I sleep?

On the train
On the train
On the train
On the train
Can I sleep?

On the train
On the train
On the train
On the train I sleep.

I Roots in other texts (in particular paying attention to the materiality of language itself and poetry)

With this poem I want to draw attention to the physicality and materiality of writing itself. However to say this, is not to uncouple it from more macro-conditions of literary production. This is merely a question of focus on my part while looking at this poem.

As Voloshinov noted, the very acts of speaking, writing, printing and the like are material acts (Voloshinov 1986: 11). They involve using energy exchanges of the human body and machines and they use up minerals and compounds. With regard to language, this means that when something is spoken, written down, or reproduced in any form, certain aspects of the language itself are involved with quantifiable material acts – amounts of energy to speak, amounts of ink and paper, amounts of electricity to run computers and so on. (It is always worth bearing this in mind when thinking of how and where writers write, publishers publish and poets perform. The specific acts (a publication, a reading to 2000 people) are only possible if certain productive capacities are in place e.g., printing presses, electricity production and so on.) However, though the quantifiable aspect is unavoidable in all conditions of literary production, I want to draw attention to a qualitative aspect within this materiality of language. Thus if, for example, I say 'mmmmmmmmmmm' this requires me to do something with my body that is distinct from if I say 'laaaaaaaaaaah'. Similarly, my listeners' ears and brains will have to perform different processes in order to perceive those sounds. In between, different kinds of molecular disturbances of air, different kinds of sound waves (i.e. energy) will be involved too. In other words we are talking here about the physicality of language. This is sometimes called the 'phonology' but I am using the word 'physicality' because it connects more clearly with the material aspect.

Strictly speaking, I should be talking here of physicalities (plural), because a whole range of physical acts are involved – pitch, volume, rhythm, percussion, non-percussion Ie continuous tone, silence, cadence, slurs, unvoiced sounds, distortions of the expected. Sometimes this becomes most clear to us when we hear someone speaking in a language we don't understand, or alternatively, when we are learning a new language. Otherwise we tend to restrict our comments, in everyday conversation, to observations like 'she's got a deep voice' or 'he speaks fast' i.e. perceived exceptional circumstances. As has been noted ever since anyone has written about poetry, and probably before that even, it has meddled in this area, using the physical aspect of language beyond what everyday speech appears to do (see Weismiller 1993: 1180-1183). (Whether poetry really manifests this quality more than the oral rhetoric of joke-telling, chanting, talking to pets and the like is not proven, but the discourse around poetry certainly tells us that the physicality of poetry is important in relation to readers' pleasure). Poetry has tended over the centuries and in most cultures to create non-semantic patterns that run counter to, or in time with the unfolding of meaning. We can picture here the process of reading as involving a double-action of 'revelation' and 'harvest'. The new unit of meaning is *revealed* (or we reveal it) as we read, but at the same time we *harvest* it and carry it with us into the next revelation. There is also a process of 'dropping' and 'losing'. Meanwhile, on another track the purely physical aspects of poetry quite often have a pattern, (a text of sorts) of their own: rhythms, assonance, alliteration, rhymes and, as has been shown endlessly, the 'great' poets have been able to achieve dazzling synchronicities of the physical with the semantic such that it appears on analysis to create a 'perfect unity'. Anyone who has studied poetry formally in school or college has had their attention drawn to poetic moments like the soothing line of murmuring in Gray's 'Elegy' line 10

'The moping owl does to the moon complain'

(see Gray T. in Leeson 1980: 243-247).

My concern here though is more general, noting that poets often create patterns of sound that roll on at one level identifiable as independent of the semantic unfolding. In reality and holistically speaking, they cannot be independent in the last instance because you cannot have meaning in a word unless it has form.

This poem plays in this area. It seems logical (quite apart from the Lacanian possibilities identified by Kristeva (1984:153-154)) that young children encountering the language will foreground the physical aspects of language. This is because for quite a lot of the time, they are surrounded with language whose effect on them will be semantically weak. That is to say, they hear plenty of words, phrases and general talk that they do not understand. Yet such children could, if asked, locute most of these not-understood words and phrases. A four year old could have quite a good bash at saying 'hermeneutics' but probably not have much idea of what it means. More relevantly, parents and carers will say things to children that convey feeling through the sound of words without a child having heard it often enough in context to have a full grasp of what the word(s) mean. So a parent might shout angrily at the child with words that a child does not *understand* but the child *knows* that the parent is angry.

All this makes linguistic sound-play with children a very rich vein to mine. Their conversation is full of jokes around puns (knock-knock jokes, 'what do you get if you cross . . . ?' jokes, nonsense rhymes, verbal games in conversation where meaning collapses under relentless rhyming, and half-rhyming and so on (see Opie I and Opie P. 1959).

Certain physical processes have been used by poets where they have explored both meaning and the rhythms and sounds of the process simultaneously, one of the most celebrated being Auden's 'Night Mail' (Auden: 1976: 113-114) and one of the most gloriously over-abundant, Southey's 'The Cataract of Lodore' (Southey in Philip 1990: 168). My poem, then, is in that tradition, and given the high density of train poems it was an attempt in part not only to do what they do but also, very mildly to make fun of them. So, rather than describe all the wonderful things that a train does (see Auden's 'Night Mail' and Stevenson's 'Faster than fairies, faster than witches . . . ' from 'From a Railway Carriage' (Stevenson 1912: 24-25)), I have described what the train does to me, ie to send me to sleep. It is also a lighthearted way of looking at my frequent, existential situation as a peripatetic poet, trying to sleep on the train, wondering if I will , and then actually doing so. There is an intention there too, of coming up with an explanation in the *sound* of the poem, as to how this apparent magic of falling asleep is brought about. In this way, that seemingly independent quality of sound, actually carries meaning without it being directly articulated in the semantics of the words. To spell it out: in the poem I am saying largely (but not entirely) with the *sound* of the words: 'The rhythm of the train is hypnotic'. (Of course, this meaning is not really independent of conventional comprehension because it is not possible to know that it is sleep and trains we are talking about here unless we understand the *meaning* of those words.)

The Line

When the new school was opened we had to line up, Girl here, Boy
    there, Girl here, Boy there. Miss Wheelock, who was the
    Headmaster's Deputy Sheriff said: 'In this school, there will be
    a Boys' Playground and a Girls' Playground. I want you all
    to draw an imaginary line between the top of the steps here, over
    to the edge of the United Dairies on the other side of the
    fence up there. I don't ever want to see any boy crossing
    the Line in morning playtime, dinner-time, or afternoon playtime
    and I don't want to see anyone loitering along the line.'

In the first week I was at the new school, I got to know a girl called
    Frances who tried to teach me how to skip. This was difficult

because she had to stand on one side of the Imaginary Line
and I had to stand on the other. First of all she skipped for a bit and
then carefully making sure her feet kept to her side she passed
the skipping rope over the Line to me – where I was making sure
my feet were keeping to my side. Then I skipped.

Miss Wheelock saw this and said, 'I'm going to put a stop to this. If you
want to learn how to skip, boy, then bring your own skipping
rope. I've said: I don't want anyone crossing the line. Passing a
skipping rope over the line is just the same as crossing the line,
isn't it? Frances I'm surprised at you. I thought you knew better.'
I thought: that's funny. We've only been at the new school a
week. Why's she surprised at Frances but she wasn't surprised
at me? Not long after this, something much more serious
happened to us and the Line.

Gunter the German brought a ball to school that said 'Handball' on it.
Someone kicked it and we all went haring across the Line to
get it. The whistle went off and Miss Wheelock screamed. She
wanted everyone to stop moving. 'Everyone stop moving. Stop
moving. Stop moving. I want that ball Gunter,' she said, 'I want
that ball.'

Gunter didn't know what was going on except he wasn't going to give
the ball to anyone – least of all to her. 'I want that ball, Gunter,'
she said, 'and by God, I'll have it, boy.' So she started off
walking across the playground towards him.

There was the playground, absolutely still, with all of us standing
there, like skittles all over it, except for Miss Wheelock marching
for Gunter the German's Handball. All boys one side of the
Imaginary Line. All girls on the other. Except for a group of us,
miles over the Line. It took ages for her to get to us.

'Give me that ball, Gunter,' she said, 'I want it.' Gunter didn't say
anything. He Just held on to it a bit harder, hugging it to his
chest. He couldn't speak English. He'd only been in England a
week or two and he was still wearing his yellow shoes.

Miss Wheelock prodded the Handball. 'Ball – Gunter – Ball.' Gunter
hugged the Handball. Everyone else for miles and miles, right
the way across the playground was standing still, right up as far
as the climbing frame in the Nursery playground. No one talked.

So Miss Wheelock got her hands round the German's Handball and
heaved on it. But he wouldn't let go. It was his Handball. Miss
Wheelock and him were still heaving on it and she was still
screaming, 'Ball – Gunter – ball,' when I booed.

And the moment I booed, Harrybo booed and all of us who had run all
this way over the Line booed. But Miss Wheelock, who was
bigger than Gunter, even though she was a tiny grown-up,
actually got hold of the Handball and wrenched it out of Gunter's
hands.

Gunter started gulping in big sobs but he didn't say anything. She
turned on us and said, 'Never, never, never, in all my time–'
when suddenly up the steps at the end of the Imaginary Line,
came the Headmaster.

We stopped booing. The whole thing had got too big for booing. But
he had seen what was going on. 'You,' he says, 'You – you – you – and
you.' And, no trouble, he knew which ones of us to get,
because we were standing there, the only boys out of the whole
school, in girl-country.

'You – you – you,' he said, 'go straight to my study and no running.'
Then he turned to Miss Wheelock, his Deputy Sheriff and said, '
Are you alright, Miss Wheelock?' And Miss Wheelock took out
her hankie and dried the corners of her mouth.

It was miles and miles to his room and all the way I was thinking: I
started the booing, so I'll be the one to get it. On the way
there, there were hundreds of girls' faces right down to the
tinies, all watching. Though some of them were so good they
didn't even dare look at us. They just stared at the ground, afraid
that if they looked into our eyes, they'd catch some of our evil
spirit.

Gunter was still gulping. He didn't know what was going on. He hadn't done anything wrong. Miss Wheelock had. She had stolen his Handball. 'Come in. Come in,' said the Headmaster, breathing through his nose and quivering his nostrils. I'll make them hear me breathing. I'll make them hear every bit of breath I've got. Up and down my nose. They'll learn what it means to break my rules and boo my teachers.

'Why do we have the Line? Eh? What's it for? For fun? For my amusement? You! Why do we have the Line?' No one knew why we had the Line. 'Come on. Come on. Come on. Don't waste anymore of my time.' 'Because they're girls sir.' It wasn't what he wanted.

'You! Why do we have the Line?' 'I don't know, sir.' 'You!' 'I don't know, sir.' 'You!' 'I don't know, sir.' 'Then I'll tell you why.' He was walking about all over the place.

'Because I knew, long before we moved into these buildings that your parents have paid for, that there would be trouble from children like you. And I sat down here in this room and I thought: How am I going to stop that little group of boys – and it will be boys – and there are always some in every school – how am I going to stop them from spoiling everything for everyone else?

Well, I said to myself, maybe it does seem as if it always happens like that but it's not going to happen in my school.' And it was Miss Wheelock who put me on to it: 'The trouble' she said, 'always starts in the playground. That's where the trouble starts.' And I think she's right.

I come out on to the playground. And there you are. That little group Screaming about amongst the girls, spoiling their games, then daring to catcall Miss Wheelock: the school's Deputy Head Teacher. You must think we're mad to even– 'At my last school, sir, we–' 'But you're at this school, boy.'

So he gave us the cane three times for going into girl country and three times for booing. He did the cane with a bamboo stick, bringing it down on our hands as fast and as hard as he could. 'I'm putting this down in a book,' he said, 'where it will never be forgotten.'

1) Roots in other texts (my own)

In this section I want to consider a piece of personal intertextuality and show how a poem can evolve through several forms within a writer's oeuvre.

This piece has a long history in my own writing. When I was about twenty, as I mention several times in this thesis, I embarked on a project inspired by the opening pages of *Portrait of the Artist as a Young Man* (Joyce 1914-15, 1916). I wanted to write a whole novel in the voice of a child. I wrote it but it came out at about 20,000 words and various people told me that it was too short to be a novel and too long to be a short story. It tells a much distorted story of my last year at primary school, a year which was, I now see, remarkable for several reasons: at the macro socioeconomic level, it was a year of great educational pressure around the 11 plus exam. At the local suburban socioeconomic level, it was a new school and the head teacher and his deputy head were (my parents have told me since) desperate to put the school on the map as a good 11 plus school. At the Reichian personal level I was duly panicked into thinking that I would fail the exam and I would lie awake at nights worrying about it. Meanwhile, I had got in with a bunch of boys who were (again on reflection) a band of middle-class hoodlums. Some of them, the inner core of which I was not a part, claimed to be up to various sexual practices – being played around with (i.e. sexually abused) by 'Old Man Harris'; going to the woods and masturbating with 'Colin', a teenager, attacking girls, and thieving from local stores.

As I wrote the piece, it occurred to me that we had lived two cultures, a highly formal, middle-class school-culture and an underground, anarchic, illegal one. One of the passages out of the original text that I first started writing in 1966 concerned 'The Line' and my being caned. At the time of writing, what I was most interested in was the fact that I was caned and that several of the middle class boys (who were even further out from the inner core of hard nuts than I was), cracked under the strain and broke out sobbing. In the context of this long text, it was important, partly for the plot, that I developed the idea of different layers of hoodlum, and the caning was a key moment in which to demonstrate this.

The text as a whole (it once had a working title 'Rapes' (!)) sits in my mind embedded in a web of emotions. It is like any other book or poem to which I can refer from memory as a resource or reference and yet no more than five or six people have ever read it. In other words, it exists for me as a piece of 'literature' yet it does not have that status. It is also shot through with memories and feelings:

1) there are the memories that are described or deliberately distorted,
2) there are the memories of writing it – the sense of excitement that could do it and that it unfolded a bizarre and troubling story,
3) the memory of the few people who read it saying that they thought it was good,
4) the disappointment and frustration that two publishers said it was unpublishable,
5) the pretence at stoicism that I muster whenever I think about that disappointment, even as I write this now,
6) a kind of defensive reflex where I say to myself: 'Oh well, it doesn't matter much, I've used parts of it as poems and stories elsewhere . . . ',
7) But another part of my mind is not fooled. It says, 'Yes, but secretly you are cheesed off, you think it explores aspects of young male suburban life that no one has ever really dared to write about, don't you?'
8) 'Yes, but if I dwelled on the failure of it then I would never be able to write anything else . . . ' (And so on).

Thinking about it yet again as I write this, its failure contributes to a channelling of my writing into the kind of poetry that has had some success. To unpick that now: it is that I discovered between about 1966 and 1973 that publishers of adult poetry, short stories and novels were not interested in the way in which I was writing about my childhood in the voice of a child. On the other hand, a BBC producer and an editor at Andre Deutsch were. It seemed to them to have potential as 'children's literature'. In other words, the very fact that we have in our literary culture an age-ranked system of delineation 'books for the very young', 'teenage' 'adult' and the like, helped condition what I would write (could write?). This, of course, corresponds quite closely to Foucault's idea in which the production of 'discourse' is controlled, selected and organised (Foucault 1972). So I 'couldn't write' 'Rapes' for the adult genres and I 'couldn't write' it tor the children's either. However, I 'could write' things *like* it, or *extracts* from it for the children's genres, which then led me to suppress the intention and effort to try and write about these difficult matters for adults whilst at the same time 'not permitting' them for a child's audience because it was too shocking. It is clear to me that the problems of this area are what Reich was describing.

This piece then is a 'permissible' extract. However, in extracting and reworking it as part of the work for this thesis, something else came up. Firstly, there is the pleasure in excavating it from the larger text and trying to make it work. I have read it to a variety of audiences and I have been pleased by the response – which I have perceived as a mixture of amusement and discomfort, (though this is how I feel about it too, so I may be projecting here.) The reworking brought about a shift in the narration, away from specific boys and whether they were more or less upset, towards a realisation, as I reread, rewrote and re-contemplated 1956, life at West Lodge County Primary, Pinner, Middlesex, that the school was obsessed with what seemed like gender but was probably sex. The deputy head in 'The Line', Miss Williams was the only primary school teacher that I knew of who called girls by their first names and boys by their second. I was always 'Rosen'. We were all surnamed apart from the boy 'Roger' who appears in another poem in this collection as the boy who wasn't allowed to play with me.

Since 1966 I have been informed by the enormous efforts that have been made in teaching, children's books and society at large to raise the question of woman's role in life (Stinton 1976, 1979; Dixon B. 1977; Barrs and Pidgeon 1993). In the wake of this there has been a knot of concern about how it is that masculinity 'happens' (Seidler 1989; Seidler 1992; Jackson 1995). This has taken off in various directions: rediscovering the 'real man' in ritual; claims that men are victims too in the construction of gender as they are forced into roles that they cannot or should not have to live up to; efforts to be 'non-sexist guys' ('new men') and take on more of what were previously thought to be 'female roles' – child-care, crying, even cleaning the toilet bowl.

So, in reworking the piece I found myself thinking about how it was that my gang of hoodlums were both intent on 'law-breaking', being 'evil', whilst at the same time, were constantly being told we were just that The opening sally of the piece over the skipping being a case in point, where Miss Williams is 'surprised' at Frances but not at me. Then at the end, in the Head's speech, when he tells us that there is always a little bunch who do the wrecking, I am incorporating several things:

1) the self-fulfilling prophecy that was expressed in the school at the time;

2) a line from a story by Gwyn Thomas that my father read to us when I was in my teens: when the new school opens, a teacher falls on a child who is doing something wrong with the comment : 'Precisely the sort of lout we've been looking for!' It became a family catch phrase (*A Frost on My Frolic* Thomas 1953);

3) a scene out of a documentary film by Nick Broomfield, that he made when I was at the National Film School with him in which a policeman visiting a school informs the children that somewhere in the room, there are criminals to be and it's his job to catch them (*Proud to be British* (Broomfield 1975).

However, there is one more twist. Since having a step-daughter who wanted to play football, I have been drawn into listening to the arguments about how the playground and playtimes should be divided up. In short, if schools do not create a special time for girls to play football on their own, most of them will never play. If and when schools do create a special time, on the lone football pitch in a cramped inner city school playground, the boys become very resentful and, if given a chance, try to wreck the girls' football games by running on the pitch. So in the head's speech, just at the very point at which he is going over the top, just as he is about to cane us (something that I do not condone) I have him making what I intend to be a valid point. In other words sometimes the wrong people say the right things, or the right things are said for the wrong reasons, or the right things are said at the wrong times and so on. I was trying to create a little maelstrom of feelings for a reader, and I wanted to write it into a structure of reception that is already gendered: i.e. upper juniors battling over territory whilst under the close supervision of teachers. Historically and autobiographically speaking, I guess that those teachers of mine were, in their own ways, trying to resolve an actual problem. The snag was that the only way they thought they could resolve it was a self-confirming criminalising of little boys.

The repressed sub-text of the whole piece, though, is the sexual activity of some of those boys, being masturbated by 'Old Man Harris' in his hut in the woods, and their attacking of girls in the same woods in the company of 'Colin'. I do not like finding myself in the role of self-censor but of course it illustrates very clearly just what are the discursive limits of 'children's literature'.

Conversation with a six year old

Do you want to come to my party?
Yes.
You'll get ice cream jelly
a punch in the belly
you can't watch telly
cos your feet are too smelly.
Thanks.

1) Roots in other texts – oral tradition

In this section I want to look at another kind of intertext: the oral tradition.

This is the transcription of a memory of a conversation with a boy from Whitechapel in about 1979. In one sense this piece is analogous with the section on found poetry, except we have here an oral find. Here though, I am not drawing attention to some unnoticed absurdity that undermines the original and official intention. Instead I am enjoying the upfront and deliberate absurdity and subversiveness belonging to a tradition already in place.

In a lot of my work with children, both in my own performances and when doing writing workshops with them, I have borne in mind what I tell myself are two kinds of oral tradition. There is the oral tradition of what I call 'fixed forms', though I have to bear in mind that they are not truly 'fixed' – more of that in a moment. And then there is the oral tradition of sociolects, culturally shaped pockets of speech habits and forms. So in the first category come the rhymes, parodies, jokes, proverbs, riddles the set pieces that have an immediately apparent structure within which new variants are constantly being made. This is the area first explored in depth by the Opies but which I have also investigated with *Inky Pinky Ponky* (1982) (with Susanna Steele and Dan Jones), *South and North, East and West* (Rosen 1992a) – (with orally collected traditional stories) – and Rude Rhymes (Rosen 1992b) and *Rude Rhymes 2* (Rosen 1994a). In the second category comes the *seemingly* free flow of conversation, banter, gossip, information, reflection that goes on in everyday speech. I say 'seemingly' because on closer examination, many of the rhythms, phrases, sequences and routines of this conversation are almost as structured as the so-called 'fixed forms' kind. However, subjectively speaking, people (and children especially) feel that there is a difference between the set-piece that they deliver ('Knock knock . . . ', 'Do you know the one about . . . '

and so on) and the conversations they have, even if conversation includes set strategies such as 'And your mother!', 'Why pick on me?' and the like.

My own writing is clearly heavily informed by the latter – in fact it feeds off it, exploiting some characteristic locutions of my own parents but also playing about with past and present children's voices. However, in various ways I have lived in the flow of the 'fixed forms'. So, when working in schools I have encouraged the children to do research projects on their family, school and local cultures collecting stories, rhymes, proverbs, riddles and the rest from people around them. As mentioned above, I have recycled various examples of these in books and on occasions in my own poetry books, I have incorporated or changed folk rhymes from my own childhood or my children's. Where these have been too rude (by the standards of 'children's literature') they have ended up in *Rude Rhymes* and its sequel (Rosen 1992b, 1994a), but sometimes they have sneaked into my own poems.

There is an ideological point here about language, literacy, literature and class. There is an unwritten assumption in our literate culture that there is an inbuilt superiority of the written word. In class terms this translates into cultural deficit theory that states that there are social groups, ethnic groups and classes of people that do not possess 'culture' or who possess less or more inferior forms of culture. This basic notion has underpinned education for over a hundred years: that working-class children in particular (but also some other groups of migrant origin), enter schools lacking in culture and/or civilisation. It is the school's job, the theory goes, to instil real culture into these children in the form of good language, good behaviour, and high art. Basil Bernstein's 'elaborated' and 'restricted' codes were only yet one more chapter in the evolution of the theory (Bernstein 1971).

I have implied with my poetry and my performances in schools that in the air around us and with the language (more accurately, the sociolects) we use, there is not only tremendous vitality and energy but also that this is the site where we play out our identities and try (partly) to shape our subjectivities. In fact, having made the distinction in my mind between the 'fixed forms' and the sociolectal flow I then make great efforts to show that there is a continuum. Or that if there is a distinction, it can be blurred. So in performances I jump from poems of my own to songs, riddles, tonguetwisters and rhymes that I have collected orally. Both in the overall output of my books (see *We're Going on a Bear Hunt* (Rosen 1989), *Little Rabbit Foo* (Rosen 1990a) and within books (as with the 'work' here) I do the same thing.

Children as a whole, but working-class children, non-standard English speaking and non-English speaking children in particular, 'learn' at school that their own day to day speech is anything on the spectrum from inadequate to wrong i.e. it is not part of the acceptable school code and they 'learn' to fail. This is one of the ways in which the class structure of society is reproduced (Bourdieu and Passeron 1977: 204). If, (as I am) we are interested in the idea that education is (amongst other things) about reflecting on who we are, where we come from and where we are going then it seems to me axiomatic that this cannot be done if the dominant pedagogic discourse puts the children's own sociolects out of bounds. In other words you cannot say, 'Tell me about your experience, your experience is valid' if at the same time you say, 'Your way of talking is useless, bad, and a hindrance.' My poetry, my work in schools, my overall range of books implies another approach that says, 'Each of our sociolects is valid, tell me about your experiences . . . ' In this way the poem is an effort in a very small way to undermine the reproductive function of devaluing-working class language.

This little tiny found oral poem is yet another example of following this path of thought into my own work, but it could just have easily ended up in one of my anthologies like *Sonsense Nongs* (Rosen 1992c) or *Walking the Bridge of Your Nose* (Rosen 1995b). I guess it is what the poet Brian Moses meant in part when he referred to my attitude to the limits and definitions of poetry as 'cavalier' [hearsay]. I would prefer to think, if we are using seventeenth-century analogies, they are more 'Roundhead' or, better still, 'Leveller' and 'Digger'.

Talking-tubes

I believe everything my brother tells me
that's why I know about talking-tubes in old houses.

Once we went to this old house
and the guide who was taking us round
told us that there were tubes
running through the massive great thick walls
so that the people in the olden days
could talk to each other.

After the guide went off
my brother explained to me

that these talking tubes were only discovered
a short while ago.
He said they were closed up
with great big corks.

He said,
when the people who discovered them
pulled the corks out
they heard
all these old words from hundreds of years ago.
They heard knights-in-armour talking.
What they said just came tumbling out of the talking-tubes.
Amazing.
I believe everything my brother tells me
that's why I know about talking-tubes in old houses.

1) Root in material (sibling relation) and within the dialogue surrounding this

One further aspect of my material conditions of life was that I was brought up with a brother. In this section I look at how that situation is yet another determinant in the production of this 'work'.

An inescapable condition of my life has been the relationship with my brother. He was one of the conditions I was born into, already there and always there. He is four years older than I and took a clearly senior role. From as early as I can remember he took on the job of teaching me whatever he was learning at school. This meant that he taught me to read before I went to school and when he was older tried to teach me calculus when he was doing A-level maths. He was a mad keen collector, model maker, train spotter and designer. My feeling about him while I was under about twelve was that he was supremely capable, much, much better than I at making and doing. When we were on our camping holidays, he kept log books, which he illustrated with what seemed to me beautiful coloured crayon landscapes and pictures of trains.

Running alongside this construction of him as someone with immense capabilities was a fairly stormy emotional life. For whatever reasons, my father was a hard taskmaster to him. My brother always felt that he was not living up to the standards my father set him. There were rows and my brother would storm about shouting. The direct effect this had on me was that once our bedroom door was closed, my brother would chew over the day's events, the latest row and his rage of feelings in a kind of dramatic extemporisation. He would try to engage my sympathies, get me on his side in whatever was going on. This meant that in very deep ways, family life for me was constantly seen as if through a prism – one side, my view; the other side, his view. He provided a running commentary, a highly charged filter through which to see the inner politics of the family.

In the past I have expressed various facets of all this: the rows, his rages, his relation with me in more 'bossing-about' mode but for some time I have been trying to find ways to express the ways in which I looked up to him. Then the episode of the talking-tubes came to me. It interests me that this is a holiday story, whilst doing that educationally sound, middle-class thing of visiting castles and listening carefully to guides (the kind of thing I inflict on my own children too). In fact, it came to me whilst doing precisely this as a parent, just as I was waving a professorial finger about at a bit of old wall. The point is that both as a boy and as a man, it is quite usual that I should have a paternal voice inside me, a voice that I have to negotiate with and around. My situation is complicated by the extent to which I also have my brother's voice inside me.

In saying that, perhaps I am not succeeding in describing here the enormous amount of hysterical humour that was involved in all this. It seemed to me that he was a brilliant mimic and mime, so that he could reproduce in the theatre of our bedroom all kinds of people: both of our parents, teachers, friends, encounters with shopkeepers, police and various local characters that he would dub with names like 'The King of Pinner' or 'Accelerating-Past-the-Dustbins'. In other words, there was with my brother a heady mixture of deadly serious studious achievement and wildly funny theatrical showmanship. He used to read and perform whole sections of the satire on public school life *Down with Skool* (Winans and Searle 1953) and later, *Beyond the Fringe* (1960). He was and still is an Arthurian freak. And he mixed all this with a strand of trickstering. Another indication of that mixture was the fact that he called the camp latrines we dug at our camp sites, the Arthurian name 'Siege Perilous'. He could have been no older than thirteen when he came up with that one.

So my brother is an inescapable presence in my life and writing. He is a force of dominance, he is a commentating eye, a web of voices – some analytic, some theatrical – and, in a disconcerting way, he is a focus of my sympathy. All this strikes me as a powerful example of the way in which human relations are both actual (real); are to a great extent expressed in language (conversation between people); and are represented in language (as I am doing here). However, they are also expressed in hugs, kisses, strokes, blows and, by way of response, in body development, posture and gesture. We did fight – there was a period when he hit puberty when he was a bit of a bully and would enjoy being much more powerful than I, and would go in for the conventional (culturally fixed) acts of domination and humiliation that boys at this time and place would go in for: e.g. sitting astride my chest and spitting in my face. In this poem as it appears on the page I am operating in the linguistic mode (of course), but in performance I bring to bear much more somatic and visceral elements. In some respects, I view the written forms of what I make as strangely 2-dimensional, as if they sit on the page unable or unwilling to conjure up the physical dimensions of relationships and feelings, say my brother's gestures, voices, facial expressions and motor skills. There is an interesting insufficiency about language here in trying to express these somatic experiences. Thus, the poem misses my brother's mock earnestness of tone and the professorial finger-wagging and yet I know that in performance I will try to reproduce that, treating the text as a short play script. As I re-enact these, I express something of the somatic relationship I have had with my brother, I 'become' him and for a moment (of course, completely illusorily) achieve what I had always wanted to do: be him.

Aldermaston March

I ran away from home once.
I was 13,
the second year of the Aldermaston March,
marching from Aldermaston to London
to Ban the Bomb (for evermore).

I said, I'm going on the Aldermaston March.

They both said that this was out of the question,
the boy's mad, crazy.

My mother said,
where will you stay? you'd have nothing to eat
you don't know anyone, what would you eat?
you're not going. Harold say something, he's too young,

look at him, he's packing.
You can't go without a spare pair of trousers
how can he carry a bag like that for 20 miles a day?
Stop him Harold,
what would you do in the evening?
you need to eat, you get ill If you don't eat
take a tin of beans, you can always eat beans
Harold, stop him.
There's the chicken, take the chicken
if you're taking a tin of beans, take 2,
he's thirteen Harold, go next year
wait till next year, they won't have banned the bomb by then, believe
me. There'll be another march, go on that one.
You must keep eating fresh fruit.
And you like dates. He's always liked dates, hasn't he Harold?
Just squeeze them in down the side of the bag.
Couldn't he wait till the last day
when *we'll* be there?
We can all go to Trafalgar Square together
Harold have you got the chicken?
Just because it's Easter doesn't mean it's warm.
It can snow at Easter, wear the string vest.
Who's organised the coaches?
Do we know these people Harold?
 One orange! Take five.
And raisins. He's 13. It's ridiculous. He can't go.
Keep the chicken wrapped.
Phone us If you need more food. Goodbye.

1) My reception

In this final section I want to explore how I perceive a poem. It is intended to show some aspects of the process described above, namely how it is I read a poem of my own, after the text has stabilised. However, this exemplification is also an insight into the particular sensibility, derived from the particular cultural and socioeconomic formation that I bring to bear as I write and perform.

Line by line analysis as an act of personal reception (bearing in mind my particular historical situation):

'I ran away from home once.'

It is often said that stories have beginnings, middles and ends. I do not think they necessarily do, necessarily should, or for that matter, in oral conversation very often do. That is to say, we quite often begin stories with some or all of the 'end'. We say, 'my dog died' and tell the story of how it happened. I have been repeating this heresy for some time in teachers' meetings. Though it was not a conscious choice when I wrote this, I read that first line as one such 'ends in beginnings'. Rhetorically speaking, they are attention-grabbers. They are essentialised, headlining statements to draw the mind of the reader to wonder what the possible explanation of such a statement could possibly be. So I read this line as an attempt to write a headline.

'I was 13,'

More of the same.

'the second year of the Aldermaston March
marching from Aldermaston to London
to Ban the Bomb (for evermore).'

This is a way of simultaneously explaining, referring and patterning. It tries to incorporate necessary referential detail in a way that is pleasing and gently ironic. (The bomb was not banned for evermore). This last phrase is a quotation from the anthem we sang on the marches ('The H-Bomb's thunder', Brunner 1982). However, as a result of readings in front of children and adults I have come to see that it is an excluding phrase. Whereas adults of my age, older and a bit younger know the references, children are confused and baffled. (This explains why it will not appear in the final published version of this 'work')

'I said I'm going on the Aldermaston March'

This expresses my wilful, stubborn, dogmatic style of the time. It feels to me when I read this out in public that I am celebrating it. I enjoy the certainty of it I can also remember the sensation of saying it at the time, the flush of excitement about the mixture of defiance and dare.

'They both said that this was out of the question the boy's mad, crazy.'

This is a deliberate compression because I wanted to get on with the meat and purpose of the poem: my mother's dramatic monologue. But reported speech compression can have an amusing undertow if you insert idioms, or isolated specifics into it. It conjures up minutes, even hours of conversation with one or two dabs. I can hear (rehear) the certainty of 'their' refusal. The use of 'they' is deliberately impersonal – or more accurately – highly personal because it assumes knowledge of the referents. It is overly familiar. This is one of the ways in which I incorporate orality into my poems.

'My mother said,'

Now we are into it. This is where the poem 'begins'.

'where will you stay? you'd have nothing to eat
you don't know anyone, what would you eat?
you're not going.'

This is my mother speaking and it is also me now as a parent. And perhaps it is most parents. It is a quite reasonable set of objections. The strange act of writing about childhood while being a parent oneself is that I can hear justifiable logics on all sides.

The 'eat' trope is how my mother actually spoke and is intertextually linked to the 'Jewish mother', part caricature, part stereotype. But as is often the case in such conditions, it has a basis in culture. My mother genuinely believed that for much for my life I did not eat enough or properly. The house was always full of food, she provided vast amounts to friends and relations. On one occasion we left a tape recorder running when some friends came over and when we played the tape back we found that my mother was punctuating the conversation every few minutes or so with 'Have an apple.' 'Have a sandwich'. As I observed earlier, it is not difficult to see that the syndrome lies in the fact that home-based Jewish mothers bore the total burden of domestic arrangements in times of poverty and persecution.

'Harold say something, he's too young,'

My parents had a way of invoking each other in times of argument. They needed each other for support. They had been together since the age of 16 and saw everything they did as a kind of joint activity. I have written this with deliberate shifts and changes. I see my mother turning and twisting physically as well as rhetorically, always busy.

'look at him he's packing.'

Stage direction disguised as monologue. But it is also the mannerism of Jewish speech to dramatise what is going on, as a statement of feeling: 'look at him dancing there, the little fellow' and the like.

'You can't go without a spare pair of trousers
how can he carry a bag like that for 20 miles a day?'

The first fatal shift. She has now been drawn into contemplating the reality of the very thing that she has forbidden. She is in effect considering what it will be like if I go. There is the delivery of the rhetorical question, also a Jewish mannerism as in the joke: 'Why do you Jews always turn everything into a question?' 'Why do you ask?'. In writing, I seek out these mannerisms in my oral repertoire.

'Stop him Harold'

I connect here with my father being strangely mute. In certain domestic arguments, when my mother got under full steam ahead, he would take a back seat. I have deliberately invoked this here. I am also invoking the fact that secretly I think he approves. One of my fondest memories of my father is of him coming to meet me at Bow Street police station at about 2 in the morning after I had been arrested at Grosvenor Square in 1968. He sympathised, nay approved, of my political activity and here is just keeping his head down to see what will happen.

'what would you do in the evening?'

More fatal imagining.

'you need to eat, you get ill if you don't eat
take a tin of beans, you can always eat beans'

She has conceded too much. Through the metaphor of food, she has conceded that I am going but she can express her concern now into making sure that I will go well provided. This was so typical of my mother. She worried about the risks I took in life, sometimes did not want to express those in case she was interfering and so displaced them on to food. Yet there was a genuine worry about how I would eat.

'Harold stop him.'

Still mute, still biding his time.

'There's the chicken, take the chicken
if you're taking a tin of beans, take 2,'

I am fully aware that this is now beginning to sound like caricature but in fact I did take a chicken on this Aldermaston March and friends of theirs who I met, were amazed and commented for years on how 'Connie fed the Aldermaston March'.
Again, I ended up taking a whole stack of tins.

'he's thirteen Harold, go next year'

She is pulled back into realising the enormity of what is going on here. I reinsert 13 into the monologue partly for shock value.

'wait till next year, they won't have banned the bomb by then believe me.'

Though I do not remember if my mother actually said this, it is intended to be typical. She came up with hundreds of these kinds of statements. It is difficult to describe them. They are logical but inappropriate. Though sometimes they were illogical and appropriate. When there was a typhoid scare in the corned beef coming in from Argentina in the early 1960s, she once went to the cupboard, took down a can of corned beef, stopped herself and said, 'Oh no, I'd better not open that until the typhoid outbreak is over.' Though the statement in the poem is in a sense its mirror image (logical but inappropriate), I see it as how my mother's rhetoric worked. I find these phrases through excavating the memories and oral formulae of my family.

There'll be another march, go on that one.'

She's right. There was. And I did.

'You must keep eating fresh fruit'

This is my mother turning advice into generalities about well-being. It was never sufficient for her to give a specific line of help, it had to be generalised into a whole state of mind, or a suitable way of life.

'And you like dates. He's always liked dates, hasn't he Harold?

To be absolutely honest, this is why I loved my mother and father. They knew me. Part of parenting is a simple business of saying who you think you're children are. The only problem is that as your children get older, it keeps getting out of date. You say that they like things when they don't anymore. At this stage though I had liked dates, she was right, and I still liked dates. I am glad that she knows that. But it is also what infuriates.

'Just squeeze them down the side of the bag.'

She has blown it. She has finally admitted, (and I have revealed it to the reader) that I am going. It is also a stage direction. We can now see the bag. It was in fact a weird object, a kind of army kitbag that my father had made out of an old army blanket which he had used for our camping holidays.

'Couldn't he wait till the last day
when we'll be there?
We can all go to Trafalgar Square together'

The sub-text of the poem is that they did not disapprove of the march and its politics, they would not have minded me going next year, or with them. The problem, is of course, am I old enough? It would have been incredible and impossible for very nearly all my friends in the neighbourhood to have come with me, not only because they were too young, but much more importantly that their parents would have deeply disapproved of the march.

'Harold have you got the chicken?'

If Harold is doing the chicken, what is she doing? She's 'faffing.' She's expressing her anxiety by pulling at my clothes, and getting in the way as I am trying to stuff things into the kitbag. Harold is still mute.

'Just because it's Easter doesn't mean it's warm,
It can snow at Easter, wear the string vest.'

'Wrap up warm' was one of my mother's slogans. She knitted jumpers for us, and seemed to live in a perpetual worry about the cold. The death of a child through whooping cough and pneumonia and my brother's pneumonias and chilblains provided plenty of evidence for why she should worry.

'Who's organised the coaches?
Do we know these people Harold?'

She did know them, they were friends of friends in the political circles they moved in. It is a totally reasonable question. But in this context it is already too late. Meanwhile I am not saying anything. I am just pressing on. This is how the episode went into the family folklore: that there was something weirdly directed and stubborn about my behaviour. Whether this became or has become a self-confirming bit of conditioning, I am not sure. Did I become more wilful, more directed, more stubborn as a result of my parents observing that I was? Did I take pride in the fact that I could see that my father's re-enactment of the episode was tinged with a little bit of pride that I

1) should want to go and

2) actually went in spite of their discouragement.

But then there was a bit of pride on his part that they were liberated enough parents to allow me. I think he took the back seat on this occasion to see whether I really did have the ego-strength to carry the whole thing through. When I showed that I did, then it became a facility that I could draw on in the future. A facility partly produced by the way my parents behaved at the time, and in retelling the story.

'One orange! Take five. And raisins.'

The over-provider.

'He's 13. It's ridiculous. He can't go'

This is the trope of the dramatic monologue whereby the person speaking reveals contradictions to the reader but not to themselves Technically it is, of course, a form of 'dramatic irony.' That it is here at all, is largely because of my initiation into the mode of dramatic irony through education.

'Keep the chicken wrapped.'

The chicken is becoming mythic. Chickens were mythic in Jewish homes that would scrimp and save all week, in order to have a chicken on the sabbath or at least on a feast day. When I was a child, there were families I knew that only had chicken at Christmas, whereas my mother bought one at least once a month.

'Phone us if you need more food.'

Is it likely that I will need more food? They gave me a stack of money as well.
   When they did appear on the last day, their friends called out to them, 'we need more food, Connie. More chicken.' She enjoyed the joke. She enjoyed being known as a food person.

'Goodbye.'

I've gone. Silently, unstoppably, determinedly.
   The poem seems to me to be a commemoration of one side of my mother, but dissatisfies me because I still have not caught her philosophical, penetrative side. I keep reducing her to this over-solicitous creature, not quite aware of what she is saying. There was one side of her that was like that, but it is no means the whole picture. A poem like this acts as a stimulus for other writing because it expresses to me what it does not say. As long as I have a feeling like that, I will keep trying to pin down what I have not said. So though it appears in a way complete, a scene that opens and closes, it talks to me of something unwritten, unsaid, an absence. And this is a feeling of sadness both that she is not around anymore and that I cannot recall this something that will not allow itself to be expressed.

Conclusion

Across these twelve poems I have tried to show how material existence, intertextuality and reception are the inescapable conditions of literary production. I have tried to break down these large abstract concepts into highly specific features, showing how they interlock. As I have stated, the commentaries should be taken as a whole, each of them expressing another aspect of a total picture.

Indeed, it needs to be expressed more strongly than that: the argument here is that no one element from the scheme outlined at the beginning of the chapter can be hived off from the others, but, as outlined in Chapter 2, there is a prime mover in the determining power of the ways in which we produce and reproduce our material existence, a power that is traceable in what is written. However, this material existence is constantly being framed, addressed and affected by ideas, mine included. The production of ideas, as here in the form of poetry for children, I have tried to show as having relations with other ideas, expressed as 'texts', but that these new texts of mine emerge as the consequence of a complex set of conditions, constraints and sources and not simply, or only, because, say, a predecessor wrote something similar. Moreover, I have tried to show here and in Chapter 3 how the way the access to a pre-text is made (i.e. through class and cultural formation) is part of the process by which the needs of material existence position us in society and is part of the process through which we express ourselves.

Conclusion

AT THE OUTSET OF THIS WORK I asked some questions:

1. How can a set of poems, written by a particular author, be related to the following:
i) the present, historical, economic and material context of their authoring;
ii) the past historical, economic and material circumstances of the author;
iii) the socioeconomic and emotional context of the author's family (or unit of upbringing);
iv) the literary and artistic context of their authoring;
v) the positioning of the author within a specific past and current literary and cultural context;
vi) the personally constructed narrative of the author's experiences, literary and non-literary?
2. How does this set of poems written by me exemplify these relationships?
3. What theoretical framework will provide an explanation for the form and structure of these relationships?

Looking back at the work, I can now see that the whole enterprise is in one sense an answer to matters belonging in my own formation. My literary critical construction took place under the influences of the 'New Criticism', Leavisite teachers in the Sixth Form, and the 'historical' and philological school at Oxford University. Though these approaches always proved to be absorbing, I had been aware for years that the actual process of *explanation* implied or claimed by these critical activities seemed deficient. Explanations for why a text said this or that seemed to be derived from any or all of the following sources:

1) previous texts (Influences);
2) the stage in development in the particular writer's writing;
3) universalistic values supposedly inherent in a given style, technique, allusion or meaning;
4) psychological events in the writer's life;
5) acceptance of formalist or structuralist 'givens' that are seen to lead inevitably to known but unexplained psychological effects;
6) general references to 'contemporary ideas'.

Since my own formation partly under the influence of these methods (which were already coming under attack) , there has been the massive explosion of 'Theory': structuralist, post-structuralist, psychoanalytic, 'reader-response', intertextual, archetypic, semiological, deconstructionist, ideological, and so on. Again, there are approaches that try to delineate how the reader is 'positioned' by a text, others that look solely at the syntactic structuring and so on.

This thesis cannot and does not 'answer' all these. However, it sought to make some vital connections which, both in the old criticism of my literary-critical formation, and those of 'Theory' are frequently effaced. These connections are between the literary text and the various material conditions of its production. I have tried to show that these material conditions may be:

1) the macro-economic circumstances a writer is born into and lives with;
2) the micro-economic conditions of how his or her family survived during upbringing;
3) the material conditions of a writer's formation within the given society;
4) the material circumstances of an audience being created prior to and during literary production;
5) the micro-economic conditions of how the writer (and family) survives in the process of earning a livelihood ;
6) the exact material circumstances of how a text is produced;
7) the connections between all these elements.

This has taken me on a journey looking at such matters as the nature of British post-war capitalism, the changing formation of the education system, the nature of the publishing industry and the circumstances that allow for performances in schools to take place. On a more personal level, it has led me to examine the circumstances of Jewish migration, differing kinds of teaching, performing, the experience of having had a working mother, living in a London suburb, having an older brother and so on.

However, I have also had to examine the sea of texts and ideas that has existed in and around me whilst living in these circumstances. At times I have expressed these as 'givens' but at others I have tried to show ways in which these texts and ideas only became available to me as a consequence of the specific circumstances and times I lived through. In the past, in old 'New' criticism, in post-structuralist theory and indeed in general 'common sense' conversation about literature, a false picture is often given of texts simply generating and producing new texts, or ideas producing ideas. I have tried to break into this idealist model by constantly looking at the where, how and when texts exist and the where, how and when I came across them.

I have also excavated some of the feedback processes that take place within very specific circumstances of writing and performing which were, in turn, to be found in their own specific material circumstances. Writing is not a one-way process but is part of a complex network of actual and imagined conversations. The word 'intervention' proved to be useful in picturing this. In looking at these matters I could not avoid looking at 'ideology' but again was anxious not to reduce what I write to 'ideology' or simply to show myself negotiating with 'Ideology'.

As I mentioned in the Introduction, I deliberately avoided, for reasons stated there, a psychoanalytic approach. What I think I have done, is provide some essential parts of a framework to contextualise and explain the production of some poems. These parts of a framework are readily available to anyone, writer or critic, researching the genesis of a literary work and so could be easily reproduced in further research by other students. The question remains, however, as to whether they provide anything like a theory of authorship.

This is a subject that has been examined elsewhere (see Barthes 1977; Williams 1977 192-198; Foucault 1977; Burke 1992; Caughie 1981) and is too broad and too theoretical a matter for me to claim that I have made much of an inroad on the matter. Frequently, the emphasis in the word 'authorship' has been on trying to figure out general questions: 'what are authors in the culture?'; 'what is their function?' By close examination of individual poems, in conjunction with a wider view of my socioeconomic and cultural positioning, I have, I think, given very concrete manifestations of what is, broadly speaking, a materialist approach to something different: 'what does a writer actually do?' In other words it is not so much a look at author*ship* as author*ing*.

I have tried to show in detail, some of the ways in which subjectivity and expression are constrained and produced by objective circumstances. Though in the past this has been described as being theoretically possible, and indeed often described in general terms, it is not, I think, very common for it to have been done with this kind of detail. In other words what I have done here is try to validate a theory.

This then, I hope is the ultimate value of this study: showing that a historico-materialist approach to literature and art is not a matter of dull and painful analyses of steel production and interest rates, nor of creating a model of the writer or artist trapped by the trade cycle. Instead I have tried to set up a fruitful way of looking at how some very specific items of literature (mine) are produced in a specific time and place in human existence. If there is value in this, then it would be found not so much in a new, neat, sewn-up theory, but rather, that in the process of reading the detail, the interconnections between consciousness, creativity, texts and material life would become more apparent, and so prove as explanations for:

1) the specific phenomenon of my writing poetry for children, whilst
2) offering ways in which similar and parallel approaches to other poetry, literature and art could be just as fruitful.

Bibliography

AHLBERG A. and AHLBERG J. (1981) *Peepo!* London: Kestrel

ALDERSON B. (1974) 'Leading young readers from mere verse to great poetry', *The Times* 10.4.74

ANON (1904) *Pearson's Humorous Reciter* London: C. Arthur Pearson

ALTHUSSER L (1965) *For Marx* London: New Left Books

ARCHIBALD W. P. (1989) *Marx and the Missing Link: Human Nature* Atlantic Highlands, New Jersey: Humanities Press International, Inc.

ARVON H. (1973) *Marxist Esthetics* Ithaca, London: Cornell University Press (originally 1970 *L'esthetique marxiste* Paris: Presse Universitaire de France)

AUDEN W. H. 91976) *Collected Poems* (ed Mendelson E.) London: Faber and Faber

BALIBAR E. and MACHEREY P. (1992) 'On Literature as an Ideological Form' pp. 34-54 in MULHERN F. (ed.) (1992) *Contemporary Marxist Literary Criticism* London: Longman [originally written in 1974 reprinted from pp. 4-12 in *Oxford Literary Review*, 3 (1978)]

BAKHTIN M. (1981) *The Dialogic Imagination* Austin: University of Texas Press

BARKER C., CALLINICOS A., HALLAS D. (1987) 'Three responses to Chris

Harman's account of base and superstructure' pp. 118-127 in *International Socialism* 2:34 Winter 1987

BARRS M. and PIDGEON S. (eds) (1993) *Reading the Difference. Gender and Reading in the Primary School* London: Centre for Language in Primary Education

BARTHES R. (1977) 'The Death of the Author' in *Image, Music, Text* London: Fontana, Collins, (originally 'La mort de l'auteur' *Manteia* V, 1968)

BARTHES R. (1984) *Writing Degree Zero* trans. Annette Lavers and Colin Smith, London. (originally (1953) *Le Degre zero de l'ecriture* Paris: Seuil

BENJAMIN W. (1970) *Illuminations* London: Cape

BENNETT T. (1979) *Formalism and Marxism* London, New York: Methuen

BENNETT T. (1990) *Outside Literature* London, New York: Routledge

BENNETT T. (1992) 'Marxism and Popular Fiction' pp. 188-210 in MULHERN F. (ed.) (1992) *Contemporary Marxist Literary Criticism* London: Longman [reprinted from BENNETT T. (1981) 'Marxism and Popular Fiction' pp. 138-156 in *Literature and History* 7]

BENTON M., TEASEY J., BELL R., HURST K. (1988) *Young Readers Responding to Poems* London and New York: Routledge

BERNSTEIN B. (1971) *Class. Codes and Control* Vol 1 *Theoretical studies towards a sociology of language* London: Routledge and Kegan Paul

BESTALL A. (1935-1965) *Rupert Bear* in *Daily Express*

BHASKAR R. (1989) *Reclaiming Reality, A Critical Introduction to Contemporary Philosophy London*: Verso

BOURDIEU P. and PASSERON J-C. (1977) *Reproduction in Education. Society and Culture* trans. Richard Nice, London: SAGE

BOURDIEU P. (1993 a) 'The Field of Cultural Production, or: The Economic World Reversed' pp. 29-73 in BOURDIEU P. (1993) (edited and introduced by Randal Johnson) *The Field of Cultural Production: Essays on Art and Literature* Cambridge: Polity Press [originally published in *Poetics* (Amsterdam), 1214 – 5 (1983), pp. 311-56, translated by Richard Nice (Amsterdam: Elsevier Science Publishers)]

BOURDIEU P. (1993 b) 'Field of Power, Literary Field and Habitus' pp. 161-175 in BOURDIEU P. (1993) (edited and introduced by Randal Johnson) *The Field of Cultural Production: Essays on Art and Literature* Cambridge: Polity Press

BRECHT B. (1964) *Brecht on Theatre* (ed John Willett) London: Methuen

BRITONN J. (ed) (1957) *The Oxford Books of Verse* for Juniors (4 vols) Oxford: Oxford University Press

BRITTON J.N. (1970) *Language and Learning* London, New York: Penguin

BURKE S. (1992) *The Death and Return of the Author. Criticism and Subjectivity in Barthes, Foucault and Derrida* Edinburgh: Edinburgh University Press

BROOKS C. and WARREN R.P. (1938) *Understanding Poetry, An Anthology for College Students* New York: Henry Holt and Company

BROWNING R. (1908) *Poems* London: George Routledge

BROWNJOHN A (1963) in HOLLO A. (ed) (1963) *Jazz Poems* London: Vista Books

BRUNHOFF de J. (1936) *Babar the King* London: Methuen (originally 1933)

BRUNNER J. (1982) 'The H-Bomb's thunder' in *The Anti-Nuclear Songbook* Nottingham: Peace News

BUNYAN J. (1686) *A Book for Boys and Girls, or Country Rhimes for Children* London [later (1701) entitled *Divine Emblems* London: John Marshall]

CALLINICOS A. (1985) 'Postmodernism, Post-Structuralism, Post-Marxism?' pp. 85-101 in *Theory. Culture and Society* Vol 2 No 3 1985 Victoria, Australia

CALLINICOS A. (1995) *Theories and Narratives. Reflections on the Philosophy of History* Durham, North Carolina: Duke University Press, Durham

CARPENTER J.E. (ed) (1867) *Popular Readings in Prose and Verse* London: Frederick Warne; New York: Scribner and Co

'CARROLL, LEWIS' (DODGSON C.L) (1865) *Alice's Adventures in Wonderland* London: Macmillan

CAUDWELL C. (1973) *Illusion and Reality, A Study of the Sources of Poetry* London: Lawrence and Wishart (originally 1937 London: Macmillan)

CAUGHIE J. (ed) (1981) *Theories of Authorship* London, New York: Routledge and Kegan Paul

CENTRAL ADVISORY COUNCIL FOR EDUCATION (ENGLAND) (1947) *School and Life* London: HMSO pp. 9-17

CHAUCER G. (1957) *The Knight's Tale* in F.N. Robinson (1957) *The Works of Geoffrey Chaucer* London: Oxford University Press

COOK C. and STEVENSON J. (1996) *Britain Since 1945* London: Longman

COOPER M. (1744 a) *Tommy Thumb's Song Book* London: Mary Cooper

COOPER M. (1744 b) *Tommy Thumb's Pretty Song Book* Voll.[sic] II (i.e. 2) London: Mary Cooper

COPELAND J.S. (1993) *Speaking of Poets. Interviews with Poets who write for Children and Young Adults* Urbana, Illinois: National Council of Teachers of English

COPELAND J.S. and COPELAND V.L. (1994) *Speaking of Poets 2. More Interviews with Poets who Write for Children and Young Adults* Urbana, Illinois:

National Council of Teachers of English

CORCORAN B. and EVANS E. (eds) (1978) *Readers, Tests, Teachers* Portsmouth, New Hampshire: Boynton/Cook Heinemann

CROMPTON R. (1922) *Just William* London: George Newnes

CULLER J. (1975) *Structuralist Poetics* Ithaca: Cornell University Press, Routledge and Kegan Paul

cummings e.e. [sic] (1991) (ed George J. Firmage) *Complete Poems 1904-1962* New York: Liveright

CUNNINGHAM H. (1991) *Children of the Poor. Representations of Childhood Since the Seventeenth Century* Oxford: Basil Blackwell

DE LA MARE W. (1912) *The Listeners and Other Poems* London: Faber and Faber

DE LA MARE W. (1913) *Peacock Pie* London: Faber and Faber

DE LA MARE W. (ed) (1923, enlarged 1928) *Come Hither, A Collection of Rhymes and Poems for the Young of all Ages* London: Constable

DE LA MARE W. (1944) *Collected Rhymes and Verses London*: Faber and Faber

DE LA MARE W. (1979) *The Collected Poems of Walter de la Mare* London, Boston: Faber and Faber

DE MAN P. (1983) *Blindness and Insight: Essays in the Rhetoric of Contemporary Criticism* ed Wlad Godzich, London: Methuen (originally 1971)

DEMETZ P. (1967) *Marx, Engels and the Poets* trans. J.L. Sammons, Chicago, London: University of Chicago Press (originally 1959 *Marx, Engels und die Dichter*)

DERRIDA J. (1978) *Writing and Difference* trans. Alan Bass, Chicago, London:

University of Chicago Press

DEUTSCHER I. (1968) *The Non-Jewish Jew and other Essays* London: Merlin Press

DEWEY J. (1902) *The Child and the Curriculum* Chicago: University of Chicago Press

DICKENS C. (1860-61) *Great Expectations* London: Chapman and Hall. (Edition used here – 'Penguin Classics' (Dickens 1996) London: Penguin Books

DIXON B. (1977) *Catching Them Young, Volume 1 Sex, Race and Class in Children's Fiction: Volume 2 Political Ideas in Children's Fiction* London: Pluto Press

DOOLEY M. (1983) 'Poetry Books for Children' pp. 7-9 in *British Book News* (Autumn 1983)

DRABBLE M. (ed) (1985) (Fifth edition) *The Oxford Companion to English Literature* Oxford, New York, Tokyo, Melbourne: Oxford University Press

EAGLETON T. (1976a) *Marxism and Literary Criticism* London: Methuen

EAGLETON T. (1976b) *Criticism and Ideology. A Study in Marxist Literary Theory* London, New York: Verso

EAGLETON T. (1983) *Literary Theory, An Introduction* Oxford: Basil Blackwell

EAGLETON T. (1991) *Ideology. An Introduction* London, New York: Verso

EAGLETON T. (1997) 'Self-undoing subjects' in PORTER R. (ed) (1997) *Rewriting the Self, Histories from the Renaissance* London, New York: Routledge

EAKIN P.J. (1985) *Fictions in Autobiographical Studies in the Art of Self-invention* Princeton, New Jersey: Princeton University Press

ECO U. with RORTY R., CULLER J. AND BROOKE-ROSE C. edited by Stefan Collini (1992) *Interpretation and Overinterpretation* Cambridge: Cambridge University Press

EBERT T.L. (1995) '(Untimely) Critiques for a Red Feminism 'pp. 113-149 in *Transformation. Marxist Boundary Work in Theory, Economics, Politics and Culture* 1 Spring 1995 'Post-ality: Marxism and Post Modernism Washington DC: Maisonneuve Press

ENGELS F. (1890) 'Engels to Bloch' 21.9.1890 pp. 381-383 in (193?) *Karl Marx Selected Works in Two Volumes* ed V. Adoratsky London: Martin Lawrence

EVANS E. (1992) Young Readers. New Readings Hull: Hull University Press

FINE A. (1997) 'Enid Blyton "Why Did We Love Her So?"' pp. 1-16 in TUCKER N. and REYNOLDS K. (eds) (1997) *NCRCL Papers 2, Enid Blyton: A Celebration and Reappraisal* Roehampton, London: National Centre for Research in Children's Literature

FINKELSTEIN S. (1947) *Art and Society* New York: International

FISCHER E. (1959) *The Necessity of Art* Harmondsworth: Penguin

FISH S. (1980) *Is There a Text in this Class?* Cambridge Mass., London: Harvard University Press

FOUCAULT, M. (1972) *The Archaeology of Knowledge* London: Tavistock Publications

FREEMAN M. (1993) *Rewriting the self, History, memory, narrative* London, New York: Routledge

FREUD S. (1985) 'Writers and Day-Dreaming' pp. 130-141 in *Art and Literature* Volume 14 Harmondsworth: Penguin (originally 1908)

FREUND E. (1987) *The Return of the Reader, Reader-Response Criticism* London, New York: Methuen

FROW J. (1986) *Marxism and Literary History* Oxford: Basil Blackwell

FROW J. (1990) 'Intertextuality and Ontology' pp. 45-55 in WORTON M. and STILL J. (1990) *Intertextuality: theories and practices* Manchester: Manchester University Press

GEIPEL J. (1982) *Mame Loshn, The Making of Yiddish* London and West Nyack: The Journeyman Press

GENETTE G. (1982) *Palimpsestes, Palimpsestes, La Littérature au second degré* Paris: Seuil

GILES G.C.T. (1946) *The New School Tie* London: Pilot Press

GINNETT L (ed) (1916?) *Light and Humorous Verse* London: George Routledge and Son

GIROUX, H.A. (1983) *Theory and Resistance in Education. A Pedagogy for the Opposition.* London: Heinemann Educational Books

GRAMSCI A. (1971) *Selections from the Prison Notebooks*, ed. and trans. Quintin Hoare and Geoffrey Nowell Smith London: Lawrence and Wishart

GRANT J.C.B. (1958) *A Method of Anatomy. Descriptive and Deductive* London: Balliere, Tindall and Cox

GRAVES R. (1975) *Collected Poems* London: Cassell

GRAY T. (1980) 'Elegy written in a Country Churchyard' in LEESON E. (ed) *The New Golden Treasury of English Verse* London: Macmillan

GREENBERG F. (1967) *Jewish Cookery* Harmondsworth: Penguin (originally 1947 published by Jewish Chronicle Publications)

GROSS R.E. (ed.) (1965) *British secondary education* Oxford: Oxford University Press

HARLAND J. and WILKINSON T.T. (eds) (1882) *Ballads and Songs of*

Lancashire, Ancient and Modern Manchester, London: John Heywood

HARMAN C. (1986) 'Base and Superstructure' pp. 3-44 in *International Socialism 2:32* Summer 1986

HAYHOE M. and PARKER S. (eds) (1990) *Reading and Response* Milton Keynes, Philadelphia: Open University Press

HEANEY S. and HUGHES T. (eds) (1982) *The Rattle Bag, An Anthology of Poetry* London: Faber and Faber

HEANEY S. and HUGHES T. (eds) (1997) *The School Bag* London: Faber and Faber

HILL J. (1979) 'Ideology, Economy and the British Cinema', in *Ideology and Cultural Reproduction* ed. M. Barrett, P. Corrigan, A. Kuhn and J. Wolff London: Groom Helm

HOLLAND N. (1968) *The Dynamics of Literary Response* New York: Oxford University Press

HOLLINGWORTH B. (ed) (1977) *Songs of the People. Lancashire dialect poetry of the industrial revolution* Manchester: Manchester University Press

HOLUB R.C. (1984) *Reception Theory, A Critical Introduction* London, New York: Methuen

HOPKINS G.M. (1953) (ed W.H. Gardner) *Poems and Prose of Gerald Manley Hopkins* Harmondsworth: Penguin

HUGHES S. (1982) *Alfie Gets in First* London: Bodley Head

HUGHES T. (1967) *Poetry in the Making. An Anthology of Poems and Programmes from 'Listening and Writing'* London: Faber and Faber

HUGHES T. (1997) *By Heart. 101 Poems to Remember* London: Faber and Faber

ISER W. (1974) *The Implied Reader: Patterns of Communication in Prose Fiction from Bunyan to Beckett* Baltimore: The John Hopkins University Press

ISER W. (1978) *The Act of Reading: A Theory of Aesthetic Response* Baltimore, Maryland: John Hopkins University Press

JAMES A. and PROUT A. (eds) (1990) *Constructing and Reconstructing Childhood, Contemporary Issues in the Sociological Study of Childhood* London, New York, Philadelphia: The Falmer Press

JACKSON D. (ed) (1978) *Ways of Talking* London: Ward Lock Educational

JACKSON D. (1983) *Continuity in English Teaching* London: Methuen

JACKSON D. (1995) *Destroying the Baby in Themselves: Why did the two boys kill James Bulger?* Nottingham: Five Leaves Press

JACKSON L. (1994) *The Dematerialisation of Karl Marx, Literature and Marxist Theory* London, New York: Longman

JOHNSON P. (1994) *Twentieth Century Britain* London: Longman

JOYCE J. (1914-1915) *A Portrait of the Artist as a Young Man* (serialised in The Egoist'; published in one volume in 1916)

KAKUBOWSKI F. (1990) *Ideology and Superstructure in Historical Materialism* London, Winchester Mass.: Pluto Press

KARIER C.J. (1976) 'Liberalism and the quest for orderly change' pp. 90-97 in *Schooling and Capitalism, A Sociological Reader* edited by Roger Dale, Geoff Esland and Madeleine MacDonald (1976) London and Henley: Routledge, Kegan and Paul in association with the Open University

KEELE C.A., NEIL E. collaboration with JEPSON J.B. (1965) *Samson Wright's Applied Physiology. Eleventh Edition* London, New York, Toronto: Oxford University Press

KRISTEVA J. (1984) *Revolution in Poetic Language* trans. Margaret Waller

New York: Columbia University Press

KRISTEVA J. (1986) 'Word, dialogue and novel' in Toni Moi (1986) *The Kristeva Reader* Oxford: Oxford University Press (originally 'Bakhtin, le mot, le dialogue et le roman' in *Critique* 239, 1967 (438-65)

LACAN J. (1982) *Ecrits: A Selection* trans. Alan Sheridan, New York: W.W.Norton

LAING D. (1978) *The Marxist Theory of Art*, An Introductory Survey Sussex: Harvester Press

LAWRENCE D.H. (1977) (eds V.de Sola Pinto and Warren Roberts) *The Complete Poems* Harmondsworth: Penguin 1977

LCC (1950) *Trends in primary education* London: London County Council

LE GROS CLARK W. E. (1965) *The Tissues of the Body, An Introduction to the Study of Anatomy* Oxford: Clarendon Press.

LEONARD P. (1984) *Personality and Ideology. Towards a Materialist Understanding of the Individual* London: Macmillan

LESSING D. (1995) *Under My Skin, Volume One of My Autobiography To 1949* (1995) London: Flamingo, Harper Collins (originally 1994 London: Harper Collins)

LESTER J. (1971) *Search for the New Land, History as Subjective Experience* London: Allison and Busby

LEVI-STRAUSS C. (1976) 'Jean-Jacques Rousseau, founder of the Sciences of Man' in *Structural Anthropology* Vol 2: 33-43 1976 New York: Basic Books

LEVY C. (1991) *I'm Going to Pet a Worm Today and Other Poems* New York: McElderry/Macmillan)

LEVY C. (1994) *A Tree Place and Other Poems* New York: McElderry/Macmillan

LEWIS C. Day (1944) *Poetry for You, A Book for Boys and Girls on the Enjoyment of Poetry* London: Basil Blackwell

LEWIS C. Day (1947) *The Poetic Image* London: Jonathan Cape

LEWIS C. Day (1957) *The Poet's Way of Knowledge* Cambridge: Cambridge University Press

LIFSHITZ M. (1973) *The Philosophy of Art of Karl Marx* London: Pluto Press (originally 1933)

LINDSAY J. (1981) *The Crisis in Marxism* Bradford-on-Avon, Wiltshire: The Moonraker Press

LOWE R. (1988) *Education in the Post-War Years: A Social History* London: Routledge

LUKACS G. (1970) *Writer and Critic and other* essays (ed and trans. Professor Arthur Kahn) London: Merlin Press

MACCABE C. (1978) *James Joyce and the Revolution of the Word* London: Macmillan

MACCOBY H. (1986) *The Mythmaker, Paul and the Invention of Christianity* London: Weidenfeld and Nicolson

MACHEREY P. trans. Wall, G. (1978) *A Theory of Literary Production London*: Routledge and Kegan Paul. (1966, *Pour une theorie de la production litteraire* Paris: Librairie Francois Maspero)]

MACNEICE L. (1988) Selected Poems London: Faber and Faber

MANY J. and COX C. (eds) (1992) *Reader Stance and Literary Understanding, Exploring the Theories. Research and Practice* Norwood, New Jersey: Ablex Publishing Corporation

MARQUIS D. (1951) *Archy and Mehitabel* London: Faber and Faber (originally 1931)

MARX K. (1954) *Capital, A Critique of Political Economy* trans. Samuel Moore and Edward Aveling, Moscow: Progress Publishers (reprint with corrections of original English edition 1887 edited by Friedrich Engels)

MARX K. and ENGELS F. (1965) *The German Ideology* London: Lawrence and Wishart [written 1845-46]

MARX K. (1965) 'Feuerbach, Opposition of the Materialistic and Idealistic Outlook' pp. 27-96 in 'Critique of Modern German Philosophy According to its Representatives Feuerbach, Bruno Bauer and Stirner' in MARX K. and ENGELS F. *The German Ideology* London: Lawrence and Wishart [written 1845-46]

MARX K. (1965) 'Theses on Feuerbach' pp. 665-667 in MARX K. and ENGELS F. *The German Ideology* London: Lawrence and Wishart [written 1845]

MARX K. (1970a) Economic and Philosophical Manuscripts of 1844 (ed. Dirk J. Struik, trans. Martin Milligan) London: Lawrence and Wishart

MARX K. (1970b) 'Preface' pp. 19-23 in *A Contribution to the Critique of Political Economy* (trans. S.W. Ryazanskaya, edited by Maurice Dobb) Moscow: Progress Publishers; London: Lawrence and Wishart (originally 1859)

MARX K and ENGELS F. (1976) *On Literature and Art* Moscow: Progress Publishers

MEDVEDEV P.N. (1928, 1934) *Formal'nyj metod v literaturovedenii* [The formal method in literary scholarship] (1928, p. 42 in 1934 edition titled *Formalizmi formalisty* [Formalism and the formalists]) in TITUNIK I.R. (1986) Appendix 2: The Formal Method and the Sociological Method' (M.M. Baxtin, P.N. Medvedev, V.N. Voloshinov) in Russian Theory and Study of Literature' pp. 175-200 in VOLOSHINOV V.N. (1986) *Marxism and the Philosophy of Language* tr Ladislav Matejka and I.R. Titunik Cambridge Mass., London: Harvard University Press, [originally 1929; tr. 1973 Seminar Press]

MEEK M. (1988) *How Texts Teach What Readers Learn* Stroud, Glos.: The Thimble Press

MILNE A.A. (1965a) *When We Were Very Young* London: Methuen (originally 1924)

MILNE A.A. (1965b) *Now We Are Six* London: Methuen (originally 1927) 332

MILNE A.A. (1926) *Winnie-the-Pooh* London: Methuen

MILNE A.A. (1928) *The House at Pooh Corner* London: Methuen

MITCHELL A. (1968) *Out Loud* London: Cape Goliard Press

MORRIS M. (1950) in *Times Educational Supplement* 24 November 1950

MORRISON R.C.H. (1901) (ed) *Chambers's New Reciter* Edinburgh: W. and R. Chambers

MULHERN F. (1979) *The Moment of 'Scrutiny'* London: New Left Books

MULHERN F. (ed) (1992) *Contemporary Marxist Literary Criticism* London: Longman

NEVILLE R (1970) *Playpower* London: Cape

NEWBERY J. (1744) *A Little Pretty Pocket Book* London: John Newbery

NORRIS C. (1981) *Deconstruction: Theory and Practice* London: Methuen

OKELY J. (1978) 'Privileged, Schooled and Finished: Boarding Education for Girls' in ARDENER S. (ed) (1978) *Defining Females* London: Croom Helm

OPIE P. and OPIE I. (1959) *The Lore and Language of Schoolchildren* Oxford: Oxford University Press

PARKER E.W. (ed) (1949) *A Pageant of Modern Verse* London: Longman

PHILIP N. (ed) (1990) *A New Treasury of Poetry* London: Blackie

PRINCE G. (1988) *Dictionary of Narratology* Aldershot: Scolar Press

PRYER N. (9.9.1992) 'Schools to put English first, Patten orders big teaching shake-up' pp. 1-2 in *The Evening Standard* 9.9. 1992

REES N. (ed) (1981) *Eavesdroppings* London, Boston, Sydney: Unwin Paperbacks

REES N. (ed) (1982) *Foot in Mouth* London, Boston, Sydney: Unwin Paperbacks

REICH W. (1972) 'Preface to First Edition' (originally 1933) in *Character Analysis* (third enlarged edition) newly translated by Vincent R. Carfagno, ed Mary Higgins and Chester Raphael, New York: The Noonday Press, Farrar Straus and Giroux

RENZA LA. (1980) The Veto of the Imagination: A Theory of Autobiography' in OLNEY J. (ed) (1980) *Autobiography: Essays Theoretical and Critical* Princeton, New Jersey: Princeton University Press

RICHARDS I.A. (1924) *Principles of Literary Criticism* London: Routledge and Kegan Paul

RICHARDS I.A. (1929) *Practical Criticism. A Study of Literary Judgment* London: Routledge and Kegan Paul

RIFFATERRE M. (1990) 'Compulsory reader response: the intertextual drive' pp. 56-78 in WORTON M. and STILL J. (1990) *Intertextuality: theories and practices* Manchester: Manchester University Press

ROBINSON J. (1993) *The Individual and Society, a marxist approach to human psychology* London: Index Academic

ROSE N. (1997) 'Assembling the modern self' in PORTER R. (ed) (1997) *Rewriting the Self, Histories from the Renaissance* London, New York: Routledge

ROSEN H. (1993) *Troublesome Boy. Stories and Articles* London: The

English and Media Centre.

ROSEN M. (1969) *Backbone* London: Faber and Faber

ROSEN M. (1974) *Mind Your Own Business* London: Andre Deutsch

ROSEN M. (1977) *Wouldn't You Like to Know* London: Andre Deutsch

ROSEN M. and McGOUGH R. (1979) *You Tell Me* Harmondsworth: Kestrel Books, Penguin

ROSEN M. (1981a) *You Can't Catch Me* London: Andre Deutsch

ROSEN M. (1981b) *Wouldn't You Like to Know* (revised edition) Harmondsworth: Puffin

ROSEN M. and STEELE S. (eds) (1982) *Inky Pinky Ponky, Collected Playground Rhymes* London: Granada

ROSEN M. (1983) *Quick Let's Get of Here* London: AndreDeutsch

ROSEN M. (1985) *Don't Put Mustard in the Custard* London: Andre Deutsch

ROSEN M. (1989) *We're Going on a Bear Hunt* London: Walker Books; New York: McElderry

ROSEN M. (1990a) *Little Rabbit Foo Foo* London : Walker Books

ROSEN M. (1990b, 1997) *The Golem of Old Prague* London: Andre Deutsch; Nottingham: Five Leaves Press

ROSEN M. (ed) (1992a) *South and North , East and West, The Oxfam Book of Children's Stories* London: Walker Books; Boston: Candlewick

ROSEN M. (ed) (1992b) *Rude Rhymes* London: Signet, Penguin

ROSEN M. (ed) (1992c) *Sonsense Nongs* London: A and C Black

ROSEN M. (ed) (1994a) *Rude Rhymes* London: Signet, Penguin

ROSEN M. (1994b) *You are, aren't you?* Nottingham: Mushroom Bookshop/Jewish Socialist Publications.

ROSEN M. (1995a) 'Robert Louis Stevenson and Children's Play: The Contexts of A Child's Garden of Verses' pp. 53-72 in *Children's Literature in Education* Vol 26 no 1 March 1995

ROSEN M. (ed) (1995b) *Walking the Bridge of Your Nose* London: Kingfisher

ROSEN M. (1996) *You Wait Till I'm Older Than You* London: Viking

ROSENBLATT L. (1978) *The Reader. the Text. the Poem, The Transactional Theory of the Literary Work* Carbondale, Illinois: Southern Illinois University Press

ROSENBLATT L. (1985) 'Transaction versus interaction – a terminological rescue operation' pp. 96-107 in *Research in the teaching of English* 19 (1)

SANDBURG C. (1950) *Complete Poems* New York: Harcourt Brace and World

SARLAND C. (1991) *Young People Reading: Culture and Response* Milton Keynes, Philadelphia: Open University Press

SAUSSURE de F. (1959) *Course in General Linguistics* trans. Wade Baski New York: Philosophical Library

SCHOLTE B. (1972) 'Toward a Reflexive and Critical Anthropology' in HYMES D. (ed) (1972) *Reinventing Anthropology* New York: Pantheon Books

SCHOOLS' CURRICULUM AND ASSESSMENT AUTHORITY (May 1994) *English in the National Curriculum* London: Schools Curriculum and Assessment Authority and Central Office of Information

SEARLE J. R. (1995) *The Construction of Social Reality* New York: Free Press

SEIDLER V.J. (1989) *Rediscovering Masculinity* London, New York: Routledge

SEIDLER V.J. (ed) (1992) *Men, Sex and Relationships, Writings from Achilles Heel* London, New York: Routledge

SEIDLER V.J. 1994) *Recovering the Self, Morality and Social Theory* London, New York: Routledge

SEVE L (1975) *Marxism and the theory of human personality*, London: Lawrence and Wishart

SEVE L (1978) *Man in Marxist theory and the psychology of personality* Sussex: The Harvester Press trans. John McGreal [orig., *Marxisme et theorie de la personnalite*, Editions Sociales 1974]

SHAKESPEARE W. (1988) 'The History of Henry the Fourth (I Henry IV)' pp. 453-481; 'When icicles hang by the wall' in 'Love's Labour's Lost' Act 5 scene 2 p. 307 in *The Complete Works* eds Stanley Wells and Gary Taylor, Oxford: Clarendon Press

SHOTTER J. (1993) *Conversational Realities, Constructing Life through Language* London, Thousand Oaks, New Delhi: SAGE Publications

SINFIELD A. (1989) *Literature, Politics and Culture in Postwar Britain* Oxford: Basil Blackwell

SINGER I.B. (1980) *A Day of Pleasure, Stories of a Boy Growing up in Warsaw* London: Julia MacRae Books, A division of Franklin Watts (first published 1970, New York: Farrar, Straus and Giroux)

SLAUGHTER C. (1980) *Marxism, Ideology and Literature* London: Macmillan

SOUTHEY R. 'The Cataract of Lodore' pp. 168-169 in PHILIP N. (ed) 1990 *A New Treasury of Poetry* London: Blackie

STEPHENS J. (1992) *Language and Ideology in Children's Fiction* London, New York: Longman

STEVENS F. (1952) *Times Educational Supplement* 4 Jan 1952

STEVENSON R.L (1912) *The Works of Robert Louis Stevenson* Volume XIV including 'A Child's Garden of Verses', 'Underwoods', 'Ballads', 'Songs of Travel', 'Additional Poems', London: Chatto and Windus (originally 1885)

STYLES M. (1996) 'Poetry for Children' pp. 190-205 in HUNT P. (ed) (1996) *International Companion Encyclopedia of Children's Literature* London, New York: Routledge

SUMMERFIELD G. (ed) 1968 *Voices* (Three volumes and Teachers' handbook) Harmondsworth: Penguin

SUMMERFIELD G. (ed) (1970) *Junior Voices* (Four volumes and Teachers' handbook) Harmondsworth: Penguin

THE NEW ENGLISH BIBLE (1970) *The New English Bible* Swindon: The Bible Societies

THOMAS D. (1966) *Dylan Thomas. Miscellany Two, A Visit to Grandpa's and other stories and poems* London: J.M. Dent and Sons

THOMAS D. (1995) *The Dylan Thomas Omnibus* London: Phoenix Giants

THOMAS E. (1964) (ed R.S. Thomas) *Selected Poems* London and Boston: Faber and Faber

THOMAS G. (1953) *A Frost On My Frolic* London: Gollancz

THOMSON G. (1941) *Aeschylus and Athens, A Study in the Social Origins of Drama* London: Lawrence and Wishart (not for public sale).

TITUNIK I.R. (1986) Appendix 2: 'The Formal Method and the Sociological Method' (M.M. Baxtin, P.N. Medvedev, V.N. Voloshinov) in Russian Theory and Study of Literature' pp. 175-200 in VOLOSHINOV V.N. (1986) *Marxism and the Philosophy of Language* tr Ladislav Matejka and I.R. Titunik Cambridge Mass., London: Harvard University Press, [originally 1929; tr. 1973 Seminar Press]

TOWNSEND J.R. (1974) 'Life Lines' *The Guardian* 3.4.74

TROTSKY L (1960) *Literature and Revolution* University of Michigan Press

TROTSKY L (1970) *On Literature and Art* (ed Paul N. Siegel) New York: Pathfinder Press

TUNNICLIFFE S. (1984) *Poetry Experience. Teaching and Writing Poetry in Secondary Schools* London, New York: Methuen

'TWAIN, MARK' (CLEMENS S.L.) (1876) *The Adventures of Tom Sawyer* Hartford, Connecticut: American Publishing Company

UNIVERSITY OF NORTH LONDON (1996) *Research Degrees, Regulations and Notes for Guidance,* London: University of North London

UNTERMEYER L (ed) (1942) *Modern American Poetry. Modern British Poetry, Combined Edition. A Critical Anthology* New York: Harcourt Brace

USHER R. (1996) 'Textuality and reflexivity in educational research' in SCOTT D. and USHER R. (eds) (1996) *Understanding Educational Research* London, New York: Routledge

[VARIOUS] 'Beacon Readers' (1922 and thereafter) Aylesbury: Ginn

VERNON P.E. (1957) *Secondary School Selection* London: Methuen

VAIZEY J. (1958) *The costs of education* London: George Allen and Unwin

VOLOSHINOV V.N. (1986) *Marxism and the Philosophy of Language* tr. Ladislav Matejka and I.R. Titunik Cambridge, Mass., London: Harvard University Press, [originally 1929; tr. 1973 Seminar Press]

WEAVER T. (1954) *Public Records Office* Ed. 147/207 1954

WEISMILLER E.R. (1993) 'Sound Effects in Poetry' pp. 1180-1182 in Preminger A., Brogan T.V.F. (eds) (1993) *The New Princeton Encyclopedia of Poetry and Poetics* Princeton New Jersey: Princeton University Press

WESTALL R.A. (1975) *The Machine-Gunners* London: Macmillan

WHITE H. (1987) 'The Politics of Historical Interpretation' in *The Content of the Form*: Narrative Discourse and Historical Representation Baltimore

WHITMAN W. (1891-2) *Leaves of Grass* Philadelphia: David McKay

WIDERBERG S. (1973) *I'm Like Me, Poems for People Who Want to Grow Up Equal* trans. Verne Moberg New York: The Feminist Press

WILLANS G. and SEARLE R. (1953) *Down with Skool* London: Michael Joseph

WILLIAMS R. (1973) 'Base and Superstructure in Marxist Cultural Theory' pp. 3-16 in *New Left Review* 'Marxist Cultural Theory' No 82, November-December 1973

WILLIAMS R. (1977) *Marxism and Literature* Oxford: Oxford University Press

WIMSATT W.K. and BEARDSLEY M. (1958) *The Verbal Icon* New York:

WORTON M. and STILL J. (1990) *Intertextuality: theories and practices* Manchester: Manchester University Press

YEATS W.B. (1933) *The Collected Poems of W.B. Yeats* London: Macmillan

NEWSPAPERS REFERRED TO

Daily Telegraph June 13 1997' "Hit squad" goes in to rescue failing schools', Liz Lightfoot

Independent on Sunday Nov 11 1995 'Poetry in need: Please send money' Anon

The Evening Standard Nov 11, 1996 'Why Hackney is so full of optimism', Edward Welsh

The Guardian April 4 1974 John Rowe Townsend review

The Sun Sept 19 1997 'That'll teach you a lesson' Dave Wooding

The Times April 10 1974 'Leading young readers from mere verse . . . ' Brian Alderson

Times Educational Supplement Jan 5 1951

FILMS AND SHOWS REFERRED TO

Beyond the Fringe premiered Edinburgh Festival 1960 Bennett, Cook, Miller, Moore

Fiddler on the Roof (1971) USA Norman Jewison

Hamlet (1964) USSR Grigori Kozintsev

Proud to be British (1975) UK Nick Broomfield

The Battleship Potemkin (1925) USSR Sergei Eisenstein

COMICS MENTIONED BY NAME

The Beano

The Dandy

Rupert Bear

JOURNALS MENTIONED BY NAME

Achilles Heel

Books for Keeps

BIBLIOGRAPHY

Children's Rights Bulletin

Dragon's Teeth

International Times

Jewish Socialist

Language Matters (from the Centre for Language in Primary Education)

New Statesman

Oz

Private Eye

The English Magazine (from the English and Media Centre),

Appendix

Contents

Note: whether the initial letters of the words in the titles of the poems are lower or upper case is fairly random and a matter of my taste. I have preserved the form used in the particular poems as first presented as the work of this thesis and to the editors at Puffin Books.

Motto 276
Butter or margarine 277
Running 278
Found Poem: a reading wall-chart for children in about 1840 279
Found Poem: Safety instructions on United Airlines 1994 280
Who started it? 281
Butcher 282
Never-ending poem (for Sam Hurd) 283
Useful Instructions 285
Stealing 286
Raw Food 289
The Deal 292
Harrybo 294
Calculator 296
Hospital 297
On the question of whether it is possible to sleep on a train 298
Great Day 299
Eddie and the Supermarket 300
Never Have 304

Miss Stafford 306
Northumberland 307
My children's rules 309
The Nest 310
The Torch 317
Robin Hood's Bay 320
The Line 325
Talking tubes 329
Trousers down 330
Adverbs 334
My Books (forty years ago) 336
Teachers' Helper for end-of-assemblies 338
Invisible Ink 339
Berwick-on-Tweed 340
The Wedding 341
Gypsy 342
Mr Vassar the newsagent 343
Aldermaston March 344
What politicians mean when they say they are against other
    countries having nuclear weapons 345
Moishe 347
Muss i' den 348
Sam 350
The Shop Downstairs 351
Top Board 352
Stobs 353
Don't tell your mother 356
Leosia 358
Ted 360
Australia 361
Eddie and the car 372
Mr Baggs 381
My friend Roger 382
Mum's School 383
The cupboard 385
Essex 387
Pneumonia 388
Sweetshop 389

For Naomi 390

Three year old boy says.. 391

Conversation with a six year old....................................... 392

The Langham Cinema... 393

Proverbs 394

Sandwich... 396

Sultanas... 397

Trying to find out what my kid's homework is............... 398

Shirt... 399

Motto

The motto on the wall said,
'Seek and ye shall find'.
I looked for it everywhere
but it was stuck to my behind.

Butter or margarine

Row, row, row your boat
gently down the stream
merrily, merrily, merrily, merrily,
life is but a –
no it's not, it's margarine.

Running

Above the tap it said
'Run a long time
to get hot water.'

So I ran round the room for a really long time
but I didn't get any hot water.

Found Poem: a reading wall-chart for children in about 1840

"A man met a mad ram.
Do not let a fat cat sit on a bed.
Do not let it do so.
A fat cat ran at a rat and fed on it.
A red rod is for me, and a fat cat is for me.
A fan is for a man.
A lad ran for a bat for me.
A red rod is for a bad lad, and for me if I am bad.
A red rod and a fat cat."

Found Poem: Safety instructions on United Airlines 1994

"If you are sitting in an exit row
and you cannot understand this card
or cannot see well enough
to follow these instructions
please tell a crew member."

I thought:
But if I can't understand the card
how can I understand it
to tell someone I can't understand it?

Who started it?

When me and my brother have a fight
my mum says:
'Stoppit – someone'll get hurt'

and we say:
'He started it.'
'I didn't He started it.'

I say:
'Mum, who started the very first fight
between me and Brian?'

And she says:
'You.'

'Me? But I'm four years younger than him.
How could it have been me?'

And she says:
'Well, it was like this . . .

You were about two years old
and Brian was six
you were sitting in your high chair
eating your breakfast
and Brian walked past
You leaned forward
and banged him over the head with your spoon

'There you are,' says my brother,
'you started it
you started it
I always knew you started it.'

Butcher

In the butchers
there are
rows and rows
of bits of animals
bits of leg
bits of belly
bits of neck.
The butcher goes
chop
chop
chop
and the bits get smaller.

When he opens his mouth
I see all his teeth
and his tongue is as red
as a bit of animal's leg.

Never-ending poem (for Sam Hurd)

What's the name?
Sam
Sam who?
Sam Hurd
Sam heard what?
Sam Hurd nothing
You heard nothing?
Hurd's the name
What's the name?
Sam
Sam who?
Sam Hurd
Sam heard what?
Sam Hurd nothing
You heard nothing?
Hurd's the name
What's the name?
Sam
Sam who?
Sam Hurd
Sam heard what?
Sam Hurd nothing
You heard nothing'?
Hurd's the name
What's the name'?
Sam
Sam who?
Sam Hurd
Sam heard what?
Sam Hurd nothing
You heard nothing?
Hurd's the name
What's the name?
Sam who?
Sam Hurd
Sam heard what?

Sam Hurd nothing
You heard nothing?
Hurd's the name
What's the name?
Sam who?
Sam Hurd
Sam heard what?
Sam Hurd nothing
You heard nothing?
Hurd's the name
What's the name?

Useful instructions

Wipe that face off your smile
Don't eat with your mouthful
When you cough, put your ear over your mouth
Don't bite your nose
Don't talk while I'm interrupting
How many tunes do I have to tell you?!

Stealing

Harrybo says:
'That's the best toy car you've nicked yet,
it's—'
My dad walks in behind him.
'What did you just say, Harrybo?'

Great! he didn't hear Harrybo properly.

Harrybo turns round ' . . . about the car – the – er . . . '
'What car?'

Oh no! the questioning.

'Whose car is it?'
Together we say:
'It's Harrybo's.' 'It's Michael's.'
'Where's it from?'
'Woollies'
'So who paid for it?'
Together we say
'Him.' 'Him'
'It couldn't have been you, Michael,
you haven't got any money.
Where did you get the money from, Harrybo?'
'I didn't have the – er actually . . . '

It's all just about to blow up

'Look, tell me if I got this wrong
did I or did I not hear Harrybo say:
'it's the best toy car you've nicked yet?' '

There's no escape.

'Yiss.'
'What do you think Harrybo meant

286

when he said that?'

Play dumb.

'I'm not really sure.'
'Harrybo, what did you mean
when you said:
'It's the best toy car you've nicked yet.'?'
Silence.

'Do you think Michael nicked the car?'
'Oh no. I wouldn't think he'd do a thing like that.'

Fool, Harrybo. He'll pounce on that.

'See, Michael, even your best friend . . .

My best friend!

thinks you're not the sort of person
who'd do a thing like that.
Aren't you really sick of yourself?'

Course Harrybo doesn't think that.
He's got a Bluebird racing car
that he nicked
in his trouser pocket.

'Yes.'
'Well, you know what you're going to do,
don't you?'
'Yes.'
'What?
'Take it back'
'Exactly. And when you get back here
you, me and your mother
are going to have a long talk about this,
aren't we?'

I thought we just had

'Aren't we?'
'Yiss'

Raw Food

Harrybo's dad grew hundreds of vegetables
and Harrybo used to say:
'Let's go down the garden . . . '
and he'd attack his dad's broad beans.
'Come on, you have some,' he says,
and he's munching through five of them.
I didn't like them very much.
Maybe I'd just have one
to show I wasn't feeble.

Then he'd go for the peas.
'These are GREAT,' he says,
'really sweet
And he'd stick his thumb in the pod
and squirt a row of raw peas into his mouth.

Sometimes he'd pull up radishes and carrots,
wipe the mud off them
bite the tops off
and munch up the rest

'You want to try potatoes, Michael,' he says,
and he'd heave one of his dad's potatoes up,
wipe the mud off that too
and –
crunch –
he'd eat a raw potato
then
red currants
black currants
gooseberries.

I said the red currants
smelt like cat's pee
Didn't bother him.
He'd gobble these till his chin

ran red.

And the apples.
His dad grew the hardest, bitterest apples
you've ever seen, with knobbly, leathery skins.

'Great!' says Harrybo,
'let's get at the apples.'
And he'd munch them up:
the whole thing –
the core
the pips
the little hairy bits at the ends.
He left nothing.

He even found some little green pip things.
'Stursham seeds', he called them.
'Try these,' he says.
They were sour, peppery beans.
Horrible.
'I love these,' he says
and he'd scoop handfuls of them into his mouth.

It was incredible watching him
roaming round the garden
grabbing at anything growing.
He chewed grass.
He ate dandelion leaves.
'These are just great, Michael,' he says.
'You ought to eat them, you know.

That was years ago.
Nowadays people write books about healthy eating
and fresh food
and they're called things like:
'Raw Energy' and
'Get Healthy – Eat Trees!'

People sit there very carefully nibbling at
one raw mushroom
thinking they're doing something
danngly healthy.

Harrybo would have munched up twenty.

The Deal

My brother once told me that
Mum and Dad had a deal about
telling off.

He said that
if one of them was telling one of us off
then the other parent
wouldn't join in.
He said that they'd said
it wasn't fair on a kid
if both parents had a go
at the same time.

It worked like that most of the time.

My dad would get angry about something.
Like the time I stuck toothpaste
in his shaving soap:
'What did you think?
I wouldn't notice?
The little fool!
He spends hours and hours in that bathroom
and we think he's washing himself!
But this is the sort of monkey business
he's getting up to
This is my shaving soap.
Not yours
If you want to play about with shaving soap
buy your own.'

And Mum wouldn't say a word. Not a word.
But somehow when it was Mum's turn

it didn't quite work out the same way.
She'd be telling me off
for not cleaning my shoes:

'How can you go out like that?
You look like a tramp.
I don't want to be seen in the street with you.
All I'm asking is that you give them a wipe.
A little wipe.
That wouldn't harm you, would it?'
And out of the corner of my eye
I could see my dad
twitching about
itching to join in.
He's nodding and tutting
and coming in with:
'Quite!'
and
'You're right there, Connie.'

Then when Mum went out the room
he'd burst out with:
'You've pushed your mother to the edge this time.'

Never mind her,
he was well *over* the edge.

Harrybo

People often say to me
'What's become of Harrybo,
the boy in your poems?'

And I say:
'When I was 11
we had to do an exam
called the 11-plus.
I passed and went to a Grammar School.
Harrybo failed
and went to a Secondary Modern School.

So though up till then
we used to see each other every day
– weekends as well
after that,
we didn't see much of each other at all.
I'd see him from the bus
talking with his new friends
and I was with mine
One time when we met
he told me that once
him and his girlfriend were snogging
in his front room
and his mum was looking in
through the window.
It sounded very different from exploring
the ponds
and making go-karts.

When I was 17
we moved
and I didn't see him again.

When I was 38
I visited my old school

and a boy said his dad knew me
from when we were children
and he would like me to come back
for tea at his place.

When I got there I found out it was Jimmy.
Giggly Jimmy, who hopped about on one foot
if he thought something was funny.
He's a truck driver now.

Jimmy said:
'Harrybo died when he was 17.
I don't know where his parents are.
They moved.'

Before Jimmy told me this
I had sometimes wondered
if somewhere some time
Harrybo had read all these things
I've been writing about him . . .
but he hadn't.

Calculator

If you turn a calculator upside down
you can make the numbers look like letters.

4 is h
3 is E
7 is L
8 is B
5 is S
6 is g
0 is O
I is I
2 is Z

so type in
8075 07734
turn the calculator round and you've got
hELLO SLOB

you can type in
BOB gIggLES
BOB gOBBLES BOILS
 LIZZIE gOBBLES OIL
LIZZIE SIZZLES
BOB gOggLES
g0 gOB
Oh BOSh BOB..

 . . . and other things just as useful.

Hospital

There's a boy on the other side of the ward
and his face is completely covered in plaster.

There's a man called Charlie and his face
has been burnt off. He's got no face. He shows
 me a picture of himself before his accident. He
used to look like Elvis Presley.

The nurse says: When you go into the
operating theatre they're going to bang
your nose straight with a rubber hammer.

I'm here because I was hit by a cricket ball.
I fell to the ground and shooting pains
went into my eyes. The teacher rushed
over and said: Did you catch it?

My mother has a shiny dent in her nose
with a little ridge down the middle of it. It
looks like someone took a bite out of her
nose and its the mark of two front teeth
with the gap in the middle. She says when
she was five she walked into a car.

In a moment I am going to be wheeled
out of here on a bed, they're going
to put me to sleep and bang my nose
with a rubber hammer.

Poor Charlie

On the question of whether it is possible to sleep on a train

Can I sleep on the train?
Can I sleep on the train?
Can I sleep?

On the train
On the train
On the train
On the train
Can I sleep?

On the train
On the train
On the train
On the train
I sleep.

Great Day

Can't find the bathroom
Can't find my socks
Can't find the corn-flakes
Can't find the lunch-box
Can't find the book-folder
Can't find the front door
Can't find school Can't find the class-room
Can't find the pen
Can't find the paper
Can't find the lunch-box
Can't find the pen
Can't find the paper
Can't find the way home
Can't find the front door
Can't find my plate
Can't find the television
Ah – find bed.

Eddie and the Supermarket

Shopping with Eddie was a nightmare.

I lift Eddie up and squeeze him into the seat
on the shopping trolley.
'In you get, little feller.'
So he goes rigid.
He turns himself into a little fat iron bar
that can't be bent. I can't push his legs through the spaces.
'In you get, Eddie.'
Push.
'I said,
in
you
(push)
get
Eddie
(squeeze)'

Slowly he lets his legs relax
and I unbend them and thread them
into the trolley

And off we go
We're wheeling past the baked beans
and he leans out and grabs a can.
'Bince. More bince '
'No, Eddie, we don t need any more beans.'
'Bince, bince, bince, bince, bince—'
'No, we don't need any beans.'
'Bince, bince, bince, bince, bince.'
'No Beans, Eddie'

Were heading now for the Kit Kats, Penguins, Topic Bars
Crunchies, Milky Ways . . .
He stops shouting, 'Bince, bince, bince . . . '
and he leans out of his seat

300

arms waving
we whizz round the corner of the
packs of chocolate wafers
and his chunky little hand grabs a packet.
'Wheeeeee – chocleet – wheeee.'
'We're going to take that packet back Eddie.
We're going to take that packet back.'
Then there's an explosion:
'My chocleet. My chocleet. My chocleet.'
He turns into the little fat iron bar again.
In front of my eyes he becomes a screaming demon,
head flung back
face going red
eyes getting swollen
back stiff
hands punching out
body heaving to and fro.

A woman is looking at me
and saying to herself:
You're a torturer.
You're horrible to babies.

'My chocleet. Bince, bince, bince, bince.'

Some people walk about pretending
nothing is going on.
But I can tell they're in pain.
The noise of Eddie is getting into their bones.

People are moving away from us.
There's a man over there
hurrying to get to the kitchen rolls.
Eddie is wrenching the bars of the trolley,
'Chocleet bince. My chocleet bince.'
I want some kitchen rolls too
So the man who's trying
to get away from me thinks

he's being hunted by Eddie.

Then one of the shelf-stackers
tries to be friendly.
He looks at the screaming blob called Eddie
and winks, does some useless trick with his finger
and says:
'Oooh it's not that bad, little one.'

Thank you, shelf-stacker, brilliant finger move.
She is making a fuss, isn't she?'
says our jolly shelf-stacker.
Eddie is veering about so much
the shelf-stacker can't even tell it's a boy.
'Bince, bince, bince. Chocleet, chocleet, chocleet.'

I head for the check-out
I'm in an old war film.
I'm the submarine commander
and the submarine is leaking . . .
but I'm brave, I stay on board
while everyone else leaves the ship.
The noise of the engines is deafening,
I look ahead with calm, sure eyes . . .
But I want to scream as well.

I want to yell my head off too.
I want to run round the supermarket
waving my arms about
screaming, 'Bince, bince, bince.'
I want to sit in someone's trolley
and bend the bars
and drop baked bean cans on the floor
and grab chocolate biscuits
and drive my dad crazy.

Then the Security Men arrive.
They've come to collect the money

from the cash registers.
There's four of them.
They're huge –
in big padded blue uniforms
with crash helmets on
and truncheons in their belts.
This is my chance:
'Eddie, look who's come to get your

He looks
he looks
and he stops howling.

All round me people relax
they smile
they chat.
I glide through paying my bill.
We all float out into the car park.
Everything feels nice and easy.

When we get home
I find that I have forgotten to get
bread, jam, toilet rolls, milk
orange juice, tuna fish and corn flakes.
'Dinner time, Eddie,' I say,
'What do you want?'
'Bince,' says Eddie
I go to the cupboard.
He was right.
We have run out of beans.
I say:
'Eddie, I'm sorry but we've run out of beans.
No beans.'
And he says:
'Bince, bince, bince, bince, bince, bince . . . '

Never Have

They said there was a badger.
We went and looked
at a hole in the ground.
There was a log, a hump
a thousand dents in the earth.
'Badgers' feet did that,' they said.
I dreamt of coming at midnight,
brave and quiet,
up a tree
to watch them sniffing about.

Years later
on the road from Strangford
there—
trapped by the headlights
bigger than a rabbit
was it a dog?
White stripe, black stripe
This wild hurrying thing
made the thousand dents?
Up a tree
brave and quiet
at midnight
I might have watched it sniffing.

Then in a daytime
passing a brown field
with all the stubble turned under
there was one
dead.
We stood beside it.
'Maybe it ate poison,' says one.
'They do poison the ground,' says another.
'I think someone shot it,' says another.
'It got old, rolled over, and just died,' says another.

A maggot moved in the gums.
Then I touched one claw of one toe
nothing more
because
I never have been brave and quiet.

Miss Stafford

We had old Bible stories in the hall
when I was at school.
Miss Stafford marched across the floor
with her box of coloured chalks.
There were the Pharaoh's dreams
and only Joseph could say what they meant.
There was Abraham holding a knife
to the neck of his beloved son.
There were the nasty brothers
who threw Joseph down a well
because they were jealous of his
many-coloured coat.

Miss Stafford marched across the floor
with her box of coloured chalks
and she drew prisons and daggers
and mountains and city walls
but best of all she drew Joseph's many-coloured coat:
green, red, blue, purple, yellow and white.
What a coat
Every chalk in the box.
No wonder the brothers were jealous.

Miss Stafford marched across the floor
with her box of coloured chalks.

Northumberland

He took me, a boy of eleven, up on the moor
and showed me sheep stuck on their backs.
'They roll over to scratch theirselves.
The wool takes up the water
they can't rise.'
He grabs a blackface and heaves it out of the hollow.
'They die if I don't do that.
You and your mum and dad don't believe in God
do you?'

He took me to the stable
and showed me a cow
with a chain round her neck.
'Milk fever,' he says.
He holds a bottle above her neck,
runs a tube down to a needle.
He jabs the needle into the cow.
A big flat bubble swells up
under the cow's skin
around the root of the needle.
Her eyes roll and whiten.
'You're afraid she'll die, aren't you?
I'm not afraid of death.
You are'

He took me into the field
and showed me a cow with her calf
lying in the pool of its afterbirth.
'If it doesn't get up
I'll have to take it away.
If I touch it too soon, mind
the cow won't have anything to do with it.
Reject it.'
We watched.
'Could you kill a man?
I had to choose.

Kill or be killed.
What would you do?
There it's up – it won't need a bottle.
The cow'll eat all that stuff now.
You wouldn't, would you?'

My children's rules

Last one to the door is a smelly.
She's not allowed in my room
when I've got my pants off.
First one to the door is a smelly.
He's not allowed to jump on my head
before I wake up in the morning.
Second one to the door is a smelly.
He can't do a poo in here when I'm in the bath.
Anyone who gets to the door is a smelly.

The Nest

Miss Goodall has this idea of having a Nature Table
and we all had to bring into school
things we'd found.

Soon the table was piled high with stuff:
brambles, acorns, worms, woodlice
dead leaves . . .

so Miss Goodall said,
No need to bring in anymore Nature things
thank you very much.
What we're going to do now
is have a Wall Chart. A Nature Watch.
I want you to write up on the chart
the date, your name
and What You Have Observed.'

It started off OK.
11/10/54, Sheena Maclean, I saw a robin
12/10/54, Melanie Baxter, Today there was a duck.
But it wasn't long before
it started turning into a competition.
14/10/54, Michael Rosen, I saw a robin *and* a duck.

Things were getting
pretty hot
round the Nature Chart.

One night while I was walking home
through the Memorial Park
I was getting to thinking about
what I could write up tomorrow
on the Nature Chart.
Wouldn't it be great
to see something really good
on the way home from school?

Like a
walrus.
Then I thought about how it would be great
to find a nest of baby animals.
Like a nest of baby vultures.
I remembered how
I had once seen a film
of a bird that lays its eggs on the ground.
Well –
I could find a nest on the ground,
couldn't I?
Trouble was
there were no nests on the ground
in the Memorial Park.
But there was plenty of dead grass lying around . . .
. . . so maybe I could pick up some of this dead grass
and make something.

I twisted the grass around
poked it about
and I made something
that looked like a bird's nest.

Then I worked out a plan
that would *prove* it was a nest.
When I got to school the next day
everyone would think I was brilliant
at Nature.

I left my nest lying on the ground
and walked home
Next morning, my friend Harrybo calls for me
and off we go to school
through the Memorial Park.

So I say to Harrybo:
'Hey, let's walk over this way, eh?'
'No,' he says.

'Go on,' I say, 'we might find *something*.'
'Oh, OK,' he says.
So I led off in the direction of the nest.

I didn't want to lead him there
and find it.
He might get suspicious
and say it was a trick.
I wanted us to see it together,
maybe him a little bit first
then he'd believe it was real.
Good plan.. .the only trouble was:
I couldn't see it anywhere.
I didn't know where to lead him.
Maybe it had blown away.
'Come on,' says Harrybo, 'or we'll be late.'
'No hang on,' I say.
'What are you doing?' he says.
'Oh, you know. Just looking for Nature,
come on over here. You look.'

Then I saw it.
The nest.
It was still there.
He wasn't going to see it.
My plan wasn't working.
So I just pretended not to look surprised
and said:
'Hey Harrybo, I don't suppose this is anything, is it?'
He comes over.
'Michael. That's a nest.
That
is
a
nest.'
'Is it?' I say
'Yep. Amazing. That's what it is alright.
That's a nest.

We could take that into school', he says
'and write it up on the Nature Chart.
No one's ever found a nest before.
Incredible

So we picked up the nest
and took it into school.
We put it on Miss Goodall's table
and all the other kids crowded round:
'Where did you find it?'
'It's brilliant.'
'It could be an eagle's.'

Harrybo put on his important voice
and said,
'Look, er, don't touch it, OK?
Its a bird's nest.
We were looking for Nature
and we spotted it.
I knew it was a nest straightaway.'

Miss Goodall looked at us
and looked at the nest.
She had a way of raising one eyebrow
and smiling
if she thought something funny was going on.
'Looks to me,' she said, 'like someone made it.
Some little fingers or other made it.'

I looked at it sitting on her table.
It didn't look much like a bird's nest at all.
In fact, it looked just like what it was:
a heap of dead grass that someone had twisted about a bit.

But Harrybo was quite cross:
'Oh no Miss Goodall,' he says.
'We found this when were looking for Nature.
It was there on the ground.

Actually Miss,
if Michael hadn't said
let's go over the grassy bit
we'd've missed it.
That was really lucky he said that.'

Miss Goodall now looked at *me* very hard.
Her eyebrow still up.
I said nothing.
'Can we write it up on the Nature Chart, now?'
says Harrybo.
'Not just now, 'says Miss Goodall,
'it's assembly time.'

Now we didn't get to writing it up
all that day.
Or the next
The nest sat on her table
getting looser and looser
until all it was
was a heap of dead grass.

I hated looking at it.
Surely everyone could see now
it was all a big trick.
Someone was bound to say
that we made it
Then I would go red
and I would be shown up
in front of everybody.
But no one said anything
and Harrybo
kept going on about
what a Great Find it was.
I started to wish he'd just shuttup about it,
or someone would steal it.

A week or two later

we got to school one day
and the nest was gone.
so was the Nature Chart.
Harrybo said,
'Miss Goodall,
why have you taken down the Nature Chart?'
'Oh,' she said, 'I thought it was time for a change.
Anyway,' she says, looking at me,
things were getting a bit
silly
don't you think?'
'Were they?' I said.
'Yes,' she said,
'they were.
But if you want your nest back, boys
I've put it under the sink.'
'That's OK,' I said.
'I haven't really got anywhere to put it.'
'I have,' said Harrybo, 'brilliant.
I'll take it home, Miss and keep it in my room.
When you come over my place, Michael
you can look at it anytime you like.'
'Thanks.'

That night he took it home
put it on his chest of drawers
and every time I went over to his place
he showed it to me.
He never let me forget the great day
we found a real bird's nest
on the ground
at Memorial Park.
He never seemed to wonder
why I didn't jump up and down
and get as excited as he did.
He just loved looking at it,
Thinking about the bird that made it.

I tried to forget about it.
I couldn't.
I haven't.
And that was forty years ago . . .
and I never did tell Harrybo the truth.

The Torch

I nagged my mum and dad for a torch.
'Oh go on. I'd love a torch.
One of those ones with black rubber round them.
Go on. Pleeeeeeese.'

It was no good. I wasn't getting anywhere.
Then came my birthday.
On the table was a big box
in the box
a torch.
My dad took it out the box 'You see that torch,' he says
its waterproof.
That is a waterproof torch.'

Waterproof. Wow!

So that night I got into the bath
and went underwater swimming with it.
Breathe in,
under the water,
switch on
search for shipwrecks
and treasure
Up breathe
under again
exploring the ocean floor.

Then the torch went out.
I shook it and banged it but it wouldn't go.
I couldn't get it to go again.
My birthday torch.
So I got out, dried myself off
put on my pyjamas and went in to the kitchen.

'The – er – torch won't work. It's broken.'
And my Dad says,

'What do you mean, it's broken?'
It couldn't have just broken.
How did it break?'
'I dunno, it just went off.

'I don't believe it. You ask him a simple question
and you never get a simple answer.
You must have been
doing something with it.'
'No. It just went off.'
'Just try telling the truth, will you?
How
did
it
break?'
'I was underwater swimming with it.'

'Are you mad?
When I said the torch is waterproof
I meant it keeps the rain off. I didn't mean you could go deep sea
diving with it.
Ruined. Completely ruined.
For weeks and weeks he nags us stupid that he wants
one of these waterproof torches
and then first thing he does is wreck it.
How long did it last?
Two minutes'? Three minutes?
These things cost money, you know.
Money.'

I felt so rotten.
My birthday torch.

At the weekend, he says,
Were going into Harrow to take the torch back.

We walk into the shop,
my dad goes up to the man at the counter

and says:
'You see this torch.
I bought it from you a couple of weeks ago
its broken.

So the man picks it up.
'It couldn't have just broken,' says the man,
how did it break?'
'I dunno' says my dad, 'it just went off.'
'Surely you must have been doing something
with it'
'No, no, no,' says my dad, 'it just went off.'
'Come on,' says the man, 'these torches don't just break down.'
So I said
'Well, actually, I was in the –'
and I got a hard kick on the ankle from my dad.
'I was in the, you know, er kitchen and it went off.'
So the man said that he would take it out the back
to show Len.
He came back a few minutes later and said that Len
couldn't get it to work either
so he would send it back to the makers.
'You'll have to have a new one,' he says.
'I should think so too,' says my Dad.
'Thank YOU.'

Outside the shop
my dad says to me,
'What's the matter with you?
Are you crazy?
You were going to tell him all about your underwater swimming,
weren't you?
Blabbermouth!'

Robin Hood's Bay

It was summertime
and it was hot.
We were on holiday in Yorkshire.
My friend Paul said:
'Why don't we go and explore the old railway tunnel?'
and I said:
'Yeah, good idea.'

So we did.
We left our mums and dads at the tents.
When we got there
the tunnel was dark
all the bricks were covered in black soot
from the smoke of the old steam engines
that used to run through.
You couldn't see the other end.
It was like a great, empty, black space in front of us.

Paul said:
'I don't think I want to go in there.'
and I said:
'What shall we do then?'
and he said
'We could walk to the station.'
and I said:
'Yeah, good idea.'

So we did
We walked along the old railway tracks
to the station.
As we walked
we jumped from sleeper to sleeper
and did horrible things to slugs.

When we got to the station, Paul said:
'How much money have you got?'

and I said:
'Two and six.' (That's about 13p nowadays)
and he said:
'Me too. We could go to Robin Hood's Bay
and back with that.'
and I said:
'Yeah, good idea.'

So we did.
On the train
by the sea
through the sand dunes
over bridges
along the cliff tops.

When we got to Robin Hood's Bay
we walked along the beach
we paddled in the sea
we diddled along in the wet sand
and Paul said:
'There are fossils here, you know.'
and I said:
'Are there?'
and he said:
'Let's look for some.'
and I said:
'Yeah, good idea.'

So we did.
We picked up hundreds and hundreds of stones.
They were a sort of grey-blue colour.
We didn't find any fossils.
There was a stream though
and we piled up stones in the river
to make a dam
Hundreds and hundreds of stones.
It didn't dam the river
it made a kind of bridge.

Then Paul said:
'I think we ought to go back soon.'
and I said:
'Yeah, good idea.'

So we did.
We caught the train back:
by the sea
through the sand dunes
over bridges
along the cliff tops.
We walked back along the tracks to the tents.

Just as we were nearly there
I saw Paul's Dad.
He had a pair of binoculars in his hand: they were muddy.
He started shouting:
'Here they are! Here they are!
Here they are!'
and he was waving his arms.
He rushed up to us.
'Where have you been?
Where have you been?'
and Paul said:
'Robin Hood's Bay. It was really good.'
and Paul's Dad said:
'Robin Hood's Bay? You must be mad.'

Just then, I saw my Mum and Dad.
They were running up the road
and shouting to Paul's Dad:
'Where did you find them?'
Paul's Dad looked up at the sky
shook his head
and raised his arms and he said:
'They've been to Robin Hood's Bay,
would you believe!'
and my Dad said:

'Robin Hood's Bay? Robin Hood's Bay?
They must be out of their minds.'
and Paul's Dad said:
'We've been hunting for you, for hours.
We've been worried sick.
We thought you were stuck in the tunnel.
I thought you may have been run down
by a train.
We've been all over the cliffs looking for you.
We thought you might have fallen down the cliffs.'

My Dad said:
'Why did you go to Robin Hood's Bay?
Whose idea was that?'
and Paul said:
'It was my idea. All my own idea.'
and my Dad and Paul's Dad looked at me and said:
'Paul's idea? Paul's idea?
What did *you* say to Paul
when he came up with this idea?'
and I said:
'I thought it was a good idea.'
and they said: 'A good idea? A good idea?
for goodness sake, You're older than him.
He's only seven. You're ten years old.
You know better than that.
We've got to go and phone the police now.'
and Paul said:
'Can I come?'
and Paul's Dad said:
'No you can't.
I've got to go and tell them
that we've found you
and they don't have to get the helicopter out
looking for you
and Paul said:
'OK Dad'
I just stood there.

After that we went off to have something to eat.
It wasn't lunch
because it was after lunch-time
it wasn't tea
because it was after tea-time.

Paul's Dad didn't speak to me for the rest of the holiday.
Actually he's scarcely spoken to me ever since.
That was forty years ago.

The Line

When the new school was opened we had to line up, Girl here, Boy there, Girl
here, Boy there. Miss Wheelock, who was the Headmaster's Deputy Sheriff
said: 'In this school, there will be a Boys' Playground and a Girls'
Playground. I want you all to draw an imaginary line between the top of the
steps *here*, over to the edge of the United Dairies on the other side of the fence
up *there*. I don't ever want to see any boy crossing the Line in morning playtime,
dinner-time, or afternoon playtime and I don't want to see anyone loitering
along the line.'

In the first week I was at the new school, I got to know a girl called Frances who
tried to teach me how to skip. This was difficult because she had to stand on on
one side of the Imaginary Line and I had to stand on the other. First of all she
skipped for a bit and then carefully making sure her feet kept to her side she
passed the skipping rope over the Line to me – where I was making sure my
feet were keeping to my side. Then I skipped.

Miss Wheelock saw this and said, 'I'm going to put a stop to this. If you want to learn
how to skip, boy, then bring your own skipping rope. I've said: I don't want
anyone crossing the line. Passing a skipping rope *over* the line is just the
same as *crossing* the line, isn't it ? Frances I'm surprised at you. I thought you
knew better'

I thought: that's funny. We've only been at the new school a week. Why's she
surprised at Frances but she wasn't surprised at me? Not long after this,
something much more serious happened to us and the Line.

Gunter the German brought a ball to school that said 'Handball' on it. Someone
kicked it and we all went haring across the Line to get it. The whistle went
off and Miss Wheelock screamed. She wanted everyone to stop moving.
'Everyone stop moving. Stop moving. Stop moving. I want that ball Gunter,'
she said, 'I want that ball.'

Gunter didn't know what was going on except he wasn't going to give the ball to
anyone – least of all to her. 'I want that ball, Gunter,' she said, 'and by God, I'll
have it, boy.' So she started off walking across the playground towards
him.

There was the playground, absolutely still, with all of us standing there, like skittles all over it, except for Miss Wheelock marching for Gunter the German's Handball. All boys one side of the Imaginary Line. All girls on the other. Except for a group of us, miles *over* the Line. It took ages for her to get to us.

'Give me that ball, Gunter,' she said, 'I want it.' Gunter didn't say anything. He just held on to it a bit harder, hugging it to his chest. He couldn't speak English. He'd only been in England a week or two and he was still wearing his yellow shoes.

Miss Wheelock prodded the Handball. 'Ball – Gunter – Ball.' Gunter hugged the Handball. Everyone else for miles and miles, right the way across the playground was standing still, right up as far as the climbing frame in the Nursery playground. No one talked.

So Miss Wheelock got her hands round the German's Handball and heaved on it. But he wouldn't let go. It was *his* Handball. Miss Wheelock and him were still heaving on it and she was still screaming, 'Ball – Gunter – ball,' when I booed.

And the moment I booed, Harrybo booed and all of us who had run all this way over the Line booed. But Miss Wheelock, who was bigger than Gunter, even though she was a tiny grown-up, actually got hold of the Handball and wrenched it out of Gunter's hands.

Gunter started gulping in big sobs but he didn't say anything. She turned on us and said, 'Never, never, never, in all my time—' when suddenly up the steps at the end of the Imaginary Line, came the Headmaster.

We stopped booing. The whole thing had got too big for booing. But he had seen what was going on. 'You,' he says, 'You – you – you – and you.' And, no trouble, he knew which ones of us to get, because we were standing there, the only boys out of the whole school, in girl-country.

'You – you – you,' he said, 'go straight to my study and *no* running.' Then he turned to Miss Wheelock, his Deputy Sheriff and said, 'Are you *alright*, Miss Miss Wheelock?' And Miss Wheelock took out her hankie and dried the corners of her mouth.

It was miles and miles to his room and all the way I was thinking: I started the booing, so I'll be the one to get it. On the way there, there were hundreds of girls' faces right down to the tines, all watching. Though some of them were so good they didn't even dare look at us. They just stared at the ground, afraid that if they looked into our eyes, they'd catch some of our evil spirit

Gunter was still gulping. He didn't know what was going on. He hadn't done anything wrong. Miss Wheelock had. She had stolen his Handball. 'Come in. Come in,' said the Headmaster, breathing through his nose and quivering his nostrils. I'll make them hear me breathing. I'll make them hear every bit of breath I've got. Up *and* down my nose. They'll learn what it means to break my rules and boo my teachers.

Why do we have the Line? Eh? What's it for? For fun? For my amusement? You! Why do we have the Line?' No one knew why we had the Line. 'Come on. Come on. Come on. Don't waste anymore of my time.' 'Because they're girls sir.' It wasn't what he wanted.

'You! Why do we have the Line?' 'I don't know, sir.' 'You!' 'I don't know, sir.' 'You!' 'I don't know, sir.' 'Then I'll tell you why.' He was walking about all over the place.

'Because I knew, long before we moved into these buildings that your parents have paid for, that there would be trouble from children like you. And I sat down here in this room and I thought: How am I going to stop that little group of boys – and it will be boys – and there are always some in every school how am I going to stop them from spoiling everything for everyone else?

Well, I said to myself, maybe it does seem as if it always happens like that but it's not going to happen in my school.' And it was Miss Wheelock who put me on to it: 'The trouble' she said, 'always starts in the playground. That's where the trouble starts.' And I think she's right.

I come out on to the playground. And there you are. *That little group.* Screaming about amongst the girls, spoiling their games, then daring to catcall Miss Wheelock: the school's Deputy Head Teacher. You must think we're mad to even–' 'At my last school, sir, we–' 'But you're at *this* school, boy.'

327

So he gave us the cane three times for going into girl country and three times for booing. He did the cane with a bamboo stick, bringing it down on our hands as fast and as hard as he could. 'I'm putting this down in a book,' he said, 'where it will never be forgotten.'

Talking-tubes

I believe everything my brother tells me
that's why I know about talking-tubes in old houses.

Once we went to this old house
and the guide who was taking us round
told us that there were tubes
running through the massive great thick walls
so that the people in the olden days
could talk to each other.

After the guide went off
my brother explained to me
that these talking tubes were only discovered
a short while ago.
He said they were closed up
with great big corks.

He said
when the people who discovered them
pulled the corks out
they heard
all these old words from hundreds of years ago.
They heard knights-in-armour talking.
What they said just came tumbling out of the talking-tubes.
Amazing

I believe everything my brother tells me
that's why I know about talking-tubes in old houses.

Trousers down

My best friend Mart said that
we could take rucksacks and drinks
and sandwiches and raisins and chocolate and
go and climb The Sugarloaf.

I said that it was miles and we might get lost
but he said he knew how to read maps
and we had walked 15 miles in a day before
when we went with our parents.

So we did,
we climbed The Sugarloaf
all on our own
with our rucksacks.

It's a mountain with one bit in Wales
and one bit in England.
We were so pleased when we got to the top
we said we ought to celebrate.
We discussed this as we sat at the top
eating our sandwiches and raisins and chocolate.

'I know,' said Mart
I've got it.
You see that path down there?
that's the way we go to get home.
Somewhere along that path
is the border between Wales and England.
We leave Wales and we go into England.
What we do,' he said
is we celebrate by walking into England
with our trousers down.'

'But how will we know where the border is?'
I said.
Well,' he said,

'I don't know exactly where it is
but by looking at the map
I've got a pretty good idea.
So when I say we're getting near
to the border
we take our trousers down.
Then for the next few minutes
we walk along with our trousers down
until I reckon from the map
that we're in England.
What do you think?'

I said I thought it was a brilliant plan

So we packed up our stuff
and headed down the mountain.
Mart was studying the map
and then he suddenly said,
'We're getting there
Trousers down!'

So we took our trousers down
and our underpants
and we started walking on down the path.
It wasn't very easy because you can't take
very big strides with trousers and pants
round your ankles
but we kept on.

I said,
'What if we see someone, Mart?'
'We'll have to pull our trousers up
and wait till they've gone,' he says,
then we take our trousers down again
and carry on.
We can t give up Just because some people
turn up.'
'That's true,' I said

So we walked on and Mart started singing
We're walking into England with our trousers down
with our trousers down
with our trousers down
We're walking into England with our trousers down
with
Our
trousers
down – yeah!'

Nobody did turn up
and after quite some time
I said,
'Are we in England yet, Mart?'
And he studied the map and said,
'Yeah we must be by now.'
So we pulled our pants and trousers up
and headed back to the campsite.
When we got back
our mums and dads asked us how we got on:
'Did you climb right to the top of The Sugarloaf?'
'Oh yes,' said Mart, 'no problem.'
'But you must have walked something like fifteen miles,'
my dad said.
'That's it,' said Mart
'Well done, boys,' said Mart's dad.
And I was feeling really proud so I said,
'And we walked into England with our trousers down.'

There was silence.
'You what?' said my dad.
'We walked into England with our trousers down.'
'Why in heaven's name did you do that?' he said.
'To celebrate. We had climbed The Sugarloaf.'

'Do you understand that, Connie?'
my dad said to my mum,
'Do you?'

He turned to Mart's parents:
'What have we done'?
We've brought up two completely crazy children.
They go out they climb a mountain,
they walk fifteen miles,
they read maps
they carry their own food and drink
they show themselves to be really capable,
responsible boys
and then what do they do?
They walk all over the countryside
with their trousers down.
How come we've produced two complete idiots.
Where did we go wrong?'

I thought,
wrong? wrong?
You haven't gone wrong.
Me and Mart
did something really brilliant today.
I mean,
I bet there's not many people in the world
who can say that they've walked into England
with their trousers down.

Adverbs

Today we have adverbs.
As you can hear an 'adverb'
is something to do with a verb.
You remember the 'verb' from last week?
The adverb tell us how the word we call a 'verb'
does its business.
Except you remember the verb doesn't only 'do'
it also 'is' and 'feels'.
So the adverb tells the verb how.
But also remember a verb isn't strictly speaking
a word.
It can be two, three or even four words.
And also – strictly speaking –
we can't always be certain which of these words
the adverb is telling 'how' to.
OK?
Now the adverb is also a word
that describes adjectives.
You remember adjectives describe nouns.
So really these kind of adverbs should be called
ad-adjectives.
But they're not
Sorry about that
but there's nothing I can do about that.
Same word – adverb –
doing its stuff to verbs
doing its stuff to adjectives.
But watch out here:
don't go calling any old word
hanging in there next to an adjective
an adverb.
It could be another adjective.
Watch out for that one.
Are you still with me?
Great,
because this gets even more interesting.

334

Sometimes there are words that
do things to adverbs.
You know what we call them?
Adverbs.
They could
it's true
be called ad-adverbs
but they're not
my hands are tied.
And we might as well
do the job properly here:
there's even another kind of adverb
that is really all on its own but
in a kind of way
does things to the whole of the rest of the sentence.
Don't ask me just for the moment to remind you
what a sentence is
but just remember there is this word
(not actually called an ad-sentence)
that is doing some business for the whole sentence.
And it's an adverb.

So there you are.
Get reading
and look out for adverbs
changing all sorts of things
all over the place.
It's a useful word isn't it?
Adverb.
Once you get the hang of them
they're good fun:

'Well, honestly, –
they're really dead easy.'

well, adverb
honestly, adverb
really, adverb
dead, adverb

My Books (forty years ago)

Oh 'Wonder Book of Machinery'
Oh 'Wonder Book of Knowledge'
Oh 'Thrills of the Iron Road'
you were excited by wheels.

You were photos of submarines
locomotives, escalators and racing cars
things that went vroom and clang
a crane
a dome
a hole in the ground
dug by diggers

Oh 'Wonder Book of Machinery'
Oh 'Wonder Book of Knowledge'
Oh 'Thrills of the Iron Road'
you were so hopeful
If you could,
you would make us
love engines nowadays
and we would sing
long live bulldozers
hurrah for rockets
three cheers for the bullet-train.

But the bulldozers bulldozed forests
the rockets rocketed bombs
and the bullet-train never got there
because they closed the line.

So now when it's: Bulldozers,
It's:
Oh yeah.
It's:
Rockets? No thanks
And:

Bullet-train? You wish.

Oh 'Wonder Book of Machinery'
Oh 'Wonder Book of Knowledge'
Oh Thrills of the Iron Road'
you wanted it all to be auto-speedo-wizzo-wonderful.
And it wasn't.

Teachers' helper for end-of-assemblies

No need to shout
no need to yell
no need to have a riot.

Shut your eyes
shut your mouth –
oh! you've gone all quiet.

Invisible Ink

Dad?
Yup.
What can you use for invisible ink?
Lemon juice.

(He gets lemon juice,
match stick,
piece of paper,
he writes something)

Dad?
Yup.
I can't read it.

Berwick-on-Tweed

The sign in the window said,
'Bargain basement upstairs.'

The Wedding

Uncle Ronnie got married in *shul*,
my dad was the best man,
there they all were standing under the *khuppe*,
and the Rabbi is talking,
and *Bubbe* is watching from her wheelchair,
and it's time for my dad to hand Ronnie the ring.

Out it comes and just as my dad gives it to him,
Ronnie faints.
Out cold.
Bubbe starts crying
and everyone in the shul starts talking and tutting.
So the bride's brother got his shoulder in tight on Ronnie
on one side
and my dad got his shoulder in tight on Ronnie
on the other
and the *shammes* propped him up from behind
and that was how Uncle Ronnie got married.

Bubbe said later it was a terrible shame
he missed it

shul = synagogue
khuppe = canopy for wedding ceremonies
Bubbe = grandmother
shammes = synagogue helper

Gypsy

My mother looked in the mirror
and said, there's gypsy in me.
She pulled a red scarf
tight over her head
and tied it at the back of her neck.
How could she be a gypsy? we said.

When Uncle Ronnie got married
an old woman who I'd never seen before
sat next to *Bubbe*. She had gold earrings and a gold tooth
her skin was dark
she laughed at the food
and pointed at me saying
who's this? somebody tell me who this young man is?

Who was she? I asked later.
Bubbe's sister, they told me.
I never saw her again.
She was wearing a scarf
tight over her head tied at the back.

Mr Vassar the newsagent

He thought I was my brother
and said,
'Hallo Brian, er, Michael, Brian? is it Michael?'
but sometimes he gave up
and just called me
laddy.

He thought my brother was me
and said,
'Hallo Michael, er, Brian, Michael? is it Brian?'
but sometimes he gave up
and just called him
laddy

So my brother made up a chant
and sat up in bed
going
'Michael Brian Brian Michael
laddy!
Michael Brian Brian Michael
laddy!'

So when mum said,
'Pop over the road to get the paper,'
my brother would say,
'Michael Brian Brian Michael
laddy!
Michael Brian Brian Michael
laddy!'

Aldermaston March

I ran away from home once.
I was 13,
the second year of the Aldermaston March,
marching from Aldermaston to London
to Ban the Bomb (for evermore).
I said, I'm going on the Aldermaston March.
They both said that this was out of the question,
the boy's mad, crazy.
My mother said,
where will you stay? you'd have nothing to eat
you don't know anyone, what would you eat?
you're not going
Harold say something, he's too young,
look at him, he's packing.
You can't go without a spare pair of trousers
how can he carry a bag like that for 20 miles a day?
Stop him Harold,
what would you do in the evening?
you need to eat, you get ill if you don't eat
take a tin of beans, you can always eat beans
Harold, stop him.
There's the chicken, take the chicken
if you're taking a tin of beans, take 2,
he's thirteen Harold, go next year
wait till next year, they won't have banned the bomb by then,
believe me There'll be another march, go on that one.
You must keep eating fresh fruit.
And you like dates. He's always liked dates, hasn't he Harold?
Just squeeze them in down the side of the bag.
Couldn't he wait till the last day
when we'll be there?
We can all go to Trafalgar Square together
Harold have you got the chicken?
Just because it's Easter doesn't mean it's warm.
It can snow at Easter, wear the string vest.
Who's organised the coaches?

Do we know these people Harold?
One orange! Take five. And raisins.
He's 13. It's ridiculous. He can't go.
Keep the chicken wrapped.
Phone us if you need more food
Goodbye

What politicians mean when they say they are against other countries having nuclear weapons

we've got a bomb
it keeps the peace
you can't have a bomb
you'll start a war
our bomb's clean
your bomb's dirty
our wars are nice
yours are horrid
we're sensible
you're mad

Moishe

One time Moishe,
my friend Chris's dad,
put on a science show
in the laundry-room in the basement of his flats.
It was packed out with friends and relatives.
Moishe was crazy about plastic.
I think I heard him say that one day
everything could be made of plastic.

In the science show,
Moishe poured mercury into liquid oxygen
and the mercury went solid.
He put a soft rubber ball into liquid oxygen
fished it out, threw it on the floor
and it broke into bits.
Then he poured liquid oxygen in the sink
and it boiled.
It was magic. Everybody clapped
and somebody's aunt said,
'So this is why you spent all that time at college, Moishe!'

I didn't think Chris's mum, Rene,
was quite so passionate about plastic
until one day she served me up fried egg and mushrooms
with a plastic egg

Why didn't I have a father who could make break rubber balls
and a mother who played tricks with plastic eggs?

Muss i' den

Our giggly German teacher, Miss Joseph said:
'This year I want to teach you a little Austrian folk song
hee hee hee . . . '

And she began singing:
'Muss i' den, muss i'–'

There was sudden rush of air on the back row
and Pat Phipps screamed:
'YAAAAAAAAAAAAA!'
Miss Joseph was appalled:
'Pat, really! how unlike you. What is going on?'
'Miss, it's Elvis,' said Pat.

Miss Joseph had been teaching Muss i' den'
to her German classes for 20 years.

She didn't know that Elvis Presley, the King,
the greatest rock singer ever
the man who was God to Pat Phipps
and very nearly every other girl in the world
was at that very moment stationed in Germany.

She didn't know that Elvis Presley, the King,
the greatest rock singer ever
the man who was God to Pat Phipps
and very nearly every other girl in the world
had that week,
given the world the song 'Wooden Heart'.
A song, that had the chorus and the tune of
Miss Joseph's little Austrian folk song:
Muss i' den.

That's why Pat Phipps screamed:
'YAAAAAAAAAAAAAA!'

348

Pat Phipps explained all this to Miss Joseph.
Miss Joseph was still appalled.
Pat Phipps was still trembling.
So Miss Joseph said,
'Well, class, perhaps we won't do
Muss i' den this year.
Open your books at page 71 . . . '

Sam

My father told us that when he was a boy
he used to share a bedroom with his Uncle Sam.
They weren't on speaking terms though.
He said Uncle Sam once wrecked a soldier's cap
that my father had brought back from the market.
Sam pulled it apart at the seams.
My father wouldn't talk to him after that.
For about seventeen years.

So who turned out the bedroom light?
we asked him.
We didn't have one, he said.
It was a candle.
So who blew out the candle?
He did, he said.

The Shop Downstairs

We lived in a flat over a shop.
It was an estate agents called Norman and Butt.
My father told me that Norman was the talkative one.
'He's full of big ideas. He rushes in
and starts gabbling away with what they're going to do,
things like:
'We could open a new shop,
we could buy new desks
we could be millionaires'
and then Mr Butt says:
'But—'
and so nothing happens.
'That's them, Norman and Butt,'
says my dad.
'Is that true?' we said
'Sure it is.'

Top Board

After three weeks of swimming lessons
Mr Hicks the swimming teacher said,
'OK Michael I want you to dive off the top board.'
WHAT?!
Is he crazy? I can't do that.
The board is miles up in the air.
When people dive off there
they drop through the air
at a hundred miles an hour.

I had only ever dived off the side before.
Just lean forward and flop.

'Up you go lad, just pretend it's the side
and just go, lad, go,' says Mr Hicks.

Up I went
I stood on the board . . .

. . . the big clock at the other end of the pool
is just the same height as me.
The paint is peeling off the ceiling.
It's hotter up here
and the air is full of shouting.
Underneath my feet it feels like sandpaper . . .
. . . 'Just pretend it's the side and just go, lad, go . . . '

So I did. It felt like doing a handstand on nothing.
It felt like my belly was going into my legs.
When I hit the water
it was like someone walloping me in the face.

'Well, done, 'said Mr Hicks.
'I want five more of those before the end of the lesson.'

Stobs

My best friend at the new school was Stobs.
We got together because I used to sit at the back of the class
making faces.
He already had a best friend, Staff
but all three of us got on really well.

Me and Stobs had this idea of making a book about London.
We'd collect post-cards and take pictures, we said, yeah.
And we'd go places like reporters and say what we'd seen, yeah.
You know, like under Charing Cross Bridge and interview tramps.
Or we could go to posh places like Harrods or the Ritz
and write down what they said when they chucked us out, yeah.

We went out and bought a scrap book
and stuck in it a post card of Westminster Abbey
and Stobs drew a picture of the coat of arms of London.
He said I could do the writing and he could do the pictures
because he was really good at drawing, yeah
and we could go to Hampstead Heath,
like we were on safari and report back from there.

Next day at school, I was telling Staff about how me and Stobs
were making a London scrap book thing.
Later that day Stobs came up to me
his face all glowering and furious.
'You told Staff about the London thing, didn't you?'
'Yep,' I said
'Right, that's it,' he said. 'Right.'
And he walked off.

I thought, what's going on? I haven't done anything wrong.
All I did was tell Staff about the London thing

I ran after him.
'Look Stobs, all . . . '
He cut me dead.

He just looked straight through me.
He didn't want to talk to me.
I remembered feeling kind of desperate.
All tight round my chest.
I mean
he was the person I'd decided to be my friend
at the new school
and now he was like an enemy.

I tried talking to him
I tried saying sorry.
I tried saying, what was wrong with telling Staff?
All I got was this fat sulky look.
He just ignored me.
I hated him for making me feel so bad.

Staff quickly sussed that something was wrong
and he grabbed me and said,
'What's going on, what's all this about?'
'Nothing,' I said, 'no, no, no, nothing.'
I was too embarrassed to say.
I thought the whole thing had got too daft to talk about.
'Come on, 'he says, 'tell me, is it to do with Stobs?'
'Yes, he's not talking to me.'
'Why not?'
'I don't want to say,' I said.
'Just tell me,' says Staff.
'He's really angry I told you about the London thing.'
'And he's not talking to you just for that?' he says.
'Yep.'
'Oh that's rubbish,' says Staff, 'he's always like that.'
'You mean he's done that sort of thing to you?'
'Oh yeah,' he says, 'loads of times.'

That got me thinking.
I had thought it was all to do with me.
That there was something I had done wrong.
That it was bad of me to have told Staff about the London thing.

Now I realised it was all in Stobs.
All it was, was something that Stobs did to his friends.

From that moment on
I didn't try to talk to him.
I didn't even give him the chance to ignore me
and cut me dead.
I went off and knocked around with some of the other guys,
Rodge and Nell.

A day later
I'm packing my bag at the back of the class
and Stobs is there and he says,
'Don't forget your maths book,
he wants the work in tomorrow.'

Don't tell your mother

When my mum went to evening classes
my dad would say,
'Don't tell your mother – let's have *matzo bray*. *
She always says:
"Don't give the boys that greasy stuff.
It's bad for them."
So don't tell her, alright?'

So he broke up the *matzos*
put them into water to soften them up.
Then he fried them
till they were glazed and crisp.

'It tastes best like this,
fried in *hinner shmaltz*,' **
he says,
'but olive oil will do'

Then he beat up three eggs
and poured it on over the frying *matzos*
till it was all cooked

It tasted brilliant
We loved it
Then we washed everything up
absolutely everything
and we went to bed

Next day,
Mum says to us
'What did your father cook you last night?'

Silence

'What did your father cook you last night?'
Oh you know . . . stuff
. . . egg on toast, I think

* *matzo bray* = the Yiddish name of a dish made of matzos and egg. Matzos is the word for unleavened bread and tastes like water biscuits

** *hinner shmaltz* = the Yiddish word for chicken fat, which is skimmed off the top of chicken soup

Leosia

I went to see my father's cousin Michael.
He was born in Poland.

When the Nazis came in the west
his parents put him on a train
going east
and he never saw them again.
They died in a Nazi death camp.

When the Russians came in the east
he was arrested, put on a train
and sent to one of the Russian camps.
But he lived.

When I went to see him
he wouldn't tell me any of this.
When he went out of the room
his wife said he can't bear to talk about it.
When he came back into the room
he said, 'Tell him the story about my cousin Leosia.'

So they told me the story about cousin Leosia.

When the Nazis came in the west
Leosia pretended to be a Christian.
She put a crucifix round her neck
and then she fetched her grandmother's brooch
and took the diamonds off it.
She took the soles off the heels of her shoes
put the diamonds inside the heels
and put the soles back on.
She thought if there were going to be any problems
she would be able to sell them.
Then she went west
into Germany.

In Germany she worked in a factory.
No one ever found out that she was Jewish.

At the end of the war
she couldn't face going back to Poland.
Her parents, all her friends and all her relations
had been taken away to the camps and killed.

She went to Israel to find her brother Naftali.
She told him how she had lived
right through the war
with diamonds in the heels of her shoes.
'And here they are,' she said,
The very diamonds themselves.'

And Naftali said, 'Where did you get the diamonds from, Leosia?'
And Leosia said, 'From our grandmother's brooch.'

So Naftali said, 'Listen carefully, Leosia.
Many years ago, our grandmother wrote to me.
She said that grandfather's business wasn't doing too well
and so to help out,
she had taken the diamonds off her brooch
put in glass ones instead
and sold off the diamonds.
She didn't tell anyone about it
but she wrote to me to get it off her chest.
You went through the whole war
with nothing more than
bits of glass in the heels of your shoes.'

Ted

I went to see my father's cousin Ted.
He was born in England
but has lived all his life in America.

Ted had known my father's father.
He and Ted had lived together in America.
My dad grew up in England without his dad.

My father's father was called Morris.

Ted said that Morris was a smart dresser.
He wore spats, a straw hat and carried a cane.
When Morris got up to speak,
people listened.

Ted said that Morris
stayed with a landlady in Rochester
for quite a time

Ted said that Morns had once turned up
taken him on one side
put his hand in his pocket
and taken out a wallet
Out of the wallet
he took a picture of a boy
about nine years old.
'What do you think of him?' said Morris to Ted.
'He's a smart boy, isn't he?
Believe me, he's going to do great things.'

'Was that a picture of my dad?' I said to Ted.
'Nope,' said Ted.

Australia

We went to Australia.
It was a great time for beasties.
They were all over us:
ants, mosquitoes, spiders, stick insects, lizards
horse flies . . .
even the birds in Australia fly out of the sky out at you.
You walk under a tree where a magpie's nesting
and it dive bombs you:
eeueeeeoooooooowwwwwww.
You have to duck out the way
or you end up with a magpie stuck in your head.

In Australia
they have hundreds of different kinds of ants.
There's the little mad-harry kind
that zoom about in gangs
at nine hundred miles an hour,
little tiny ones that you can scarcely see
when one's on its own.
But they never are on their own,
they're in gangs, hunting you down
'Come on fellas, over here, quick.'
'I'm being quick'
'I'm being quicker . . . '
And they eat everything:
soap, chalk, toenails – and they love chicken poo.
Someone once told me to put talcum powder down
to keep them out of the house.
We did.
They ate it
They crawl up the wall next to your bed at night
and run all over your face.
'Quick, over here'
'What is it?'
'His eyelids.'
'Great. Eat them.'

'I am.'
When you get a letter in the morning
you have to get there straightaway
or you end up in a tug of war with them. 'Give me that.'
'No it's ours.' 'Yeah, it's ours.'

That's the tiny ones.
You go for a walk in the bush
and you see these giant ones.
I've never seen anything like them.
When you see them
you think you're in a horror film
where all the insects have got enormous
and you've shrunk.
I told my kids that they had better watch out
when they're walking out there
or the giant ants would eat their shoes off
yep just like that:
walking along,
and
ker-unch, ker-unch – no shoes.
'Wow, could they Dad?'
'Yep.'

The mosquitoes are deadly.
One of them bit me on the leg in the night.
When I woke up in the morning,
I said,
'Hey I'm growing another knee.'
Mosquitoes are dead sneaky.
They're not like wasps who tell you
they're coming to get you:
'Zzzzzzz, here I comezzzzzz
I'm going to sting your neckzzzz
gotcha zzzzzz told you zzzzz
Mosquitoes just float down on to you like a little feather
and sit on your arm, smiling.
You can't feel them

till they start sucking your blood out.
Like they're having
a really good milk shake there.
'Don't mind me – scrooooooosh.'
At night though, you hear them.
A tiny high pitched hum:
'Mmmmmmmmmmmm'
It's dark.
You can't see them.
'Mmmmmmmmmmmm'
AND THEN THE HUMMING STOPS.
That's when you know the trouble starts.
Because the mosquito has landed on YOU.
But where?
You don't know.
So straightaway you start smacking yourself.
Bang, slap, smack, clack. All over.
Ah, that's done it, you think. Then:
'Mmmmmmmmmmmmm'
It's no use trying to hit it mid-air.
It'll just bounce off your arm.
So you wait for it to stop again.
'MmmM'
Now go for it:
slap, smash, bang – it's you your hitting.
I ended up beating myself up.
Those Australian mosquitoes loved me.
Every night they were all over me.
In the morning I was covered in bites
and I could see them laughing at me,
staggering about
drunk
with my blood
all bloated, eyeballs crossed
too heavy to fly.
When I left Australia
they were at the airport,
a little gang of mosquitoes saying,

'Thanks, thanks for coming.
It's been great having you,
come again.'

We went to stay in the bush.
(You know that doesn't mean we were staying *in* a bush.
like: 'Mm, it's really prickly in here.'
No, the 'bush' means the countryside.)
We were staying in a little old house.
Next door to the house was the outside toilet
and next door to that was another little old house
where the children were going to sleep.
First night we were there I said,
'OK, off you go to the toilet,
then off to your little house
and I'll come and tuck you in in a moment.' I sat down to read something
when I heard this screaming noise from outside:
'Yeeeeee.'
'Ahhhhhh'
Oiiiiiiiiiiii'
I rushed out to see what was going on
and my kids were standing outside the toilet
screaming,
'THERE'S A SPIDER IN THE TOILET, DAD.'
I said,
'I don't believe it.
We've travelled all these thousands of miles
and first night we get there, all you can say is:
'There's a spider in the toilet, dad.'
'NO DAD, IT'S HORRIBLE
IT'S GOING TO EAT US WHILE WE'RE DOING IT.'
'OK,' I said, 'I'll go in there and have a look.'
I looked.
Up, down, round, behind.
'Nope. No spider in there.'
'IT IS. IT'S UP THERE ON THE WALL
IT'S GOING TO DROP ON US

WHILE WE'RE SITTING THERE.'
I said,
'I tell you there is no spider in there
at all–'
(I was looking all round)
'– no spider anywh–'
And there it was.
Up on the wall.
A great grey furry thing
all quivery
its beady little eyes staring at me
like it was growling.
'Grumrrrrarrurr?
I started backing off,
'Look kids, don't worry about it,
just go in there, do what you've got to do
and get our again.'
And they're pushing me back into the toilet.
'NO GET RID OF IT DAD.
IT'S GOING TO EAT USSSSSSSS.'
So I said,
'OK, OK. Course I'm not scared.
Sure I'll get rid of it.'
But as I got up to it,
I thought, how do you get rid of it?
Go up to it ? and say?
'Hi.
We're just in from England.
I'm Mike. These are my children.
OK if they use your toilet for a while?'
But it went on looking at me:
'Grrrrnrarrrrrrrurn'
So I looked round for something to get it with.
And I found it:
the toilet brush.
Perfect.
I know what I'll do:
There's a gap between the top of the wall and the roof.

I'll flick it through the gap.
So I started out towards it
stretching out with the toilet brush.
Nothing hurried.
Nice and easy.
Don't want it to jump off the wall at me.
'Course I'm not scared.
I'm doing it, aren't I?'
Then I reached it with the end of the toilet brush
and
flick!
That got rid of it.
Over the top of the wall.
Brilliant.
I'd got rid of the spider.

Then I looked down at the brush.
There it was.
Crawling up the handle of the brush
towards my hand.
'YAAAAAAAAAAAAAAAA
GET OFF, GET OFF, GET OFF.'
I shook the brush like mad.
That got rid of it.
Phew. I don't want to be bothered like that again.

Then my son Joe says,
'Dad.'
'Mmm'
'Look at your foot.'
'What's the matter with it?'
I look down,
its sitting there on my bare foot:
'YAAAAAAAAAAAAAAAA
GET OFF, GET OFF, GET OFF.'
Shake shake shake.
That got rid of it.

Course I wasn't scared of it.

The next night
we were sitting round having tea
and my Eddie (now 7 years old)
walks in from outside in his bare feet.
'Dad, dad, quick over here.
There's a scorpion over here.'
Now you know what scorpions are don't you?
Little land lobsters
with a tail that's a sting
that curls right over from the back
and wobbles about in front of them
zing, zing, zing.
And they've got two big nippers
that go
slicey, slicey, slicey. .
I said, 'Don't be silly Eddie,
they don't have scorpions in Australia.
Do you think we would let you walk about
in bare feet if we knew there were scorpions here.
You could tread on one of those
and next thing you know
it stings you
and your foot is swelling up like a football
vvvvoooooooooh.
Or even worse:
you could sit on of those things
and:
vvvvooooooooh.
You'd know about it, believe me.'
'Dad, it's a scorpion. Come over here and look.'
I said, 'I don't know what it is,
but it's not a scorpion, OK?
They're unbelievably dangerous.
One foot on one of those and –
vvvvooooooooohh.'
Dad. Listen to what I'm saying.

It's a scorpion.'
I said,
'OK, I'll come and have a look
but it won't be a scorpion, OK?'
I went over to have a look.

'Stand back everybody.
That is really dangerous.
THAT IS A SCORPION.'

'Yeah, that's what I was trying to tell you, dad.'

'Nobody go anywhere it.'
And I looked round for the biggest thing I could find.
It turned out to be
Richard Scarry's *Giantest Book Ever Ever.*
I lifted it up above my head and
blam!
Right on it.
And little bits of scorpion
went flying off in all directions.
That wasn't very Green of me, was it?
Probably wrecked the food chain in the area
for hundreds of years.
Anyway
I swept the bits of scorpion out
and I said to Eddie,
'Lucky you didn't tread on that.
One foot on it and
vvvvooooooooh.'
And he's nodding at me,
not saying anything.

Next day
he comes up to me and says,
'You know that scorpion yesterday?'
'Yep.'
'I did tread on it.'

'You trod on that scorpion?
Yesterday?
Why didn't you tell me at the time?'
And he shrugged his shoulders
and said all indignant:
'Dunnooooo'
'What do you mean, you don't know?'
'Dunnooo I dunnoooooo.'
And I've never found out
why he didn't tell me he trod on a scorpion.
Why couldn't he have said,
'Er Dad, I've trod on a scorpion.'?

One day Naomi went to the shower.
She came running out of the shower.
She was pointing back at the shower
without saying anything.
I went over and had a look.
In the corner of the shower
on the ground was this thing.
A fat grey snake-thing with legs.
When it saw me
it opened it's mouth.
And it was a huge mouth
like a little crocodile
except the mouth inside was bright red
and in the middle of the mouth
was a little blue tongue that waggled to and fro
like it was saying,
'Don't you come in here or I'll bite your leg off.'
I said to it,
'It's OK, we won't come in here.
Relax. The shower's all yours.'
When I turned round to leave
I brushed up against the shower curtain
and this one foot long stick insect
flew into my face.
It felt like a flying hand coming for me.

369

'Don't worry about them,'
my Australian friends said
when we got back to the city,
'they're nothing to worry about.'

'But what about the horse flies?' I said.
Like old second world war bombers
looming up towards you
dzzzzzzzzzzzzzzzzzzzz,
hairy bodies, bright green eyes
and a little sharp triangle that they dig into your skin.

'Don't worry about *them*' they said.
'lucky you didn't see a Red Back.'
'A Red Back,' I said, 'what's a Red Back?'
'Oh it's just a little spider with a Red Back.'
'And what does it do?'
'Bites yer.
and – er – kills yer.'
'You don't see many of them around do you?' I said.
'Oh yeah, they're everywhere.
They love outside toilets and
little old houses in the bush.
You just brush your hand across one of them
and you know about it
A few people die of them every year in Australia, you know.'
'Oh really?' I said, 'and what about those giant
grey furry spiders.
They're pretty dangerous too, aren't they?'
'Nope. Totally harmless, mate.
You can kiss them goodnight every night.
Its the little Red Back you want to watch out for.'
I felt all kind of weak.
Our little old house and our outside toilet
out there in the bush
were probably teeming with Red Backs.
They were probably in the bed.
And nobody told us.

We could all have been bitten to death
by hundreds of raving Red Backs.
All seven of us,
wiped out,
just like that.
And we never knew.

Eddie and the car

The stupidest thing I have ever done
happened in France.
We were going to have a picnic,
so we were driving along the road
in our little yellow Renault 4.
Have you ever seen a Renault 4?
It's like a little square tin box.
If you lean on it
your hand goes straight through the side of the car.

We were off to have a picnic.
Have you noticed how long it takes
parents to make up their minds where to stop for a picnic?
It takes us longer to find where to have the picnic
than it takes to eat it.
We stop, we get out, we spread the sheet
we unload the boxes and bags and bottles
we sit down and it's
sniff
sniff
sniff
what's that?
what on earth could smell like that?
a dead dog?
OK
EVERYONE BACK IN THE CAR

Drive on

We stop, we get out, we spread the sheet
we unload the boxes and bags and bottles
we sit down and it's
zzzzzzz
zzzzzzz
zzzzzzz
wasps.

Hundreds of them.
OK
EVERYONE BACK IN THE CAR.

Drive on.

In the end we got to this perfect place.
Backed the car up a little slope
laid everything out on the ground
sat down.

'Eddie do you want some chicken?'
'Na.'
'Eddie do you want some crisps?'
'Na.'
'A drink?'
'Na.'
'Right, well, you toddle off
and leave us to eat in peace.'

So Eddie (who was three at the time)
walked off to the car
and he got into the back seat.
He looked out the window
and called out:
'Look at mee-eeeee.
I'm in the car.'
Joe, who was seven,
looks over and starts giggling back at Eddie.
'Look at Eddie, dad,' says Joe.
'Turn round, Joe.
Don't take any notice of him.
It only encourages him.
Turn round.'

Then Eddie climbed into the front seat of the car.
He grabbed hold of the steering wheel
and shouted out at us:

'LOOK AT ME-EEEEEEE,
I'M DRI-VING.'
And Joe says,
'Look at Eddie, Dad
he's driving.'
I say,
'Turn round Joe,
don't take any notice of him.
It only encourages him.
Turn round.'

We went on eating.
Then Joe looked up and said,
'Dad.
The car's moving.'
I said, 'Don't be silly, Joe,'
and I turned round to look at the car.

He was right.
The car was moving slowly down the slope
towards the road
with Eddie at the wheel. He is screaming:
'THE CAR'S MOVING. THE CAR'S MOVING.'

Now if you were a sensible, intelligent person
at this moment
you might perhaps go over to the car
open the door
get Eddie out
jump in
jam on the brakes
and stop the car.

That would be a sensible thing to do.

Slightly less sensible
but still quite sensible
would be to

374

go over to the car
open the door
get Eddie out
close the door
and wave goodbye to the car.

At least Eddie would be safe.

What I did was
try to stop the car.
I rushed over
and grabbed hold of the pillar between the two doors
and tried to stop the car going down the slope.
Eddie was screaming out the window:
THE CAR'S MOVING!'
And I'm grunting back at him,
'I know it's moving.
All the time the car is moving down the slope
and I'm hanging on.

On the roof of the car is a tray of peaches
so Joe is calling out,
'Dad, look at the peaches.
the peaches are flying off the roof of the car.'
and I'm saying, 'Never mind the peaches,'
And Eddie is shouting,
'The car's moving.'
'I know it's moving.'

Now I know that what we've got coming up next
is the road.
So I think, it'll be flatter there.
The car will slow down.
I'll be able to stop the car.
We get to the road.
The car doesn't slow down.
I am not able to stop the car.
'Dad, look at the peaches.'

'Never mind the peaches.'
'The car's moving.'
'I know it's moving.'

We are now heading for a twelve foot ditch.

The car nosedives down the ditch
with me still hanging on.
it bounces once, twice on its nose
and lands up stuck head first in a hedge
with its wheels spinning in midair.

I opened the door, grabbed hold of Eddie
got him out
and he jumped into his mother's arms
and bit her.
He sunk his teeth right into her arm.
Joe is walking around saying,
'Look at the peaches
look at the peaches.'

Eddie is OK
now to get the car out of the hedge.
Get in
start up
into reverse
and
nothing.
The little yellow Renault 4 has front wheel drive.
The front wheels are turning over and over
in midair
and nothing else is moving.

What to do?

I got out the car and looked round and there is no one anywhere.
We're in the middle of the French countryside.
Were stuck in a hedge

miles from home.

Then I looked again
up the road
and I could see in a field
someone's backside.
A man was bending down
digging potatoes.
So I ran up the road and spoke to him.
'Excusez-moi, monsieur,
je suis anglais et je suis stupide.'
(I'm English and I'm stupid)
and my little boy got on the front seat of the car
and the car went down the hill
and
BLUP
it's stuck.

The man stood up
and slowly wagged his finger at me.
'Jamais, jamais, jamais–'
(Never, never, never)
Never let a child on to the front seat of a car
they can easily–
'Yeah I know that *now*,' I said
but how do I get the car out?
He then raised both hands by his side and said,
'Bof!'
This is French for:
'I haven't got a clue
you're on your own, mate.'

Try it:
raise both arms
by your side
hands upwards
and as you say it
buff your cheeks out:

'Bof!'

So now what?

Far away in the distance
I see a man ploughing a field
so I started off running up the road
towards him.
As I am running along
I start to realise that I am only wearing my underpants.
When we had the picnic
I thought I would sunbathe.
So here I am running down the road
in my underpants.
No matter.
Must press on.

As I got nearer to the field
where the man was ploughing
I started thinking,
how *do* you get someone to stop ploughing a field?

So I climbed over the fence
and stood in front of the tractor
held up both my hands
and started waving.
I don't suppose the farmer
had ever seen a large hairy bloke
in his underpants
standing in front of his tractor waving his hands.
But he brought the tractor up to me and stopped it.
And he said,
'Ey bein?'
which is French for:
'Well? Have you got something to say or not?
Or are you completely stupid?'
As you say it you have to nod your head upwards
leaving your mouth open after you've said it.

The 'bein' bit sounds like 'bang' said through your nose.
Try it.

So I said,
'Excusez-moi, monsieur,
je suis anglais et je suis stupide.'
(I'm English and I'm stupid)
and my little boy got on the front seat of the car
and the car went down the hill
and
BLUP
it's stuck.

The man looked at me
and slowly wagged his finger at me and said
'Jamais, jamais, jamais,'
(Never, never, never)
let a child get into the front seat of a car
because they can easily –
'Yeah, yeah, yeah, I know that now
but do you think you could help me?
I could pay you . . .
it would be very nice if . . .'

So three hours later
after he had lunch
he came along with his tractor
his wife
his dog
and a long chain.
They tied the chain round the back bumper of the car
and they pulled and they heaved
and they heaved and they pulled
(just like the story of The Enormous Turnip)
and they pulled and they heaved the bumper
right off the car.

Thanks

Well, in the end
they got the little yellow Renault 4 out of the bush
and out of the ditch.
After we had kicked it a few times
it worked.
It was a bit difficult going round corners
but it worked
We've got a photo of the
little yellow Renault 4
stuck in the ditch
in our photo album.
It's great.
It reminds me of
the stupidest thing I have ever done.

Mr Baggs

I was walking home from school
with Mr Baggs
the teacher who took us for football
and he said:
'You see Michael what we need in the team
is a really good centre-half,
someone who can control the game from midfield
collect the ball in the middle
distribute the ball to the front players.
A good centre-half can turn a game.
He can make all the difference.
Now who have we got playing in the middle?
– oh, my goodness it's you
I forgot
I'm sorry
I wasn't thinking
no hard feelings, OK?'

My friend Roger

My friend Roger said
that I couldn't walk up the road with him
in case his parents saw me
so I used to say goodbye to him
at the corner of the road.
But sometimes I would just
lean
round
the
edge
of the wall on the corner
and watch him walk up the road
on his own.

Mum's School

My Mum was a teacher
and once she had to take me to school with her.
Her children lined up in the playground
ready for games.
I was at the back.
It was all quiet,
we were waiting to begin.

I looked up
and then I skipped round to the front of the line
in a great big circle
round to the front
round to the back
skip skip skip.

Then Graham thought he would do the same
and he started to skip round
round to the front
round to the back
skip skip but my Mum sent us in.

We sat in the classroom
and Graham taught me
Inky pinky ponky,
the farmer bought a donkey,
the donkey died,
the farmer cried,
inky pinky ponky.

That night at home
Mum said that I had let her down
and it made her sad
what was I trying to do?
show her up in front of her children?
well?
what have you got to say for yourself?

well?

and I didn't say anything
I just looked at the floor
feeling hot

well? she said
and I said
er –
inky pinky ponky.

The cupboard

At the top of the stairs
there's a landing
that's where the bedrooms are
our bedroom
and mum and dad's bedroom

At the top of the stairs
there's a landing
that's where the bedrooms are
our bedroom
and mum and dad's bedroom
and the cupboard.

The walk-in cupboard
with no floor at the back
where the walls slope down
with the roof of the house
down to narrow grey corners.

The walk-in cupboard
with no light
where the old brown metal trunk
and the old grey metal trunk
stand on end
tall and empty
like caves
that would welcome you in
and shut tight behind you.

The walk-in cupboard
where two gas-masks
lie between the timbers
like crazy skulls
and dad's army jacket talks of tanks
and dead heads.

The walk-in cupboard
where my brother showed me
behind the trunks
was a little low door
leading into a lightless nothing
where
With a wriggle
he said you could get through
– go on
and I did
and once in,
there was nothing
and nothing
and nothing
until
my head hit a box.

A slit of light leaked through a slipped slate
in the roof.
I opened the box
it was stacked to the top
with sheets of paper
written on
letters to mum from dad
when he was away
as the war was ending
when my brother was small
and he was coming home
and he was leaving home
and he was coming home
just before I was born.

Essex

When you drive along the road in Essex
there are signs up by the side of the road
telling you to come in and buy things.
We saw signs for:

Bird cages, bird seed
rustic poles, a yellow van
paving slabs and mopeds.

Horse boxes, incubators
horse manure, picture frames
roasting chickens, country wear
young budgies all colours

Wavy edge panels
dried flower baskets
chimney pots
collie dogs and greenhouses
chinchillas,
sheds,

reptiles

Pneumonia

My brother has pneumonia
and the house is quiet.

I am allowed in his room
FOR A SHORT TIME ONLY.

My brother has pneumonia
and the house in quiet.

When I go in he shows me
a little row of glass bottles with rubber lids
that go pop pop pop pop pop

he shows me a tiny cardboard locomotive he's made
and we go digger de doo, digger de doo

I sit on his bed and – whoofff
and I spill his orange juice on his blanket

Mum comes in and says
Get out get out, look what you've done.

My brother has pneumonia
and the house is quiet.

Sweetshop

do you think there's a sweetshop here?
are we going to the sweetshop?
when are we going to the sweetshop?
will you take me to the sweetshop?
have we got enough money for the sweetshop?
will the sweets be in jars in the sweetshop?
will they have homemade sweets in the sweetshop?
will they have those soft squashy toffees with the chocolate inside
in the sweetshop?
are we going to the sweetshop?
when are we going to the sweetshop?
will you take me to the sweetshop?
have we got enough money for the sweetshop?
will you take me to the sweetshop?
when are we going to the sweetshop?
are we going to the sweetshop?
are we?

For Naomi

I'm the kind of dad
my children don't want to be seen with
because I'm the kind of dad who

shouts in shops
says hello to babies
doesn't clean the car
eats pizzas in the street
doesn't cut his moustache
sings on buses
argues with policemen
waves to old ladies
has long hair
and
writes poems

Three year old boy says:

I can't catch the air
I want to catch the air
and dump it all in my mouth

My pasta is kidnapped
and my mouth is a dungeon

O look at the cat her skin is bursting through her fur.

Does she know she's a cat?

Is a sheepdog a half-dog, half-sheep?

I hate you, Bear-poo

I like Coughed Wheat

I can't go to my party because I haven't got an invitation.

You wait till I'm older than you.

Conversation with a six year old

Do you want to come to my party?
Yes.
You'll get ice cream jelly
a punch in the belly
you can't watch telly
cos your feet are too smelly.
Thanks.

The Langham Cinema

On Wednesday afternoons
you could get into The Langham for ninepence
if you were a kid.
We didn't have a TV
so I used to go there in the holidays.
Quite often I'd be the only one in the whole cinema
and when the slushy bits came on
and they started kissing
I used to start shouting.

Then the usherette would come round
and say
'The manager says that you've got to be quiet
or you'll have to leave.'
And I said,
'But I'm the only one in here.
I'm not disturbing anyone.'
And she said,
'I'm just telling you what the manager said.
If you go on making a noise
then you'll have to leave.'
And I said,
'But I'm the only one in here.'
And she said,
'I know you are.
But if it goes on you'll have to leave.'
And I said,
'But I'm the only one in here.'
And she said,
'I know you are'
And I said,
'I know you know I am.'
The usherette went away
and I watched the rest of the film.

Quietly.

Proverbs

On the wall in our house
we've got a picture called 'Flemish Proverbs'.

There are hundreds and hundreds of people in it
acting out different proverbs and fables like
'It's no use crying over spilt milk.'
'Big fish eat little fish.'
and the story of the fox and the stork.

There are ones we don't have like
one about someone trying to tile his roof with pies
and one about someone trying to cut wool off a pig.

The picture is full of kings and hats and snakes and fires
and rivers and knights in armour
all in one huge picture
on our front room wall.

My friends come over and look at it.

They come to look at the rude bits.
There's an inn-sign of a moon
and there's a man looking out of the window
peeing on it
The proverb is about a show-off –
He thinks he's so clever, he can pee on the moon.

There's one where all the men have got their trousers off
and they're bending down
walking backwards into a little house.
The proverb is about several people trying to do something
that only one person can do.
They think they can all do a poo in the same toilet.

My friends have got pictures in their houses:
'Elephants at Dawn'

and
'Brixham Harbour'
I quite like them
but they say,
'Let's go over to Michael's place
and look at the rude bits on his parent's picture.'

Sandwich

He's not putting jam on his tuna fish, is he?
He is putting jam on his tuna fish.
Why is he putting jam on his tuna fish?
Why are you putting jam on your tuna fish?
He says he likes jam on his tuna fish.
No one likes jam on their tuna fish.
But he is someone who is going to have jam on his tuna fish.
OK, OK, he can have jam on his tuna fish.
I'm not going to stop him putting jam on his tuna fish.
But have you ever heard of anything like it?
Jam on tuna fish?
Now I've heard of it.
First he puts the tuna fish on
then he puts the jam on.
That's how he has it.
Jam on his tuna fish.

I can't believe it.

Sultanas

Where are the sultanas?
Why are there no sultanas?
Who's eaten the sultanas?
The children must have eaten the sultanas.

Dad?
Mm?
You've eaten all the sultanas.

Trying to find out what my kid's homework is

So what's your homework?
Nothing much.
Sure, I know it's not much
    but what is it?
Stuff.
What stuff?
You know. Stuff.
Stuff about what?
History stuff.
What history stuff?
The West.
What West?
The American West.
Oh yeah ? What about it?
You know. The West and what happened.
When?
Ages ago. It's history isn't it?
So what's your homework?
Nothing much
Sure, I know it's not much
    but what is it?
Stuff.
What stuff?
You know Stuff
Stuff about what?
History stuff.
What history stuff?
The West.
What West?
The American West.
Oh yeah? What about it?
You know. The West and what happened.
When?
Ages ago. It's history isn't it?
So what's your homework?

Shirt

Whenever my mum got me some horrible shirt
that I didn't want to wear
she would say,
'It's good. Have it. It's nice.
They're wearing them like that now.'

So I would wear it to school.

And whenever I came home from school
she would say,
So? Did they like the shirt?'

Sometimes I used to go off a favourite food
and my mum would say,
'What's the matter him?
He used to love apricot jam.
Why don't you want the apricot jam?
I got it in specially for you.
You said you liked it.
So I bought it.
You've always liked apricot jam
I can remember a time
when the only thing you would have on your bread
is apricot jam
and now you're telling me you don't like it
its good Have it. It's nice.'

So I would have the apricot jam.

And when I had eaten it
she would say
So? Did you like the apricot jam?'

Printed in June 2019
by Rotomail Italia S.p.A., Vignate (MI) - Italy